The Feminist Aesthetics of Virginia Woolf
Modernism, Post-Impressionism and the Politics of the Visual

In this book, Jane Goldman offers a revisionary, feminist reading of Woolf's literary Post-Impressionism. Focusing on Woolf's engagement with the artistic theories of her time, Goldman traces the feminist implication of her aesthetics by reclaiming for the everyday world of history and politics what seem to be private, mystical moments. Goldman analyses Woolf's fascination with the aesthetic possibilities of the Post-Impressionist exhibition of 1910 and the solar eclipse of 1927, by linking her response to wider literary and cultural contexts. She argues that Woolf evolves a kind of 'feminist prismatics' through which she is able to express and develop both the challenge and pessimism of her feminist vision. Lavishly illustrated with colour pictures, this book will appeal not only to scholars working on Woolf, but also to students of Modernism, art history and women's studies.

Jane Goldman is Lecturer in English at the University of Dundee. She is co-editor of *Modernism: an Anthology of Sources and Documents*, and author of the forthcoming *Image to Apocalypse: 1910–1945*, and *The Icon Critical Guide to Virginia Woolf's 'To the Lighthouse' and 'The Waves.'*

The Feminist Aesthetics of Virginia Woolf
Modernism, Post-Impressionism and the
Politics of the Visual

JANE GOLDMAN

CAMBRIDGE
UNIVERSITY PRESS

PUBLISHED BY THE PRESS SYNDICATE OF THE UNIVERSITY OF CAMBRIDGE
The Pitt Building, Trumpington Street, Cambridge, United Kingdom

CAMBRIDGE UNIVERSITY PRESS
The Edinburgh Building, Cambridge CB2 2RU, UK
40 West 20th Street, New York, NY 10011–4211, USA
10 Stamford Road, Oakleigh, VIC 3166, Australia
Ruiz de Alarcón 13, 28014 Madrid, Spain
Dock House, The Waterfront, Cape Town 8001, South Africa

http://www.cambridge.org

First published 1998
First paperback edition 2001

Printed in the United Kingdom at the University Press, Cambridge

Typeset in 11/13pt Adobe Garamond (GC)

A catalogue record for this book is available from the British Library

ISBN 0 521 59096 5 hardback
ISBN 0 521 79458 7 paperback

For my mother
In memory of J.H.S.
All honour to my father and his art

Contents

Illustrations

The author and publisher gratefully acknowledge the Carnegie Trust for assistance towards the cost of colour illustrations.

Thanks are also due to Geoff Ward, Head of English at the University of Dundee, for finding the funds to supplement this award.

Acknowledgements

I am especially grateful to Suzanne Raitt and George Hyde for their very helpful and detailed reader's responses to the later drafts of this book. I would also like to thank for their comments those who, as part of their academic duties or out of sheer scholarly friendship (sometimes both), read (and sometimes re-read) its numerous earlier and less polished forms between thesis-proposal, thesis, and book: Leila Brosnan, Aidan Day, Kate Flint, Martin Hammer, Philip Hobsbaum, Vassiliki Kolocotroni, Pam Morris, Colin Nicholson, Faith Pullin, Randall Stevenson, Jim Stewart, Karina Williamson. Others have helped me enormously in a number of other ways from sound advice to practical assistance: Lesley Atkin, Kirstine Burnett, Ian Campbell, Ronnie Jack, Gail Low, Paddy Lyons, Geraldine Prince, Polly Rewt, Olga Taxidou, Geoff Ward, Marion Wynne-Davies, Julian Wolfreys. For his advice and patience I also thank my editor, Ray Ryan. I confess eternal gratitude for a truly generous and learned introduction to the pleasures of elegiacs (and much else) at the table of Paul Edwards. My 'without whom' (and whose books) is Gus McLean. I thank him for his love *and* his library.

Abbreviations

AROO	*A Room of One's Own* (London: The Hogarth Press, 1929)
BERG	[Microfilm] *The Virginia Woolf Manuscripts: from the Henry W. and Albert A. Berg Collection at the New York Public Library* (Woodbridge, Conn.: Research Publications International, 1993)
CDB	*The Captain's Death Bed and Other Essays* (London: The Hogarth Press, 1950)
CE	*Collected Essays*, 4 vols. (London: The Hogarth Press, 1967)
CR	*The Common Reader* (London: The Hogarth Press, 1925)
CSF	*The Complete Shorter Fiction of Virginia Woolf*, New Edition, ed. Susan Dick (London: The Hogarth Press, 1989)
D I–V	*The Diary of Virginia Woolf*, 5 vols., ed. Anne Olivier Bell and Andrew McNeillie (London: The Hogarth Press, 1977–84)
DM	*The Death of the Moth and Other Essays* (London: The Hogarth Press, 1942)
E I–IV	*The Essays of Virginia Woolf*, vols. 1–4, ed. Andrew McNeillie (London: The Hogarth Press, 1986–94)
F	'Foreword', *Recent Paintings by Vanessa Bell*, The London Artists' Association, Cooling Galleries (London, 1930); *The Bloomsbury Group: A Collection of Memoirs, Commentary and Criticism*, ed. S.P. Rosenbaum (London: Croom Helm, 1975), pp. 169–173
F2	'Foreword', *Catalogue of Recent Paintings by Vanessa Bell*, Lefevre Galleries (London, 1934)
GR	*Granite and Rainbow* (London: The Hogarth Press, 1958)
JR	*Jacob's Room* (London: The Hogarth Press, 1922)
L I–VI	*The Letters of Virginia Woolf*, 6 vols., ed. Nigel Nicolson and Joanne Trautmann (London: The Hogarth Press, 1975–80)
LAW	*Life As We Have Known It*, by Co-Operative Working Women, ed. Margaret Llewelyn Davies (London: The Hogarth Press, 1931)
M	*The Moment and Other Essays* (London: The Hogarth Press, 1947)

MB	*Moments of Being*, Second Edition, ed. Jean Schulkind (London: The Hogarth Press, 1985)
Mrs D	*Mrs Dalloway* (London: The Hogarth Press, 1925)
N&D	*Night and Day* (London: Duckworth, 1919)
O	*Orlando* (London: The Hogarth Press, 1928)
PA	*A Passionate Apprentice. The Early Journals 1897–1909*, ed. Mitchell A. Leaska (London: The Hogarth Press, 1990)
RF	*Roger Fry: A Biography* (London: The Hogarth Press, 1940)
RN	*Virginia Woolf's Reading Notebooks*, ed. Brenda Silver (Princeton: Princeton University Press, 1983)
TL	*To the Lighthouse* (London: The Hogarth Press, 1927)
VB	*Selected Letters of Vanessa Bell*, ed. Regina Marler (London: Bloomsbury, 1993)
VO	*The Voyage Out* (London: Duckworth, 1915)
W	*The Waves* (London: The Hogarth Press, 1931)
WS	*Walter Sickert. A Conversation* (London: The Hogarth Press, 1934)

1   Introduction: interrupted moments

> . . . to catch and enclose certain moments which break off from the
> mass, in which without bidding things come together in a combination
> of inexplicable significance, to arrest those thoughts which suddenly, to the
> thinker at least, are almost menacing with meaning. Such moments of vision
> are of an unaccountable nature; leave them alone and they persist for years;
> try to explain them and they disappear; write them down and they die
> beneath the pen.[1]

The elusive qualities of Virginia Woolf's 'moment' have exercised critics for
some time, yet her phrase 'menacing with meaning' has not survived into the
common lexis of debate: rather, the Woolfian moment is considered a moment
of pure being, a mystical experience beyond the everyday, beyond history, and
beyond meaning. I would like to place the Woolfian moment in the context
of 'the real world',[2] that is in the material and historical realm beyond merely
the personal and subjective; to understand some of the feminist implications
of Woolf's aesthetics. In the continuing debate over the relationship between
Woolf's aesthetics and her politics, I suggest that some of those elements critics
have identified as Woolf at her most abstract, aestheticized, and philosophically
remote, may alternatively (and paradoxically) be read, and reclaimed, in relation to an historically aware, materialist and feminist Woolf. This is not to deny
the former in favour of the latter, but to suggest their intimate interrelation.

From the mass of Virginia Woolf's writing I have chosen to focus on two
'moments' of significance to Woolf which might well be considered 'almost
menacing with meaning': June 1927, and November/December 1910. My study
falls into two parts, 'Eclipse', and 'Prismatics', each of which takes one of these
dates as its point of departure. If linear chronology were to dictate, we would
begin with the prismatics of the Post-Impressionist Exhibition of 1910 and build
up to the solar eclipse of 1927, but this would be to dispel the very qualities of
Woolf's 'moment' my argument explores.

> Yet what composed the present moment? If you are young, the future lies
> upon the present, like a piece of glass, making it tremble and quiver. If you
> are old, the past lies upon the present, like a thick glass, making it waver,
> distorting it. All the same, everybody believes that the present is something,

seeks out different elements in this situation in order to compose the truth of it, the whole of it.[3]

By beginning with a focus on 1927, we encounter Woolf *in medias res*, at the heart of her writing career. In 1910 it had barely begun. The events of 1910 gain significance in the first part of my study as a 'waver' upon the moment of 1927, before being explored in the second part from a different perspective. Whereas Part One comprises an extensive and comparative close reading of samples of Woolf's writing (focusing on a diary entry and an essay, with excursions into other texts), Part Two adopts a more varied approach. Beginning with a contextualizing account of the emergence and development of theories of Post-Impressionism in 1910 and 1912, it concludes by returning, in the light of these theories, to Woolf's writing of the late 1920s and early 1930s, with readings of two novels, *To the Lighthouse* and *The Waves*. My exploration of the moment in 1927, therefore, necessitates an excursus into the earlier moment of 1910: the impetus for the investigation of Post-Impressionism arises from Woolf's reflections on it in the 1920s (after all it was 'on or about' 1924 that Woolf declared the significance of 1910). Part One's discussion of the 1927 eclipse, accordingly, makes some preliminary connections with the events of 1910; and Part Two's survey of Post-Impressionism prompts further consideration of aspects of the eclipse. The nature of Woolf's moment, then, enables (and encourages) us to explore other, past and future moments in ways that obedience to linear chronology would make less accessible.

As the choice of material suggests, I am not attempting a comprehensive reading of Woolf's œuvre, nor a systematic reading of her novels: I will tend to investigate writings and events *between* novels. Nor are my findings necessarily to be considered a paradigm for such a reading (although my study closes with readings of two novels). Nor do I claim to establish a totalizing Woolfian philosophy. I do, however, seek to understand some of the feminist implications of Woolf's aesthetics at the heart of her writing career.

Woolf's much cited essay, 'The Moment: Summer's Night' (c.1929), provides an appropriate point at which to interrupt the broad issues of Woolf criticism I contest. Under its rubric of one moment (albeit the duration of a 'Summer's Night'), the essay unfolds a series of moments and explores the moment itself as a site of many other moments, of intersecting narratives, of physical sensation, of imaginative realization, individually and collectively experienced. 'The present moment', Woolf tells us 'is largely composed of visual and of sense impressions.' (*M* 9) In response to the heat of the day,

> the surface of the body is opened, as if all the pores were open and everything lay exposed, not sealed and contracted, as in cold weather. . . . Then the sense of light sinking back into darkness seems to be gently putting out with a

damp sponge the colour in one's own eyes. . . . But this moment is also composed of a sense that the legs of the chair are sinking through the centre of the earth, passing through the rich garden earth; they sink, weighted down. Then the sky loses its colour perceptibly and a star here and there makes a point of light.

(*M* 9)

Hermione Lee's observation, with reference to this essay, that Woolf's moments so often involve images of illumination and reflection,[4] is confirmed here by the 'sense of light sinking back into darkness', and the sensual references to colour and points of starlight. Differing somewhat from Lee's emphasis, my study will examine Woolf's manipulation of an imagery of light, dark and colour.

Fleetingly, in 'The Moment', the moment is registered as something beyond human control, something we may witness but not affect: 'One becomes aware that we are spectators and also passive participants in a pageant. And as nothing can interfere with the order, we have nothing to do but accept, and watch.' (*M* 9–10) With reference to this material, Woolf's art is often characterized as impressionistic – 'a process of strenuously fixing such moments and trying to turn them into narrative'[5] – and her much quoted literary dictum to 'look within' is also often considered to support such interpretations. The process of 'fixing' is one that 'Modern Fiction', the essay in which it appears, addresses:

Look within and life, it seems, is very far from being "like this". Examine for a moment an ordinary mind on an ordinary day. The mind receives a myriad impressions – trivial, fantastic, evanescent, or engraved with the sharpness of steel. From all sides they come, an incessant shower of innumerable atoms. . . . Is it not the task of the novelist to convey this varying, this unknown and uncircumscribed spirit, whatever aberration or complexity it may display, with as little mixture of the alien and external as possible?

(*CR* 189)

There is a paradox here in the dual aim of showing both the fluid and the fragmentary nature of experience, both the flow of time and one instant. The process of writing becomes a struggle to capture the subjective flux of experience and reproduce it for the reader in a fixed moment or image. 'To render these moments of being in their entirety', it has been suggested, 'to describe them so that the reader was placed in the very center of the consciousness experiencing the moment – receiving from all sides the shower of atoms as they fell, those myriad impressions of perception and emotion – was [Woolf's] task as she saw it.'[6]

Such critical responses are imbued with the theories of Henri Bergson which have been widely and variously employed in the characterization of the Woolfian moment. While not every one would go so far as Shiv Kumar's large claim that 'all her literary experiments as a novelist can be explained in terms of Bergson's *la durée*', the parallel remains strong in much work on Woolf.[7] *La durée* may be briefly defined as subjective, psychological, non-spatial, time. True time is, then, impenetrable and seamlessly continuous, only existing within, subjectively: 'Outside ourselves we should find only space, and consequently nothing but simultaneities.' Bergson speaks of 'two different selves . . . one of which is . . . the external projection of the other, its spatial and . . . social representation'; but the more 'fundamental' of which is connected to *la durée* and is therefore 'free'. It is reached 'by deep introspection'. Bergson emphasizes that only in 'rare moments' do we have access to *la durée* and to our true selves, and that only in such moments may we 'act freely'.[8]

Such a concept of freedom is at odds with theories which seek political freedom in the spatial, the historical and 'the real world'. Bergsonian readings of Woolf, then, risk discounting such elements in her work. But it is sensible to acknowledge that Bergson's 'rare moments' of introspection do often seem similar to Woolf's; and his suggestion of an inner illumination casting its 'colourless shadow' into the external world may also inform Woolf's 'luminous halo' imagery (*CR* 189).[9] Such similarities, I suggest, may cause us to overlook more materialist aspects. To characterize all of Woolf's writing in terms of the 'continuous movement of inner life' and the 'laval flow' of 'perceptions, memories and sensations'[10] is to risk its homogenization into an unbroken record of life as inner flux, and of existence primarily as passive, subjective and ahistorical. James Hafley, who finds Woolf 'a better artist than Bergson is a philosopher', in his sustained Bergsonian interpretation of her work, nevertheless, cautions: 'Woolf is not to be explained away by one word, "Bergsonism" or any other.'[11] Indeed, Tony Inglis in 1977 notes that for some time in Woolf studies 'pondered reading and critical accounts [have] tended to show that Woolf's novels are better read as weapons against flux than as inert surrenders to it.'[12] But these are not necessarily historical or materialist in approach; and Inglis does not mention in his optimistic survey the then emergent feminist slant in Woolf studies.

It is not my concern to establish the accuracy or otherwise of Woolf's, or of Woolf criticism's, understanding of Bergson, but rather to comment on how the invocation of Bergson has more often tended to encourage readings of Woolf's work which neglect its feminist import, for all that the gendered metaphysical dualisms[13] of this 'feminine philosopher of the flux'[14] may anticipate her fraught concept of androgyny.[15] Bergson's *durée* denies 'genuine historical experience', as Walter Benjamin observes, and is 'estranged from history.'[16] Bergson locates 'freedom' in subjective intuition, which although potentially inspiring as a site of utopian vision, remains cut off from the spatial, material and historical 'real world', the site in fact of feminist struggle.

Woolf herself, furthermore, brings to bear an emphatically materialist ana-lysis in her feminist tract, *A Room of One's Own*, the very title of which suggests a concern with the *spatial* location of the self. If her demand for 'a room of one's own' seems to cast Woolf as a literary Greta Garbo, it is not necessarily to be taken as a demand for the non-spatial introspective solitude of Bergsonian duration, which is at odds with the essay's inquiry into the material and external factors in the production of writing by women. Fiction is characterized spa-tially and materially: it is a web 'attached to grossly material things, like health and money and the houses we live in' (*AROO* 62–63). Art, according to Karl Kraus, 'can come only from denial. Only from anguished protest.'[17] Similarly, fiction for Woolf is the 'work of suffering human beings' (*AROO* 62–63). She also declares that in a room of one's own 'interruptions there will always be' (*AROO* 117): introspective solitude, then, is broken into by 'an abrasive external world'.[18] This sense of material intervention (rather than retreat into isolation), I suggest, is central to an understanding of Woolf's luminous moment.

At one point in 'The Moment' (interestingly, not one critics have examined closely), Woolf exposes a moment of illumination as also one of oppression, and as, therefore, one to be interrupted:

> Then a light is struck; in it appears a sunburnt face, lean, blue-eyed, and the arrow flies as the match goes out:
> "He beats her every Saturday; from boredom, I should say; not drink; there's nothing else to do."
> The moment runs like quicksilver on a sloping board into the cottage parlour; there are the tea things on the table . . . and Liz comes in and John catches her a blow on the side of her head as she slopes past him, dirty, with her hair loose and one hairpin sticking out about to fall. And she moans in a chronic animal way; and the children look up and then make a whistling noise to imitate the engine which they trail across the flags; and John sits himself down with a thump at the table and carves a hunk of bread and munches because there is nothing to be done. A steam rises from his cabbage patch. Let us do something then, something to end this horrible moment, this plausible glistening moment that reflects in its smooth sides this intolerable kitchen, this squalor; this woman moaning; and the rattle of the toy on the flags, and the man munching. Let us smash it by breaking a match. There – snap.

> (*M* 12)

In advocating the smashing of this 'horrible moment' of illumination, Woolf seems also to advocate the rupture of the oppressive social and familial relations it brings: there must be an end to 'this woman moaning', and an end in a wider sense to the subjugation of women. The passage is introduced by the striking and extinguishing of a match, perhaps suggesting that its light not only illuminates or reveals the scene, but also in some sense causes it. Enlightenment, then, is seen to cause, or even to be constructed out of suffering (its dark side, perhaps); and here seems dominated by male violence. Snapping the match, the pun on which suggests the ending of the marriage, may be interpreted as a refusal to see what the light reveals, but also perhaps as a veto on its very construction. The children's imitation of 'the engine which they trail across the flags' insidiously suggests the possibility (or even likelihood) of their imitating also the violent habits of their father and the bleak submission of their mother. It is this oppressive tradition (figuratively and literally) that the reader is invited to join in stopping, in terms which also dramatize the very act of reading: 'Let us smash it by breaking a match. There – snap.'

For Jean Guiguet, however, this scene is 'a finely graphic, realistic sketch, the suggestive power of which in its squalor is just as intolerable to the reader as to those in whose mind it has risen'. His reasons for finding it 'intolerable' remain unclear: Guiguet seems to suggest that its lack of aesthetic appeal causes the scene's banishment, while offering no discussion of its social and political impact. Woolf's sense of collective agency signalled in 'Let us smash . . .' is neutralized by Guiguet's emphasis on the moment's passive dissolution: 'Thus it dissolves as it was born and the moment smoothly ebbs to its original mood of muffled sounds and blurred shapes, fraught with peace and harmony.'[19] Guiguet reduces the depiction of the woman's suffering to an exercise in aesthetic technique; the injunction to end it correspondingly signals his failure to acknowledge the political import of the very realism he admires. As alarmingly, Madeline Moore, ignoring John's violence towards his wife, suggests this passage as an example of 'the negative moment when one becomes aware of the obduracy of matter and material objects'.[20]

'In every era', observes Benjamin, 'the attempt must be made anew to wrest tradition away from a conformism that is about to overpower it.'[21] Woolf's writing here may be viewed as just such an attempt, for it does more than record subjective impressions, or represent the Bergsonian flow of life: it seeks to intervene in life, and change it. My interpretation rests on close and detailed attention to Woolf's writing practice. The pun on 'match' in the passage above, for example, may be regarded as pivotal in locating Woolf's proposed site of change in the social, 'real world', and not just in the aesthetic vision. The injunction to 'smash the moment' is nevertheless one which speaks clearly to both realms (art and life), and in so doing connects them.

The tension between spatial or social experience and that of the life flux is subtly exploited by Jane Harrison, an underestimated influence on Woolf's thought and a significant, if elliptical, presence in *A Room of One's Own* ('a bent figure, formidable yet humble, with her great forehead and shabby dress – could it be the famous scholar . . . ?' (*AROO* 26)).[22] In *Themis: A Study of the Social Origins of Greek Religion*, Bergson's *durée* is acknowledged as bringing definition to the author's understanding of Dionysos as 'the attempt to express . . . that life which is one, indivisible and yet ceaselessly changing.' Harrison understands ancient Greek religion in terms of social structure and convention, distinguishing between the 'poles' of 'Natural Order' and 'Social Order'. 'Social Order, morality, "goodness" is not in nature at the outset', she warns, and, citing Bergson, questions their location in the *durée*:

> The mystic will claim that life is one indivisible movement, one, if he prefers it, ever accumulating snowball. We gladly agree. But to say that Alpha is Omega, the end is as the beginning, that life and force are the same as moral good . . . is to darken counsel. It is to deny that very change and movement which *is* life, it is to banish from a unified and sterilized universe "l'Évolution Créatrice".[23]

The social and moral pole in Woolf's alleged 'Bergsonism', I am suggesting, has not received the attention shown to her celebrated allusions to the flux; and with this in mind we might interpret her 'Bergsonism' rather differently. For example, an early and hostile critic of Woolf, characterizing her technique as 'essentially static', also finds what we might identify as Bergsonian qualities in her prose, and takes exception in terms which, emphasized differently, are relevant to the development of my argument:

> A single moment is isolated and forms a unit for the sensibility to work on. The difficulty lies in relating the various moments. . . . Everything receives the same slightly strained attention: the effect is not unlike that of a tempera painting, where there is exquisite delicacy of colour, but no light and shade. (The connection of this with the refusal to assent to a statement absolutely is too obvious to need any stressing.)[24]

M.C. Bradbrook focuses on Woolf's depiction of the single moment, which according to Bergsonian readings (for which Bradbrook appears to have little sympathy) paradoxically allows us special access to *la durée*; hence she sees in Woolf's prose a pointless subjective 'intensity'. Woolf offers no plot, that is no narrative impetus and, therefore, no sense of historical movement or morality. Bradbrook likens Woolf to a fastidious, 'myopic', painter capable of fine detail but with no overall sense of design: infatuated with technique, she has no 'statement' to make. 'Woolf refuses to be pinned down', she finds, '. . . and consequently she is debarred from narrative technique, since this implies a schema of values, or even from direct presentation of powerful feelings or major situations.'[25] Woolf's writing so focuses on the present moment, it remains outside narrative progression, and, therefore, seems without historical awareness and without a sense of value (moral or aesthetic). We may find, however, history and value not 'debarred' from Woolf's moment but actually signalled in the very imagery Bradbrook finds so static.

Bradbrook's painting simile alludes to the aestheticism she finds distasteful in Woolf's work, but it also identifies an important point about Woolf's management of light, shade and colour which my study will explore more fully. She finds stylistically flattening Woolf's replacement of the traditional handling of light and shade (chiaroscuro) with a mosaic of colour. In this analogy Bradbrook assumes a 'schema of values', that is the combined moral and aesthetic evaluations of light and shade, traditionally inscribed in Western thought: light denotes positive or good values, shade negative or evil. She censures Woolf's use of colour as evading this traditional 'schema of values'. This compositional neglect of light and shade for myriad pinpoints of exquisite colour may not necessarily constitute 'the refusal to assent to statement' that Bradbrook finds it. On the contrary, Woolf's deployment of colour may, I contend, offer the basis of a coded articulation of historical intervention. Furthermore, when light and shade are evaluated with reference to gender and subjectivity, Woolf's departure from traditional chiaroscuro, as I will explore, may be seen as a positive and feminist statement.

Woolf's work is often cited to exemplify a dominant view of modernism as an impressionistic, Bergsonian approach to art, identified in narrative techniques engaged with 'the uninterruptible, indistinguishable flow of time'.[26] Malcolm Bradbury and James McFarlane, who do acknowledge Woolf's understanding that 'the modern stylistic revolution came from the historical opportunity for change in human relationships and human character, and that modern art therefore had a social and epistemological *cause*', conclude, not that Woolf's work is bound up with historical change or interested in historical intervention, but, on the contrary, that she 'nonetheless believed in the aesthetic nature of the opportunity':

> it set the artist free to be more himself, let him move beyond the kingdom of necessity to the kingdom of light. Now human consciousness and especially *artistic* consciousness could become more intuitive, more poetic; art could fulfil *itself*. It was free to catch at the manifold – the atoms as they fall – and create significant harmony not in the universe but within itself (like the painting which Lily Briscoe completes at the end of *To the Lighthouse*).[27]

The artistic freedom they identify seems close to Bergson's rare moments of subjective freedom which allow the self 'to get back into pure duration'. In their reading, Woolf's art, like that of James Joyce, comprises 'the means to transcend both history and reality'.[28] With the phrase 'significant harmony', moreover, Bradbury and McFarlane link this Bergsonian idea of aesthetic withdrawal from the world to an echo of the aesthetics of Roger Fry and Clive Bell, commonly summarized under the heading of 'Significant Form'.

This Bergsonian connection with Bloomsbury aesthetics, which may tend to foreground Woolf's aesthetics at the expense of her politics (and indeed to see it as a retreat from politics altogether), is not unusual in Woolf criticism, as Allen McLaurin's work demonstrates.[29] Relating Woolf's work primarily to the theories of Roger Fry, he invokes as a link the Bergsonian study by Woolf's sister-in-law, Karin Stephen.[30] Interestingly, McLaurin focuses on Stephen's discussion of colour and change in relation to Bergson's theories to reinforce his own reading of Woolf's psychological and impressionistic use of colour.[31] My argument will discover in Woolf's writing the possibility of an interventionist and feminist understanding of colour, more readily associated with aspects of Post-Impressionism than Impressionism.

There remain views of modernism which contend with those such as Bradbury's and McFarlane's; and Woolf's smashing of the moment may find a more appropriate fit with notions of 'modernist disruption or interruption'.[32] Her fragmentary texts, then, may be read not merely as passively reflecting fragmentary experience, but also as actively engaging in fragmentation and intervention. Woolf's interruption of the moment is not one which characterizes subjectivity as grounded according to exclusive sexual identity: it does not intervene on a purely masculine subjectivity, replacing it with a purely feminine one. Her inclusive plea 'let us smash it' is signalled, not as an invitation to women only, but as a collective impetus to alter the moment and thus alleviate women's suffering. This 'horrible moment' shows not the previous exclusion of the feminine from the patriarchal domain, but its occlusion and oppression within it. Woolf dramatizes this point in *A Room of One's Own*, where she does describe an intervention by a woman:

> One goes into the room – but the resources of the English language would be much put to the stretch, and whole flights of words would need to wing their way illegitimately into existence before a woman could say what happens when she goes into a room. . . . One has only to go into any room in any street for the whole of that extremely complex force of femininity to fly in one's face. How should it be otherwise? For women have sat indoors all these millions of years, so that by this time the very walls are permeated by their creative force.
>
> (*AROO* 131)

For Peggy Kamuf this passage 'creates a disturbance on both sides of the threshold of subjectivity', as Woolf shows how the entering woman encounters femininity 'fly[ing] in one's face'. It is a 'double figure of self-interruption':

there is both a recognition and an infringement of the place of a creative subject which is no longer or not yet a "one". The feminine "subject" is here constituted through illegitimate intervention in the language since its "one-ness" resides already in the other's place, its unity derives retrospectively from an infraction which flies in the face of the grammatical order of subject and predicate.[33]

The intervention of a woman, then, described by a woman, requires the invention of new literary codings – which may yet derive from the spaces already marked out by patriarchy for (and as) the feminine. Out of the ruins of the smashed legitimate language of subjectivity emerges a new language of feminism, winging its way with 'whole flights of words . . . illegitimately into existence'.

I will investigate Woolf's handling of the basic vocabulary of such a language, that is, its central tropes of subjectivity – light, shade and colour – at two important moments: first, in her depictions of the solar eclipse of 1927, which emerges not so much as a moment in touch with the Bergsonian *durée*, but as a transitional moment of feminist challenge and change; second, in her engagement with the theories of Post-Impressionism which are examined contextually with an emphasis not on abstract aesthetics and significant form but on materialist, interventionist, feminism. I identify two interrelated spheres of colourism informing Woolf's aesthetic: suffrage art and English Post-Impressionism. This undertaking, I should warn any latter-day Bradbrooks among prospective readers, necessitates a non-linear approach and involves some fairly intensive phases of close-reading, but does not, I hope, result in myopia. Close attention to Woolf's language is rewarded by vistas onto Bradbrook's requisite 'powerful feelings' and 'major situations'. Exploring closely Woolf's new language of feminism in relation to the new colourist languages of suffragism and Post-Impressionism, this study concludes with readings of *To the Lighthouse* and *The Waves* as (different) moments in a modernist discourse of interruption.

PART ONE

Eclipse

2 Virginia Woolf: heliotropics, subjectivity and feminism

At the back of us were great blue spaces in the cloud. These were still blue. But now the colour was going out. The clouds were turning pale; a reddish black colour. Down in the valley it was an extraordinary scrumble of red & black; there was the one light burning; all was cloud down there, & very beautiful, so delicately tinted. Nothing could be seen through the cloud. The 24 seconds were passing. Then one looked back again at the blue; & rapidly, very very quickly, all the colours faded; it became darker & darker as at the beginning of a violent storm; & we thought now it is over – this is the shadow when suddenly the light went out. We had fallen. It was extinct. There was no colour. The earth was dead. That was the astonishing moment: & the next when as if a ball had rebounded, the cloud took colour on itself again, only a sparky aetherial colour & so the light came back. I had very strongly the feeling as the light went out of some vast obeisance; something kneeling down, & low & suddenly raised up, when the colours came. They came back astonishingly lightly & quickly & beautifully in the valley & over the hills – at first with a miraculous glittering & aetheriality, later normally almost, but with a great sense of relief. It was like a recovery. We had been much worse than we had expected. We had seen the world dead. This was within the power of nature. Our greatness had been apparent too.

(*D* III 143–144)

Shortly after dawn on Wednesday 29 June 1927 Virginia Woolf witnessed the total eclipse of the sun. In personal and professional terms this 'astonishing moment' came very much *in medias res*: Woolf was then approaching the zenith of her literary career – she had just published *To the Lighthouse* a month before, and was already making preparations for *Orlando, A Room of One's Own,* and *The Waves.* Her reputation as an essayist had been consolidated with the publication of *The Common Reader* two years earlier. The eclipse of the sun was clearly of great significance to Woolf: she recorded it in her diary, drew upon it for an essay, 'The Sun and the Fish',[1] and rewrote it (in many drafts) for her closing meditation on 'the world seen without a self' in *The Waves* (*W* 310ff.). A landscape described in *Orlando* also seems to be drawn from the event (*O* 21). More intriguingly, in 'Sympathy', a story apparently 'written in the spring of 1919',[2] Woolf makes an extended simile of 'an eclipse of the sun' (*CSF* 109) which bears many resemblances to 'the astonishing moment' described here. I begin with this moment because it focuses Woolf's engagement with light, the central concern of this study. Part One will compare and closely reflect on two eclipse texts by Woolf: her diary entry and the essay, 'The Sun and the Fish'.

Photology and feminism

Jacques Derrida has called 'the metaphor of darkness and light (of self-revelation and self-concealment), the founding metaphor of Western philosophy as metaphysics. The founding metaphor not only because it is a photological one – and in this respect the entire history of our philosophy is a photology, the name given to a history of, or treatise on, light – but because it is a metaphor'.[3] Woolf has said that 'metaphors are necessary directly you deal with thought' (*RN* 109), but it seems that to discover a photological trope is merely to discover a commonplace. Yet in Woolf's work 'the heliotrope'[4] is much more than this:[5] her novels *Night and Day* and *To the Lighthouse* pay it eponymous homage; Rachel Vinrace's death is linked to the heat of the sun in *The Voyage Out*; the refrain 'Fear no more the heat o' the sun',[6] haunts *Mrs Dalloway*; solar passages punctuate *The Waves*; and Woolf's famous dictum conforms to it: 'Life is not a series of gig lamps symmetrically arranged; life is a luminous halo, a semi-transparent envelope surrounding us from the beginning of consciousness to the end.' (*CR* 189) Singled out in her notebook is Sir Thomas Browne's observation (in *Urn Burial*): 'Life is pure flame – we live by an invisible sun within us.' (*BERG* 13, *RN* 1.25) Woolf's writing seems extraordinarily photological; her predilection for the luminous is everywhere debated.[7]

Woolf's evaluative description of light, dark and colour at the moment of solar eclipse, furthermore, comprises a challenge to some deconstructive interpretations of her work. Her diary entry depicts the world without the sun, without light, and without colour: a condition not cherished by the author. Darkness, it seems, is not to be celebrated – except as a foil against which to revel in the re-emergence of light and colour. Reinscribed here is a traditional hierarchical binary opposition: light/dark (where light is positive, dark negative). It complies with the most traditional primary order of binary oppositions identified by some feminists as complicit with 'the death-dealing binary oppositions of masculinity and femininity'.[8] These oppositions originate in the first sublime moment in Genesis when 'God said, Let there be light: and there was light. And God saw the light, that it was good: and God divided the light from the darkness.'[9] From this first act of division, Julia Kristeva demonstrates, follow all other divisions, including that between the sexes:

Yahweh Elohim created the world and concluded alliances by *dividing* (*karath*) light from darkness, the waters of the heavens from the waters of the earth, the earth from the seas, the creatures of the water from the creatures of the air, the animals each according to their kind and man (in His own image) from himself. It's also by division that He places them opposite each other: man and woman. . . . Divided from man, made of that very thing which is lacking in him, the biblical woman will be wife, daughter or sister, or all of them at once, but she will rarely have a name.[10]

In asking '*Where is she?*', Hélène Cixous has questioned woman's traditional place in the binary oppositions proliferating from this first:

> Activity/passivity,
> Sun/Moon,
> Culture/Nature,
> Day/Night,
>
> Father/Mother,
> Head/heart,
> Intelligible/sensitive,
> Logos/Pathos.
>
> Form, convex, step, advance, seed, progress.
> Matter, concave, ground – which supports the step, receptacle.
>
> Man
> ———
> Woman[11]

Light, and particularly its first source, the sun, is traditionally the province of the masculine, never the feminine. Freud held the 'view that the sun is a symbol of the father', so much so that 'symbolism overrides grammatical gender – at least so far as German goes, for in most other languages the sun is masculine. Its counterpart in this picture of the two parents is "Mother Earth" as she is generally called.'[12] This binary opposition, deeply embedded in all our cultural practices, is fundamental to our thought processes: 'Always the same metaphor: we follow it, it transports us, in all of its forms, wherever a discourse is organized.'[13] Genevieve Lloyd has examined Western philosophy from Plato to Sartre for its treatment and construction of the 'feminine' as something excluded and transcended by (masculine) reason: 'the feminine has been associated with what rational knowledge transcends, dominates or simply leaves behind'.[14] She charts the subtle variations and developments of philosophy's exclusion of the feminine from reason's light.

Inspired by Derrida's 'critique of binary logic [and of] . . . the static closure of the binary opposition', feminists are encouraged to deconstruct binary oppositions and celebrate *différance* and the free play of the signifier: 'Against any binary scheme of thought, Cixous sets multiple, heterogeneous *difference.*' Woolf, furthermore, has been rediscovered as a deconstructor of binary oppositions *par excellence.*[15] She subversively disrupts all fixed oppositions; her texts exemplify and celebrate the free play of the signifier. Toril Moi recommends, therefore, a cocktail of Derridean and Kristevan theories to assist feminist literary criticism in reconciling Woolf's aesthetic practice to her politics.

Makiko Minow-Pinkney also reads Woolf's work through the theories of Kristeva and Derrida, and finds Woolf's 'concept of androgyny' compatible with deconstructive notions of subjectivity. Woolf argues against 'an Enlightenment universalism which defines humanity as disembodied Reason and reduces sexual difference to a merely phenomenal form'. Woolf's concept of androgyny is 'the rejection of sameness. It aims to cultivate difference on an individual level, in the teeth of a cultural impulse to reduce the two sexes into something which is seemingly neither, but in actuality male.'[16] But while Kristeva's and Cixous's engagements with binary oppositions make useful analytical tools, we would have to read considerably against the grain of Woolf's texts, I suggest, in order to concur with Moi's and Minow-Pinkney's findings. Just as I have found Derrida's identification of photological tropes a critical stimulus without necessarily adopting a 'Derridean' reading, so I have also found useful some aspects of 'French feminism' in the interrogation of Woolf's texts: but I come to a different understanding of Woolf's manipulation of oppositions than any predicted by Moi. This is where Woolf's account of the solar eclipse becomes so significant – and so intriguing. Although my choice of this apparently ephemeral piece as a way into Woolf may be thought of as a typically deconstructive tactic, my reading is not deconstructive: it pays attention to context as much as textuality.

The sun may be regarded as the primary metaphorical instance of patriarchal supremacy (perhaps 'the Absolute Subject'),[17] as the very light of masculine subjectivity which, from Genesis on, has cast femininity in its shadow, relegating woman to darkness and chaos. Luce Irigaray engages the solar terminology of the 'Copernican revolution' to examine subjectivity and gender:

> by centring man outside himself, it has occasioned above all man's ex-stasis within the transcendental (subject). . . . Exiling himself ever further (toward) where the greatest power lies, he thus becomes the "sun" if it is around him that things turn, a pole of attraction stronger than the "earth." Meanwhile, the excess in this universal fascination is that "she" also turns upon herself, that she knows how to re-turn (upon herself) but not how to seek outside for identity within the other: nature, sun, God . . . (woman).[18]

Woolf herself alludes to a similar Copernican model of the subject in her discussion of 'a new novel by Mr. A':

But after reading a chapter or two a shadow seemed to lie across the page. It was like a straight dark bar, a shadow shaped something like the letter "I". One began dodging this way and that to catch a glimpse of the landscape behind it. Whether that was indeed a tree or a woman walking I was not quite sure. Back one was always hailed to the letter "I". One began to tire of "I". Not but what this "I" was a most respectable "I"; honest and logical; as hard as a nut, and polished for centuries by good teaching and good feeding. I respect and admire that "I" from the bottom of my heart. But – here I turned a page or two looking for something or other – the worst of it is that in the shadow of the letter "I" all is shapeless as mist. Is that a tree? No, it is a woman. But . . . she has not a bone in her body, I thought, watching Phoebe, for that was her name, coming across the beach. Then Alan got up and the shadow of Alan at once obliterated Phoebe.

(*AROO* 149, 150; Woolf's ellipsis)

The light of the masculine 'I' casts the feminine into its earthy shadow: the woman-reader discerns lurking in the mists of this shadow the figure of a woman. Phoebe is associated with the object world of the landscape, the tree, and the darkness. Yet her name, which means 'the bright one', suggests she may also be a source of light. But there is only one sun in the solar system, and it is masculine: Phoebe is sometimes the name given to the moon whose light is merely a reflection of the sun's. According to optical logic, moreover, we might read the 'dark bar' of the masculine 'I' as a phallic shadow blocking the light of the (woman) reader; and this undermines the notion of masculine enlightenment, paradoxically transferring the ⌐ttribute of light from masculine to feminine in suggesting that the male ego has cut off the woman-reader from her own light, just as Alan's shadow obliterates Phoebe.

This is at once a vision of possible feminine enlightenment, and a model of oppressive solar masculinity which keeps the feminine in its shade as object. In describing woman both as a source of light and as imprisoned in shadow, this passage shows how women's place historically has been conceptually marked out (or inscribed) as shadow by the discourse of masculine enlighten-ment, and how women's emancipation yet lies with the very illumination of this shadow. Within the figure of masculine solar subjectivity, then, we may find the seeds of feminist enlightenment. (In general my argument is concerned with this conceptual (or discourse-based), rather than literal or optical, model of light and shade.)

Woolf relates Alan's overcoming of Phoebe in sexual terms: 'For Alan had views and Phoebe was quenched in the flood of his views. And then Alan, I thought, has passions. . . . It took place on the beach under the sun. It was done very openly. It was done very vigorously. Nothing could have been more indecent.' (*AROO* 150–151) Phoebe is physically overwhelmed, an object dominated by

Alan, *the* subject. Mr. A's novel is 'bor[ing]', Woolf asserts, 'because of the dominance of the letter "I" and the aridity, which, like the giant beech tree, it casts within its shade. Nothing will grow there.' (*AROO* 151) This model of solar, masculine subjectivity has no space for a feminine subject to flourish. Indeed, Woolf ironically suggests that women's attempts to change this model are responsible for Mr. A's new, reinforced, 'sex-consciousness': 'The Suffrage campaign was no doubt to blame.' (*AROO* 149)

Woolf's allusion to the historical and political context of the suffrage movement in connection with photological tropes of subjectivity will be broadly taken up in my study. I will be arguing for contextual readings of Woolf's texts, suggesting a more complicated, contextually sensitive, engagement with solar subjectivity than may follow from the notion that 'binary oppositions and hierarchies . . . are ceaselessly undone'[19] in her work.

Woolf's luminous feminism, then, is pitched against the model of subjectivity represented by the 'unjustified solar male'[20] and arid feminine darkness delineated in *A Room of One's Own*, a patriarchal viewpoint she presents as dominant in the closing passage of her first novel:

> All these voices sounded gratefully in St John's ears as he lay half-asleep, and yet vividly conscious of everything around him. Across his eyes passed a procession of objects, black and indistinct, the figures of people picking up their books, their cards, their balls of wool, their work-baskets, and passing him one after another on their way to bed.
>
> (*VO* 458)

Conceptually, the masculine solar light of St John's semi-consciousness at this moment of muted 'revelation' renders everything else – people and objects – as shadows. The novel shows how Rachel Vinrace withers to death in such solar light.

A priority for Woolf's feminism, then, might well lie in abolishing the solar model of subjectivity, in 'dispersing, piercing those metaphors – particularly the photological ones – which have constituted truth by the premises of Western philosophy'.[21] Yet in her diary account of the eclipse, Woolf does not disrupt oppositions of light and dark, as Moi would expect; nor does she seem to offer here a feminist counter to photological metaphors so much as reinforce them. When Woolf witnesses the solar eclipse, we might expect from this apparent arch-feminist deconstructor of oppositions some signal of her awareness of such implications, or at least something more positive than 'We had fallen.' This would surely be a moment to celebrate as positive the darkness, the body, the earth, and all that, alongside the feminine, has been obscured and oppressed by the light of day. It might also be a moment to release light and dark from fixed dichotomies and values, and to assert endlessly transgressive readings of these terms. Yet this is not the case. Light seems reinscribed un-problematically as positive, dark as negative.

If we are not to find Woolf in sympathy with patriarchy, then, we might rethink our analysis of her engagement with oppositions. Woolf's accounts of the eclipse provide ideal material for an investigation of this engagement since they unavoidably address the founding binary opposition of light and dark, out of which all other oppositions are seen to arise. What is of interest is whether in adopting a *hierarchized* opposition, Woolf is in fact guilty of main-taining patriarchal values. Connected to this, and of equal concern to femin-ists, are the questions of subjectivity and reason. If Woolf maintains positive photological metaphors, or engages heliotropic discourses, she may be guilty of reinscribing the notions of masculine subjectivity and reason which, from Plato to the present, have so effectively excluded the feminine. This is where deconstructive models of subjectivity are appealing. Judith Butler has argued for the political necessity of such an approach in order to resolve 'the political problem that feminism encounters in the assumption that the term *women* denotes a common identity. Rather than a stable signifier that commands the assent of those whom it purports to describe and represent, *women*, even in the plural, has become a troublesome term, a site of contest, a cause for anxiety.' Butler concludes the 'internal paradox of this foundationalism is that it pre-sumes, fixes, and constrains the very "subjects" that it hopes to represent and liberate'.[22] Woolf, however, was writing at a time when public acknowledge-ment of women as citizen-subjects was still being sought – the full enfranchise-ment of women in Britain came in 1928, the year after the eclipse.

'To the extent that feminist politics is bound up with a specific constitu-ency or subject, namely, women', Christine Di Stefano argues with understand-able disquiet, 'the postmodernist prohibition against subject-centred inquiry and theory undermines the legitimacy of a broad-based organized movement dedicated to articulating and implementing the goals of such a constituency.'[23] Feminism needs (the necessary fiction of) a stable subject to function, and to acknowledge the historical inscriptions of such subjectivities. 'Women – but are you not sick to death of the word?' exclaims Woolf: 'I can assure you that I am.' (*AROO* 167) Her desire to ditch the category, 'Women', seems to anticipate Butler's more provisional, interactive sense of subjectivity: thinking 'poetically', Woolf figures woman as 'a vessel in which all sorts of spirits and forces are cours-ing and flashing perpetually' (*AROO* 66–67). But Woolf also incorporates into her model a contrary sense of the historically and materially specific, for as well as 'poetically', we must also think of woman 'prosaically': 'she is Mrs. Martin, aged thirty-six, dressed in blue, wearing a black hat and brown shoes' (*AROO* 66).

The assertion of an entirely separate, feminine reason is also fraught with paradoxes. Although 'rationality has been conceived as transcendence of the

feminine', it is also the case that 'the "feminine" itself has been partly constituted by its occurrence within this structure'. To seek a positive feminine realm
outside the light of masculine reason, then, is also no escape: 'The affirmation
of the value and importance of "the feminine" cannot of itself be expected to
shake the underlying normative structures, for, ironically, it will occur in a
space already prepared for it by the intellectual tradition it seeks to reject.'[24]

Enlightening the Enlightenment

It is modernity (the tradition of Enlightenment) that Jürgen Habermas has
credited with the potential 'to shake normative . . . structures'.[25] Pauline Johnson focuses the argument between modernity and postmodernism on the work
and critical reception of Woolf herself. First, she identifies the common ground
of Enlightenment rationality, feminism ('itself rooted in Enlightenment thinking') and modernism: 'Like the feminist, the modernist refuses to credit the
merely traditional with the authority of a "second nature". Both, in their various
capacities, offer a provocative challenge to the supposedly self-evident certain-
ties of unquestioned existence.'[26]

With reference to the 'Bloomsbury aesthetics' of Roger Fry and Clive Bell,
Johnson outlines the feminist-modernist position she ascribes to Woolf: 'Drawing on the modernist conception of the transcendent nature of the aesthetic,
Woolf's work articulates a conception of the ideal, emancipated self which presents a critical alternative to the oppressive, restricted experience of femininity
encountered in everyday life.' But on the other hand, she notes that Woolf's
'vision of an emancipated . . . self is conceived in terms of a mere aesthetic
sensibility.' Art stands separate from life as a vantage point from which to offer
critical or idealistic commentary; yet by virtue of its removal from life, it may
also be ineffectual. Johnson concludes, however, that 'at least [Woolf's] art does
preserve the protest at an unfree, subordinated femininity essential to a feminist outlook', and this is something 'sacrificed in the relativist perspective assimilated by a post-modern feminist aesthetic'. By taking the transcendentalism of
Bell and Fry as the defining influence on Woolf, Johnson is perhaps guilty of
creating a problem where none need exist. She continues on subjectivity and
the postmodern in the same vein as Lloyd and Di Stefano.[27]

Johnson, Lloyd and Di Stefano, all seem anxious to retain some aspects of
'the Enlightenment project' as fundamental to feminism, but as they themselves
acknowledge, feminism must also revolt against the 'norms' of the Enlightenment built on the exclusion and transcendence of the feminine. Such a revolt,
however, is not launched from outside Enlightenment thinking, but may be
seen as within the remit of the Enlightenment itself. In this sense feminism may

be a project for 'enlightening the Enlightenment', in the phrase of Habermas who suggests the arguments of postmodernity are constructed within the very discourse of reason they are supposed to reject.

To enlighten the Enlightenment for feminism is to remain within it but to somehow illuminate it anew, a project requiring the retention of light as a positive trope. Alternative, feminine, sources of illumination may, then, counter the singular, universal norm of the masculine. The continued valorization of light may also necessitate the maintenance of oppositions, rather than their abolishment. Habermas sees the dangers inherent in postmodernity's advocacy of the latter: 'Now the differences and oppositions are so undermined and even collapsed that critique can no longer discern contrasts, shadings, and ambivalent tones within the flat and faded landscape of a totally administered, calculated, and power-laden world.' Declaring the 'paradigm of the philosophy of consciousness' to be 'exhausted', Habermas seeks to replace 'the paradigm of the knowledge of objects' with 'the paradigm of mutual understanding between subjects capable of speech and action'.[28] He offers a model of 'communicative reason' instead of 'subject-centred reason'. This replaces 'the sort of objectifying attitude that an observer assumes toward entities in the external world' with 'a *different* relationship of the subject to itself': intersubjectivity.

It is not just the subject's understanding of self and the external world that changes, but the subject in relation to other subjects. Habermas's own argument here remains unenlightened with regard to gender and reinscribes the norm of subjectivity as already masculine. His model of contestive, intersubjectivity nevertheless has potential for feminism in its displacing of subject-centred reason: 'The ego stands within an interpersonal relationship that allows him to relate to himself as a participant in an interaction from the perspective of alter. . . . This reflection . . . escapes the kind of objectification inevitable from the reflexively applied perspective of the observer'.[29] Habermas's subject may appear masculine, but it is one no longer constructed according to the transcendence of the object world, and this is surely of interest to feminism.[30] The feminine appropriation of this model does not entail the reinscription of the *hierarchized* opposition between subject/object, man/woman. The solar model of subjectivity has been displaced by what we might call an interstellar model. With this in mind, we might contrast Mr. A's solar 'I' with Woolf's plural use of the first person singular in *A Room of One's Own*.

Woolf begins this work by claiming that ' "I" is only a convenient term for somebody who has no real being' (*AROO* 7). She then playfully resorts to using a trinity of female personae: 'Here then was I (call me Mary Beton, Mary Seton, Mary Carmichael or by any name you please – it is not a matter of any importance).' (*AROO* 8). In the course of the book, however, these women emerge as being far from interchangeable textual gaps; for Woolf weaves fictional biographical and historical snippets about them into her text (*AROO* 28, 56, 120ff). In doing so, she is enacting the advice given by Mary Beton to Mary Carmichael: 'Above all, you must illumine your own soul' (*AROO* 135). Mary Carmichael must address 'what happens when Olivia – this organism that has been under the shadow of the rock these million years – feels the light fall on it' (*AROO* 127). The 'I' of Woolf's text is constructed, not as the dominator of an object world, but in relation to a number of subjects. This 'I' also carries the trace of its own historical, object status: Mary Beton, Mary Seton, Mary Carmichael and their elided sister Mary Hamilton have been rescued from their balladic reputation for infanticide and refigured by Woolf.[31]

The project of *A Room of One's Own*, articulated through a contestive constellation of subjects addressing each other as well as the reader, includes the revelation of feminine experience, which is presented as a feminist act of enlightenment; the trope of light is maintained as positive, but no longer focused entirely on a singular solar model. Woolf exposes, then, a patriarchal model of light and dark which keeps feminine experience shrouded in darkness; but she also recommends a feminist literary project to reclaim the light for women. 'Women are beginning to explore their own sex, to write of women as women have never been written of before', she declares in 'Women and Fiction' (1929):

> For the first time this dark country is beginning to be explored in fiction; and at the same moment a woman has also to record the change in women's minds and habits which the opening of the professions has introduced. She has to observe how their lives are ceasing to run underground; she has to discover what new colours and shadows are showing in them now that they are exposed to the outer world.
>
> (*GR* 82)

Significantly, she describes the 'dark country' of the feminine emerging into the light from 'underground' in terms of 'new colour'. It is this prismatic exploration of the newly illuminated feminine that marks Woolf's innovatory feminist aesthetic.

Woolf's engagement with the aesthetics and (gender) politics of light and colour tropes, understood in historical and political contexts, seems to retain a notion of light as positive and dark as negative, but this does not amount to the reinscription of a necessarily patriarchal model of binary oppositions. Woolf may in fact do quite the reverse in reclaiming it for feminism. Distinguishing between patriarchal oppositions and Woolf's feminist oppositions, we might think of patriarchal oppositions as 'negations', and feminist ones as 'contraries'. 'Without Contraries is no progression', Blake declares: 'Attraction and Repulsion, Reason and Energy, Love and Hate, are necessary to Human existence.'[32] 'Negation', on the other hand, rigid and exclusive, is constructed out of 'a Selfhood which must be put off & annihilated away', and like patriarchal oppositions 'must be destroy'd to redeem the Contraries'.[33] Woolf's contraries, I suggest, maintain light as a positive metaphor of subjectivity and rationality but not as fixed and masculine. I will be examining the mythopœic significance of these terms in relation to her introduction (or rediscovery) of a feminine source of light.

Woolf's photology – mystical or rational?

Some feminist critics conclude that Woolf does indeed engage a positive and feminine light, but one that is also mystical. Jane Marcus, claiming Woolf was strongly influenced by the works of 'her aunt, Caroline Emilia Stephen, a great Quaker theologian', suggests: 'Woolf's work, like her aunt's, based religious and political stances on a celebration of celibacy and remade male repressive ideology into a feminist ideology of power.'[34] From Stephen's books,[35] Woolf learned 'to speak the language of light'.

Marcus makes the paradoxical case for a rational mysticism ('those mystical meditations . . . in Woolf's novels . . . are essentially rational'), but actually emphasizes the mystical at the expense of the rational. Associating Woolf's 'rationality' with the 'emotional' and 'psychological attachment to the rational' of the men in her life (her father, Leslie Stephen, and husband, Leonard Woolf), Marcus further undermines the very notion of rationality in a puzzling turn of argument: 'the language of the light' learned by Woolf is also a ' "little language", unknown to most men'. It is 'a female language of the light, a language of silence – acts of light and acts of silence.' This essentially mystical light, Marcus insists, is most true to Woolf the feminist. 'Woolf learned,' she concludes, 'to turn her lack of education to advantage; she trained herself to trust memory and inner voices.' Woolf learns, then, from her aunt that 'the daughters of educated men . . . can be mystics'.[36]

From the fact of Woolf's exclusion from Cambridge, Marcus draws the dangerous conclusion that Woolf lacked an education altogether. Her deprivation of the same educational advantages as her brother does not mean that she had no education at all. Marcus conveniently forgets Woolf was taught classical Greek and Latin, learnt several modern European languages, and was well schooled in literature, philosophy and history. She was considered educated enough to be employed as a teacher, and as a writer of articles and reviews for the serious press from youth onwards.

The silent light Marcus attributes to Woolf is worryingly ineffectual as an expression of the author's socialist-feminist views. But newly converted to the idea of a mystical Woolf, Marcus herself bears witness: 'As a feminist critic I had avoided the subject of Woolf's mysticism, and of *The Waves*, feeling that acknowledging her as a visionary was a trap that would allow her to be dismissed as another female crank, irrational and eccentric.'[37] Marcus is shown the light by Catherine Smith who 'asks us to study mysticism and feminism together',[38] referring us to Jane Lead (1624–1704), a Protestant mystic and spiritual autobiographer. Madeline Moore is struck by the account of Lead's 'vision [in April 1670] of "an over-shadowing bright Cloud and in the midst of it the Figure of a Woman."'[39] This is Lead's prophecy in composite: 'the great Wonder to come forth, A Woman Cloathed with the Sun . . . With the Globe of this world under her feet . . . with a Crown beset with stars, plainly declaring that to her is given the Command and Power . . . to create and generate spirits in her own express likeness.'[40] Moore compares Lead's woman in the sun with the 'deified sun goddess' (Moore's tautology)[41] in the *The Waves* (*W* 5). 'If there is a feminist collective unconscious', Marcus asserts, 'this figure was passed down to Woolf from her aunt Caroline and lives in Eleanor Pargiter and Lucy Swithin.'[42] This mystical, feminist interpretation reflects orthodox, aesthetic analysis of light in Woolf's work;[43] but does not account for Woolf's 'rich yellow flame of rational intercourse' (*AROO* 17).

While I agree that Woolf does indeed colonize the figure of the sun for feminism, and may well have made use of her aunt Caroline's luminous imagery, I am not convinced that this amounts to quasi-Quakerism or mysticism in her writing. Woolf (who called her aunt 'the quacking Quaker' (*L* 1 146)) engages a positive and prismatic, rational light, I suggest, one associated with the feminist movement, and indicative of a feminist project 'to enlighten the Enlightenment'. If Woolf's art is to be considered feminist, we must seek to locate, as Moi herself indicates, 'the politics of Woolf's writing *precisely in her textual practice*'.[44] Her photological textual practices, apparent in both literary and painterly references, may be more richly understood at the figurative level of metaphor and allegory, and in relation to historical and political context. It is with some irony, given her positive and prismatic engagement with photological tropes, that we may read Woolf's comment on Fry's *Vision and Design*: 'I think it reads rudimentary compared with Coleridge. Fancy reforming poetry by discovering something scientific about the composition of light!' (*D* 11 81) In some respects, Woolf, I will be suggesting, reforms fiction and poetic language for feminism with just such a discovery.

3   The astonishing moment

Part One's epigraph is from Woolf's diary entry of Thursday 30 June 1927, the day after that of the eclipse. It begins with the rather ominous imperative: 'Now I must sketch out the Eclipse'. But before we examine what follows, let us attempt to view this momentous event from a wider perspective, for the eclipse was an 'astonishing moment' to many people besides Virginia Woolf; and her eclipse accounts reflect these broader contexts as much as the more familiar subjective, abstract aesthetics invoked by some critics. This chapter will consider Woolf's diary entry in relation to other (scientific and popular) accounts of the eclipse, and suggest how its imagery is also drawn from passages in her earlier journals as well as from a Wordsworthian model of solar subjectivity.

Press coverage of the eclipse

As contemporary news coverage reveals, both before and after the event, the eclipse captured scientific and popular imagination alike. *The Times* devotes several columns to anticipating and recording the eclipse from both these perspectives. Two days before the eclipse, for example, it reports (alongside a story on the expulsion of Trotsky and Zinovieff from the central committee of the Communist Party) on both scientific and popular preparations for the first total eclipse of the sun to be visible from Britain in two hundred years. The central line of totality was to run in diagonal from the north-east of England to the extreme north of Wales. The staff of the Astronomer Royal made their preparations to observe it from Giggleswick:

> It is about 100 years since scientific observation of solar eclipses began to be made on a serious scale, but it was not until 1860 . . . that photography was successfully employed and not until 1871 that really satisfactory photographs of the corona were secured. There is still a good deal to find out about the corona and its constitution, and the efforts of the Greenwich observers at Giggleswick will be applied to obtaining a direct photograph of the corona during the period of totality and to getting two spectroscopes in order to determine from them the physical condition of the sun's chromosphere.[1]

The paper also notes other scientific experiments and observations to be attempted, such as air observations and investigations of solar influences on wireless signals particularly 'with the change of conditions from daylight to darkness'. The eclipse provides 'the means of extending our knowledge as to what happens when the sun's rays are suddenly cut off for a period of a few seconds to a few minutes, and only over a limited portion of the earth's surface.'[2] The eclipse, then, provides a special opportunity to observe sunlight. Normally it might be said to be either totally present or totally absent, but during an eclipse these conditions are no longer absolute, and are contained within a small space and a very short period of time. The public response was more concerned with the cosmic singularity of the event:

> Apart from the scientific standpoint, the eclipse is arousing exceptional popular interest. The fact that it is only at long intervals of years that a total eclipse can be seen in England, that no living person has ever seen the phenomenon in this country, and that it is extremely unlikely that more than a few will live to the year of the next eclipse [1999], has stirred public imagination, and enormous numbers have planned to travel to some point within the limit of the totality.[3]

Special trains were run to many places lying within this belt, and Virginia Woolf, accompanied by some close friends and family, was a passenger on one of these trains. She was among the 20,000 people who gathered to observe the eclipse from Richmond, Yorkshire.

The Times' next editorial seems to pander more to popular than to scientific anticipation of the event, although it does so largely by communicating, in lay terms, its scientific significance. 'The eclipse of 1919 [not visible from Britain]', it reminds readers, '. . . was notable for the fact that the photographs taken enabled astronomers to prove to their satisfaction, by the displacement of the stars around the sun, that the Einstein theory of relativity was correct.'[4] The year of that eclipse, incidentally, is the year in which Woolf's second novel, *Night and Day*, was first published: its heroine is a closet mathematician-astronomer ('looking up through a telescope at white shadow-cleft disks which were other worlds' (*N&D* 317)). It was also in this year, apparently, that Woolf wrote her story 'Sympathy' which makes reference to a solar eclipse.

Given the enormous impact of Einstein's theories upon both the scientific community and popular imagination alike, it is worth recalling in a little more detail what it was that the eclipse of 29 May 1919 confirmed. Expeditions were made to Northern Brazil and West Africa in order to observe this eclipse. But not until November of that year did it make headline news. Einstein's Special Theory of Relativity is summarized in *The Times* under the heading 'Space Warped':

the Newtonian principles assume that space is invariable, that, for instance, the three angles of a triangle always equal, and must equal, two right angles, and that a circle is really circular. But there are certain physical facts that seem to throw doubt on the universality of these observations, and suggest that space may acquire a twist or warp in certain circumstances, as, for instance, under the influence of gravitation, a dislocation in itself slight and applying to the instruments of measurement as well as to things being measured. The Einstein doctrine is that the qualities of space, hitherto believed to be absolute, are relative to their circumstances. He drew inference from his theory that in certain cases actual measurement of light would show the effects of the warping in a degree that could be predicted and calculated.[5]

The particular circumstances of an eclipse provide an excellent opportunity to attempt measurements of light. The experiment relies upon the temporary obfuscation of the sun, which allows the light of other stars to become visible and available for calculation. It is this particular aspect of Einstein's theory which is of relevance to Woolf's aesthetic of light, since she seems to undermine, in her work, the notion of the sun as a fixed absolute and self-contained value, and to reveal (in its absence) other, multiple points of illumination: the stars. They seem to represent a distant yet desirable set of alternative possibilities, in contrast to the relentless turmoil of mundanity: 'Infinite millions of miles away powdered stars twinkled; but the waves slapped the boat, and crashed, with regular and appalling solemnity, against the rocks.' (*JR* 83) In *To the Lighthouse*, the stars try to break through from behind the leaves of a tree which is the focus of Mrs Ramsay's narrow thoughts: 'It was windy, so that the leaves now and then brushed open a star, and the stars themselves seemed to be shaking and darting light and trying to flash out from behind the edges of the leaves.' (*TL* 175)

The Times explains how the eclipse illustrates Einstein's theory:

> At each of these places . . . it would be possible to take during totality a set of photographs of the obscured sun and a number of bright stars which happened to be in its immediate vicinity. The desired object was to ascertain whether the light from these stars, as it passed the sun, came as directly towards us as if the sun were not there, or if there was a deflection due to its presence, and if the latter proved to be the case, what the amount of the deflection was.[6]

The Royal Astronomical Society met in London in November 1919 to discuss the discovery of the momentous evidence which was to topple its founding, Newtonian principles. It is little wonder that Alfred North Whitehead, who was present, describes 'the whole atmosphere of tense interest [as] exactly that of the Greek drama'. He continues:

We were the chorus commenting on the decree of destiny as disclosed in the development of a supreme incident. There was a dramatic quality in the very staging – the traditional ceremonial, and in the background the picture of Newton to remind us that the greatest of scientific generalizations was now, after more than two centuries, to receive its first modification. Nor was the personal interest wanting; a great adventure in thought had at length come safe to shore.[7]

This last metaphor of Whitehead's ('a great adventure in thought') attributes to scientific breakthroughs an epic quality; and although his references to the Greek drama suggest that Newtonian thought itself has been tragically eclipsed, this is, to an extent, tempered by the word 'modification', which suggests refinement rather than iconoclasm – or perhaps even the enlightenment of the Enlightenment.

If the eclipse of 1919 was illuminating to the enlightened (scientific community), then the eclipse of 1927 was billed as an opportunity for ordinary people to witness the discovery and confirmation of scientific laws in a dramatic spectacle: 'For the first and only time in their lives a large number of people, if the conditions are favourable, will see the solar corona. . . . They will see the shadow of the moon sweeping towards and past them at a speed of over ninety miles a minute from the southwest.' Also visible to the masses will be 'the chromosphere, or layer of red gas surrounding the sun, and also the chaplet of points of light known as Bailey's Beads, may be visible towards the tips of the thin crescent along the lower edge of the sun at mid-eclipse.' It is warned that the shadow of the moon, the umbra, rather alarmingly, has provoked a somewhat irrational response, not in lay people, but actually in 'scientific observers of previous total eclipses':

In particular the sight of the black lunar shadow seems to have stirred their imagination by its appalling grandeur. It has been variously described as "something unnatural", "horribly menacing", "producing a feeling that something material was sweeping over the earth at a speed perfectly frightful", "the most terrifying sight I ever saw". "A vast palpable presence seems overwhelming the earth". In these words there lies the horror of great darkness, the darkness of one of the plagues of Egypt. Something of that awe must surely affect the multitude of untrained observers who may tomorrow look upon the same rare conjunction of the two heavenly bodies most closely connected with the being of this earth and its inhabitants.[8]

These pieces from *The Times* provide a context of common expectation against which to read Woolf's version of the event. As we can see from her diary entry on the day after the eclipse, her response is quite similar in many respects to the 'horror' and 'awe' of the umbra predicted here (for example, compare

with these her 'some vast obeisance'); and, as we will see below, there are a
number of other points of resemblance between the newspaper's account and
Woolf's account. Also of note, of course, are the many differences between
them. The context, however, does underline for us the fact that the experience
Woolf describes, although recorded in her private journal, is neither something
highly personal nor élitist. Her immediate response seems not too different
from those responses predicted, and indeed shared, by many others. In fact, it
is this very sense of shared experience which comes across most powerfully in
her description. This does not detract from her individual powers of description, nor from the personal significance of the event, but rather suggests that
this personal significance lies in the communal experience. Woolf's diary entry
and remarks in letters (*L* III 377, 382) suggest she saw it as a very exciting adventure, worthy of careful inscription.

Woolf's diary account of the eclipse

Woolf records in her diary the journey she made with her husband Leonard
Woolf, her nephew Quentin Bell, and friends Harold Nicolson, Vita Sackville-
West (Nicolson's wife, and Virginia Woolf's lover), Ray Strachey (the feminist), Saxon Sydney-Turner, and Eddie Sackville-West (Vita's cousin). She gives
a lively, if sketchy, account of the various stages of the journey, including
glimpses of the changing landscape, recollections of odd incidents, snatches of
conversation – all narrated in an appropriately fitful style. What is of interest
here is her handling of the imagery of light, dark and colour.

The voyage to the eclipse starts as dusk turns to darkness at 'about 10 on
Tuesday night [when] several very long trains . . . left King's Cross' (*D* III 142).
Woolf records the mounting anticipation of the voyagers: 'Before it got dark
we kept looking at the sky: soft fleecy; but there was one star, over Alexandra
Park. Look Vita, that's Alexandra Park, said Harold.' Here a twilight star acts
as a co-ordinate for an urban landmark familiar to the voyagers; and the further they travel from this reassuring point of light, the more unsettling their
relation to the heavens becomes. By the time they get north of York, the first
signs of dawn can be seen in mute contrast to the artificial lights emanating
from the vehicles gathered to transport them to the observation points: 'then
here was a level crossing, at which were drawn up a long line of motor omni-
buses & motors, all burning pale yellow lights. It was getting grey – still a fleecy
mottled sky'. The artificial lights are seen as pin-points of precise colour against
the diffuse and opaque grey of the cloud-covered sky. The sense of the cloud cover
acting as a curtain lends to the general air of anticipation before revelation.

Transferred from train to bus, the passengers see 'a vast castle':

> It had a front window added, & a light I think burning. All the fields were
> aburn with June grasses & red tasselled plants, none coloured as yet, all pale.
> Pale & grey too were the little uncompromising Yorkshire farms. As we
> passed one, the farmer, & his wife & sister came out, all tightly and tidily
> dressed in black, as if they were going to church. At another ugly square
> farm, two women were looking out of the upper windows. These had white
> blinds drawn down half across them.
>
> (*D* III 142)

Here artificial light is contrasted not with that of the sky, but with that of
the land. There is introduced into this description a slight air of uncertainty;
for Woolf is not sure if she did see a light in the castle window ('a light I think
burning'); she suggests a veritable blaze of bright fierce colour, only to add that
the 'red . . . plants' are yet without colour. This remarkable conjunction of
burning with pale qualities suggests that the rippling *texture* of the plants, not
their colour, makes them seem like a (pale) fire. Like the grey clouds, they have
an almost tangible light and colour, which seems to contrast with the yellow-
ness of the car and house lights.

Woolf and her party, having 'found [them]selves very high on a moor, boggy
heathery, with butts for grouse shooting', join the many other spectators gathering for the dawn: 'One light burnt down there. Vales and moors stretched,
slope after slope, round us. It was like the Haworth country. But over Richmond, where the sun was rising, was a soft grey cloud. We could see by a gold
spot where the sun was. But it was early yet.' (*D* III 142–43) This rural setting
contrasts with (and is, in fact, an inversion of) their initial urban experience of
observing a star above Alexandra Park. Here they look down from the heights
of moorland onto a single light burning below in Richmond. The 'gold spot'
of the sun is seen as a counterpoint to this. In describing their enclosure in
natural landscape, Woolf also alerts us to the literary and aesthetic associations
of this sort of terrain: she likens it to Brontë ('Haworth') country, perhaps
intimating a particularly feminine mythopœic significance. We might connect
with this Woolf's earlier likening of Vita Sackville-West to Sappho. The presence of Sackville-West and the feminist, Ray Strachey, might perhaps suggest
to Woolf a feminine and feminist perspective on the scene. This perspective,
tentative here, I will argue below, becomes more evident in the essay version.

In the diary, the various preparatory antics of Woolf's companions are
now described, as well as the sight of 'four great red setters . . . leaping over the
moor'. Woolf also makes some enigmatic remarks about sheep, guinea pigs and
other animals. Then she returns to the main point of focus:

There were thin places in the cloud, & some complete holes. The question was whether the sun would show through a cloud or through one of these hollow places when the time came. We began to get anxious. We saw rays coming through the bottom of the clouds. Then, for a moment we saw the sun, sweeping – it seemed to be sailing at a great pace & clear in a gap; we had out our smoked glasses; we saw it crescent, burning red; next moment it had sailed fast into the cloud again; only the red streamers came from it; then only a golden haze, such as one has often seen. The moments were passing. We thought we were cheated; we looked at the sheep; they showed no fear; the setters were racing round; everyone was standing in long lines, rather dignified, looking out. I thought how we were like very old people, in the birth of the world – druids on Stonehenge: (this idea came more vividly in the first pale light though).

(*D* III 143)

Woolf conveys the human anticipation and frustration as the sun is glimpsed 'sweeping' behind obscuring clouds. *The Times* reports the next day that heavy cloud cover and rain prevented the eclipse from being seen in many parts of the country, disappointing the crowds, but it adds, rather intriguingly: 'All the crowds, even when they were quite wet, were cheery. They were composed chiefly of young women.'[9] We might begin to wonder about the attraction of this spectacle for feminine consciousness. In the above account Woolf contrasts the anxiety of the people with the total indifference of the animals: like Auden's dogs, the setters, it seems, 'go on with their doggy life'.[10] Humanity is marked out by its stillness and dignity, which leads Woolf to ponder on 'the birth of the world – druids on Stonehenge'. Here she links ancient sun-worshipping practices at Stonehenge to the origins of the whole world, yet her parenthetical remark on 'this idea' suggests the connection to be doubtful, in need of qualification. Her description, incidentally, visually recalls a plate in Blake's *Jerusalem* which shows images of Stonehenge, druids, and a solar eclipse.[11]

Stonehenge and solar myth

Woolf had actually been to Stonehenge in 1903, on two different visits, recorded in her journal: 'Stonehenge', and 'Stonehenge Again'. Her comments here prefigure the sentiments expressed in her allusion to Stonehenge at the eclipse: 'The singular, & most intoxicating charm of Stonehenge to me, & to most I think, is that no one in the world can tell you anything about it.' (*PA* 199) She is impressed, then, by its mystery, its inexplicability. She is aware, however, of the various 'theories' which seek to dispel the mystery:

The most attractive and most likely, is that some forgotten people built here a Temple where they worshipped the sun; there is a rugged pillar someway out side the circle whose peak makes exactly that point on the ruin of the earth where the sun rises in the summer solstice. And there is a fallen stone in the middle, longer & larger than the other hewn rocks it lies among which may have been the altar – & the moment the sun rose the Priest of that savage people slaughtered his victim here in honour of the Sun God. We certainly saw the dent of his axe in the stone.

(PA 199–200)

Woolf favours the theory of sun worship, which she understands as patriarchal social practice, presided over by male priests. In her second entry, foreshadowing her account of the eclipse, she imagines Stonehenge to be the centre of sun worship for the whole world: 'one can imagine why this spot was chosen by the Druids – or whoever they were – for their Temple to the sun. It lies very naked to the sun. It is a kind of altar made of earth, on which the whole world might do sacrifice.' *(PA* 205) Again, she makes much of the opposition between earth and sun. Although Woolf is much taken with the theory of Druid sun worship, she is careful to keep it as one theory amongst many: 'Set up the pillars though in some other shape, & we have an entirely fresh picture; but the thing that remains in one's mind, whatever one does, is the stupendous mystery of it all.' *(PA* 200) Not only is Woolf's fascination with sun worship here interesting in relation to her later eclipse entry, but so, too, is her refusal to keep to a singular interpretation. The ruins of Stonehenge provide the stimulus for theories 'without end' *(PA* 199); they cannot be reduced to one fixed interpretation. Allegories, for Benjamin, are 'in the realm of thoughts what ruins are in the realm of things'.[12] Woolf, too, is interested in the construction of thought out of something unfinished, partly destroyed, or in process, exuding mystery and potential:

Imagine those toiling pagans doing honour to the very sun now in the sky above me, & for some perverse reason I find this a more deeply impressive temple of Religion – block laid to block, & half of them tumbled in ruin so long that the earth almost hides them, than that perfect spire whence prayer & praise is at this very moment ascending.

It is a matter for thought, surely, if not irony, that as one stands on the ruins of Stonehenge one can see the spire of Salisbury Cathedral.

(PA 200)

Woolf prefers the pagan ruin to the perfection of Christian symbolism. Stonehenge is 'more deeply impressive' than Salisbury Cathedral, but in neither case does Woolf move from the condition of wonder to actual religious belief. What interests her is the aesthetic and imaginative potential.

In both her account of Stonehenge and of the eclipse, Woolf explores human fascination with the sun, and in being 'naked to the sun'. In the eclipse scene, the solemn stillness of the people seems a tribute to solar constancy. While the 'racing' setter dogs seem to mimic the apparent 'sweeping' movement of the sun, it is, in fact, the clouds and the earth that are moving. The people, then, seem subjectively connected to the sun, perhaps seeing it as 'the Absolute Subject'. The solemnity of the occasion arises from the prospect of witnessing the momentary extinction of its light. Woolf's account signals her awareness of the event as an optical illusion ('the sun seemed to be sailing'), but also emphasizes a more subjective perspective by describing the sun as active, personified ('we saw it crescent . . . it had sailed'), where, in fact, it is passive. Interestingly, Woolf does not gender the sun here.

Woolf's reference to pagan worship, then, is couched in hesitant enough terms to suggest a sense of wonder rather than a specifically religious experience; she makes no overt reference to the Christian significance of the eclipse (at the crucifixion). There is clearly a biblical resonance, however, to the terse, post-lapsarian statement, 'We had fallen', in the passage following this (Part One's epigraph). Here, Woolf describes the actual moment of the eclipse.

The eclipse

In this passage, Woolf carefully charts the disappearance of light, the coming of darkness, and the re-emergence of light, in terms of colour. The eclipse is heralded by a change of colour from one end of the spectrum to the other – from blue to red – and by the simultaneous fading of colour altogether. Woolf communicates a paradoxical sense of simultaneously pale and strong colour (the 'soft grey' clouds turn 'pale' yet 'reddish black'): even very weak light seems composed of strong colour. This is repeated in her description of the valley below which is 'an extraordinary scrumble of red & black' and yet is 'all . . . cloud . . . delicately tinted'. In the midst of this is noted 'the one light burning' – a sign of human consciousness in the gathering darkness. Although not mentioned again, this light is the one point of illumination remaining visible during the eclipse; and it seems to act as a counterpoint to what follows.

Woolf likens the sudden descent into darkness to 'the beginning of a violent storm' (as *The Times* similarly reports),[13] describing it in terms of the fading of colour. She strikingly conveys the spectators' assessment of the increasing darkness: 'the light sank & sank: we kept saying this is the shadow; & we thought now it is over'. Whenever they conclude that the light has finally disappeared, they discover it can still get darker: what they first see as the shadow is gradually understood as still part of the light, and still colour, however weak.

This gradual sense of increasing darkness is dramatically contrasted with the final moment when the light disappears: '& we thought now it is over – this is the shadow when suddenly the light went out. We had fallen. It was extinct. There was no colour. The earth was dead.' With the loss of the sun comes a collective fall; loss of colour signals the earth's death.

The sudden removal of light is something quite other to the previous sliding into darkness. Suddenly there is no doubt. Certain and concise statements are made: the finality of death means absolutely no light, no colour, no life. Yet as soon as this 'astonishing moment' has been apprehended, it is followed by another – death is followed by rebirth: 'as if a ball rebounded, the cloud took colour on itself again, only a sparky aetherial colour & so the light came back.' Colour and light inseparably return. The absence of light not only means the absence of colour, however, it also means the absence of shadow. Two contrary states may be discerned in 'this is the shadow' and 'the light went out'. Shadow is observed as a phenomenon of light and colour, as part of life, against which is contrasted the total absence of all of these.

Woolf describes the eclipse in terms of two contrary states: life and death, light and no light. If the eclipse is understood as symbolic of the extinction of human consciousness, then the scene presented by Woolf suggests that neither is absolute: the light re-emerges; and there is a counterpoint of light or perhaps witnessing consciousness in the presence of the single light burning in the valley. Woolf describes this 'astonishing moment' not as the experience of an individual subject, singled out from the crowd, but as one shared by many. It is a communal moment ('We had fallen'). Although she communicates her personal response at the moment of eclipse, the overwhelming impression Woolf gives is of the self as part of an inclusive 'we'.

There is a religious tone evident in such words and phrases as 'vast obeisance . . . kneeling . . . low . . . raised up', yet these reverential acts are not attributed to the human beings present but to a mysterious 'something'. Woolf describes this 'something' as performing a cosmic genuflection but does not indicate for what or whom this honour is meant, if, indeed, it is for anyone. There is something rather remote and chillingly mundane in this: as if the view is spoilt by some unknown giant bending down in front of an enormous lamp. *The Times* similarly reports, 'The sinister twilight faded away, as if some unseen hand were turning off a gas jet. The shadow, says our correspondent, enveloped us.'[14]

There are Romantic overtones to Woolf's description. Her selection of the word 'obeisance' suggests an echo of the 'auxiliar light' passage in *The Prelude*.[15]

A plastic power
Abode with me; a forming hand, at times

> Rebellious, acting in a devious mood;
> A local spirit of his own, at war
> With general tendency, but, for the most,
> Subservient strictly to external things
> With which it communed. An auxiliar light
> Came from my mind, which on the setting sun
> Bestowed new splendour; the melodious birds,
> The fluttering breezes, fountains that ran on
> Murmuring so sweetly in themselves, obeyed
> A like dominion, and the midnight storm
> Grew darker in the presence of my eye:
> Hence my obeisance, my devotion hence,
> And hence my transport.[16]

The 'auxiliar light' emanating from the poet's mind complements that of 'the setting sun', at the same time displacing it. This light, like Woolf's 'one light burning', becomes a point of illumination in the darkness created by the sun's absence ('and the midnight storm/ Grew darker in the presence of my eye'). It is not clear to what 'A like dominion' refers. The birds and breezes may also be 'Subservient . . . to external things', but then they *are* 'external things', so what is the 'like dominion', 'obeyed' by them? It is the light of the poet's mind that holds sway: 'Bestowed new splendour'. Although this light is 'auxiliar', it becomes central. The pun on 'eye' ('I') allows us to read the orientation of 'my obeisance, my devotion' and 'my transport' as self-reflexive. The intrusion of the object world serves as self-confirmation for the masculine subject. The poet, paradoxically, serves nature by subordinating it to himself. The sun itself, with all its divine and religious associations, has become the object of the poet's bestowal of 'splendour'.

Earlier, Wordsworth declares his early devotion to the sun ('a boy I loved the sun'), which he personifies as male, suggesting at the same time perhaps a Christian understanding of the term.

> Not as I since have loved him, as a pledge
> And surety of our earthly life, a light
> Which we behold and feel we are alive.[17]

Woolf certainly knew *The Prelude* well, and makes direct allusion to it in her first novel (*VO* 118). In April 1911 she wrote to Saxon Sydney-Turner: 'I am reading the Prelude. Dont you think it one of the greatest works ever written? Some of it, anyhow, is sublime; it may get worse.' (*L* 1 460) Echoing Wordsworth, she describes the loss of the sun as the loss of a sort of godhead. Wordsworth's 'obeisance' comes after the sunset, with the source of his own creative powers, his 'auxiliar light'. The sun itself does not reappear. The poet's light, in a sense, has become the new dawn. Woolf's 'obeisance', on the other hand, is felt at the moment of solar eclipse. Only after the return of the colours does she convey a sense of (*collective*) self-worth ('Our greatness had been apparent too').

What seems to move Woolf more than the light going out is the re-emergence of the colours: 'They came back astonishingly lightly & quickly & beautifully in the valley & over the hills – at first with a miraculous glittering & aetheriality, later normally almost, but with a great sense of relief.' Here the sense of wonder diminishes with the return to normality, itself all the more appreciated after the experience of the eclipse has heightened the sensibilities. The sense of refreshment and rebirth apparent at the return of colour is further emphasized in a marginal note: 'The colour for some moments was of the most lovely kind – fresh, various – here blue, & there brown: all new colours, as if washed over & repainted.' (*D* III 143). In comparison, the aeronautical correspondent for *The Times* reports that 'the colours of the patchwork countryside turned from greys and purples to greens and yellows; the aeroplane passed from a momentary night to a subdued day.'[18] Woolf's description notably steers clear of religious terminology here and instead favours an artist's vocabulary – 'washed over and repainted'. There is no sense of mystic or religious destiny; instead Woolf finds communicated in the event a sense of artistic licence to 'make it new', to re-construct. Although she and her companions witness the return to ('almost') normality 'with a great sense of relief', Woolf qualifies this with a simile: 'It was like a recovery.' It was similar to, but not actually, a relief. This suggests partial detachment.

Woolf explains: 'We had been much worse than we had expected. We had seen the world dead.' This again emphasizes not the death of the sun, lost from sight in the eclipse, but the subsequent death of the world. Again the collective nature of the experience is stressed in the communal sense of loss. Yet there is also a conflicting sense of analytical detachment. They expected to find the experience unnerving and were surprised by the extremity of their response, yet they still measure this response. The rational, scientific explanation underpins their understanding of the eclipse however much its visual effects move them. Woolf's report not only conveys the emotional splendour of witnessing the eclipse, and, in so doing, acknowledges how such an occurrence led our ancestors to mystical and religious interpretations; it also distances itself from acceptance of such interpretations. The sense of triumph informing Woolf's summarizing statements arises from the endurance of the apocalyptic moment *without* succumbing to superstition: 'We had seen the world dead. This was within the power of nature. Our greatness had been apparent too.'

Acknowledging the mythopœic significance of this moment, its aesthetic sublimity, then, Woolf does not go so far as to regard it as evidence of divine or supernatural intervention. Hers is a radically different conclusion to that of *The Times'* editorial: 'For those fleeting moments the eyes of men, women, and children had looked upon a stupendous manifestation of the works of the CREATOR. "The heavens declare the glory of GOD; and the firmament showeth His handiwork."'[19] (God has become artist here). The event confirms the Deity as the prime mover of the universe. Woolf concludes that no such absolute frame of reference is possible. There is no ambiguity or hesitation in her statement that 'This was within the power of nature'; but nor is this statement without a certain awe. Woolf's sentiments here are reminiscent of Conrad's opinions on the 'Supernatural':

> all my moral and intellectual being is penetrated by an invincible conviction that whatever falls under the dominion of our senses must be in nature and, however exceptional, cannot differ in its essence from all the other effects of the visible and tangible world of which we are a self-conscious part. The world of the living contains enough mysteries and marvels as it is; marvels and mysteries acting upon our emotions and intelligence in ways so inexplicable that it would almost justify the conception of life as an enchanted state.[20]

Woolf's celebratory assertion, 'Our greatness had been apparent too', corresponds to Conrad's sense of communal self-conscious participation in a world of near (not actual) enchantment. Woolf notes the departure from that celebratory moment by remarking: 'Now we became Ray in a blanket, Saxon in a cap &c. We were bitterly cold. I should say that the cold had increased as the light went down.' (*D* III 144) After the event the communal 'we' is atomized into separate individuals, discrete persons enclosed in garments. The matter-of-fact tone suggests an earnest attempt to remain objective, as well as marking the return of the mundane, and the remark 'it was all over till 1999' is a reminder that the writer is fully aware that what she has witnessed is part of the predictable clockwork of the solar system.

Seeing 'the world dead' was an important and moving event for Woolf, then, insofar as it reaffirmed the world of light and colour:

> What remained was a sense of the comfort which we get used to, of plenty of light & colour. This for some time seemed a definitely welcome thing. Yet when it became established all over the country, one rather missed the sense of its being a relief & a respite, which one had had when it came back after the darkness. How can I express the darkness? It was a sudden plunge, when one did not expect it: being at the mercy of the sky: our own nobility: the druids; Stonehenge; & the racing red dogs; all that was in ones mind. Also, to be picked out of ones London drawing room & set down on the wildest moors in England was impressive.

> (*D* III 144)

In order fully to appreciate the 'comfort . . . of plenty of light & colour' Woolf suggests we need to experience its contrary – the darkness. Here the word 'relief' takes on its special meaning of 'distinctness by contrast' as well as its more usual one of a 'removal of burden'. Darkness is seen as a frightening yet necessary foil to light and colour, a negative against which 'all that was in ones mind' might be examined. The sense of contrary states is continued in Woolf's awareness of the experience as a kind of pastoral one – her 'London drawing room' is set against 'the wildest moors in England'; she and her party have moved between these two states.

Woolf finds the darkness a challenge to her descriptive powers. Interestingly, it is not a static condition for her, but an event, triggering a flurry of thoughts, images, and emotions, which can only be described subjectively as 'a sudden plunge when one did not expect it'. However mysterious and unutterable the darkness, it nevertheless remains for Woolf an experience of something quite other, distinct from light and colour. This point is worth labouring because it is fundamental to an understanding of Woolf's engagement with darkness and light. In this account of the eclipse, Woolf offers precise testimony to her understanding of these phenomena as they are manifested in a rare and dramatic, yet natural, occurrence. Such a moment unavoidably moves her to focus specifically upon darkness and light, and is thus pertinent to any investigation concerned with her aesthetic command of these terms. Woolf's positive attitude to light and colour here is important.

4　The amusing game

If her diary entry is significant in my investigation, how much more so is the essay Woolf develops from it. 'The Sun and the Fish' is a highly stylized account of the same event, and as such provides a good opportunity to observe Woolf's literary polishing techniques,[1] and in particular her treatment of darkness, light and colour. This chapter looks at the feminist context of 'The Sun and the Fish', and examines Woolf's engagement of binary oppositions here and in the later, more widely known, 'A Sketch of the Past'.

The feminist context of 'The Sun and the Fish'

'The Sun and the Fish' was first published in February 1928, in *Time and Tide*, the weekly magazine founded in 1920, and later edited, by the militant feminist Lady Rhondda,[2] a prominent suffragette, active in the Woman's Social and Political Union. In the same year that Woolf's essay appeared in *Time and Tide*, Rhondda's *Leisured Women* (1928) was published by the Woolfs in the Second Series of Hogarth Essays.

Rhondda's magazine, run and staffed entirely by women, had no party associations, and offered an open-minded, progressive, feminist perspective. According to Johanna Alberti, however, 'it did not claim to put forward women's views.'[3] Commenting upon the magazine's aspirations 'to show "all sides of national life, dealing with them solely on the ground that they are interesting,"' she observes:

> The paper aimed to be "untainted by any suspicion of preconceived views". The first editorial also stated that it would be possible to lay "too much stress" on the fact that the paper was run by women, that the significance lay in women's need and demand for an "Independent Press". . . . Rhondda saw women as free from party and sectarian ties, and . . . that women wanted a paper which would "treat men and women as equally part of the great human family".[4]

Alberti does not bring out the opening editorial's implicit irony, which seems a riposte to the supposedly impartial, yet obviously male dominated, press of the establishment. If impartiality is at all possible, the interests of women must be served. An editorial seeking impartiality may still be strategically feminist.

Alberti herself cites Rhondda's reasons for founding the paper as lying in her desire ' "passionately, urgently, to change customs and influence ideas." '5 Rhondda also claims that in founding the magazine she saw 'The chance of reaching out to the people like-minded with oneself who would understand what one was trying to say. That way', she continues, 'I could find the people who were worth hearing, and see that they were heard – heard, if not by the big multitude, at least by the inner group, the keystone people who ultimately directed that multitude. I could put before the public that mattered the things that I wanted them to hear.'6 Rhondda's retrospective view suggests she may have had in mind a political agenda, one which presumably saw the views of the suffrage movement as 'worth hearing'.

Woolf herself joined the Women's Suffrage Movement in January 1910, and was actively involved in a number of ways. On New Year's Day 1910 Virginia Stephen, full of seasonal good resolve, writes to Janet Case:

> Would it be any use if I spent an afternoon or two weekly in addressing envelopes for the Adult Suffragists?
>
> I dont know anything about the question. Perhaps you could send me a pamphlet, or give me the address of the office. I could neither do sums or argue, or speak, but I could do the humbler work if that is any good. You impressed me so much the other night with the wrongness of the present state of affairs that I feel that action is necessary. Your position seemed to me intolerable. The only way to make it better is to do something I suppose. How melancholy it is that conversation isnt enough!
>
> (*L* I 421)

For Alex Zwerdling, 'These are the words of a naive and reluctant political participant who nevertheless feels outraged enough . . . to become an active suffragist.' Woolf was not a 'suffragette', he emphasizes, noting that 'the distinction between the constitutional methods of the [suffragist] and the extralegal tactics of the [suffragette] had by this time been clearly established.' Thus Zwerdling concludes, 'Woolf's decision to join the nonviolent section of the movement is characteristic and important.'7 By November 1910, however, Woolf's enthusiasm for the movement seems to have waned:

> My time has been wasted a good deal upon Suffrage. We went to two meetings, at which about a dozen people spoke, like the tollings of a bell. If they spoke faster all their words went into one. It was at the Albert Hall. The only amusement was that a baby cried incessantly, and this was taken by some as a bitter sarcasm against women having a vote.
>
> (*L* I 438)

This may imply not so much disillusion with the goals of the movement, as impatience with its interminable progress.8

The feminist context in which 'The Sun and the Fish' first appeared assists our understanding of Woolf's manipulation of her material. The feminist company of Ray Strachey, a suffragist, on the actual trip is also significant. In 1927, the year of the eclipse, Ray Strachey published *Women's Suffrage and Women's Service: The History of the London and National Society for Women's Service*, and in 1928 her feminist classic, *'The Cause': A Short History of the Women's Movement in Great Britain*. The following year came Woolf's own feminist classic, *A Room of One's Own*, excerpts from which appeared in *Time and Tide*.[9] The time of the eclipse, then, closely precedes the publication of Woolf's and Strachey's most important feminist documents, both appearing around the time of the full enfranchisement of women in Britain (1928). Although Strachey's brand of feminism appears to have sometimes met with Woolf's disapproval (*L* II 357), the two, nevertheless, collaborated on feminist projects.[10] Woolf in an earlier diary entry, actually likens Rhondda to Strachey, 'a solid bull dog' (*D* II 123)! This feminist context I will later discuss in relation to Woolf's construction of 'The Sun and the Fish'; but first, there are some matters to consider concerning the overall structure of the essay.

The amusing game

The essay's striking title, 'The Sun and the Fish', is a far from straightforward reference to the eclipse; the introductory paragraph is even more enigmatic. The essay begins not with material drawn from Woolf's diary entry but with the outline for an intellectual game which at first seems entirely without connection to it, but in fact offers a key to how we should read it. Yet out of these strange origins the story of the eclipse does emerge, only to be eclipsed itself by another story: the 'Fish' refers to the final section of the piece (describing an aquarium) which is to be read dialectically against the section on the eclipse. The title sets up this oppositional play, but equally, it seems to promise some sort of biblical parable, perhaps the feeding of the five thousand, if we take 'Sun' as 'Son' (of God);[11] and it also suggests ancient and pre-Christian mythology, such as the Apollo and Python myths. Before discussing the mythopœic resonance of this imagery, we should consider the binary opposition it erects.

'The Sun and the Fish' is written in six long paragraphs, and may be divided into three sections. The first describes 'an amusing game', the second gives an account of the eclipse, and the third shifts focus to a scene in the London Zoological Gardens. Woolf anticipates this non-sequitur by establishing its rationale according to the rules of the game set out in the opening paragraph.

> It is an amusing game, especially for a dark winter's morning. One says to
> the eye Athens; Segesta; Queen Victoria; and one waits, as submissively as

possible, to see what will happen next. And perhaps nothing happens, and perhaps a great many things happen, but not the things one might expect. The old lady in horn spectacles – the late Queen – is vivid enough; but somehow she has allied herself with a soldier in Piccadilly who is stooping to pick up a coin; with a yellow camel who is swaying through an archway in Kensington Gardens; with a kitchen chair and a distinguished old gentleman waving his hat. Dropped years ago into the mind, she has become stuck about with all sorts of alien matter. When one says Queen Victoria, one draws up the most heterogeneous collection of objects, which it will take a week at least to sort.

(CDB 193)

This 'amusing game' of associations suggests it is impossible to think of anything in isolation, that the mind only recalls things by paradoxical connection with other unrelated things. As James Ramsay discovers, 'nothing [is] simply one thing.' *(TL* 286) Queen Victoria can only be remembered against that which she is not – 'all sorts of alien matter' and 'the most heterogeneous collection of objects'. Dr Johnson's denunciation of the Metaphysical art comes to mind: 'the most heterogeneous ideas are yoked by violence together'.

The strange conjunction of things is only the start of Woolf's exercise, however, and what follows is a period of sifting and discrimination ('it will take a week at least to sort'). The game is not always stimulating or rewarding:

On the other hand, one may say to oneself Mont Blanc at dawn, the Taj Mahal in the moonlight; and the mind remains a blank. For a sight will only survive in the queer pool in which we deposit our memories if it has the good luck to ally itself with some other emotion by which it is preserved. Sights marry, incongruously, morganatically (like the Queen and the Camel), and so keep each other alive. Mont Blanc, the Taj Mahal, sights we travelled and toiled to see, fade and perish and disappear because they failed to find the right mate.

(CDB 193)

Behind the horse-play is a model of oppositional relations. Woolf has carefully drawn attention to the somewhat involuntary nature of this imaginative exercise: conscious effort is made only in initiating the game ('one says to the eye'), after which one cannot be held responsible for the mind's riposte ('a great many things happen, but not the things one might expect'). The ensuing transgressions of decorum – for example, the morganatic marriage of Queen Victoria to a camel, or the nuptial disappointment of the Taj Mahal – are communicated with childish glee.

Woolf's dominant metaphor here is, appropriately enough, marriage. Her oppositions, furthermore, do not form equal partnerships: 'Sights marry, incongruously, morganatically . . . and so keep each other alive'. This statement needs some consideration. 'Incongruously' suggests that marriage occurs between inconsistent, unsuitable, or dissimilar partners; and this may imply merely that the partners are different from each other, not that one is superior to the other. 'Morganatically', however, supplies definite connotations of a hierarchy rather than difference, since a morganatic marriage is one, according to Chambers Twentieth Century Dictionary, 'between persons of unequal rank (latterly only where one is of a reigning or mediatised house)'. Woolf's sentence structure is ambiguous: the comma between the two adverbs can mean 'and', or that the second adverb offers a clearer definition of the first. In effect, Woolf is saying either that 'some sights marry incongruously and others marry downright morganatically', or that 'sights marry incongruously, which is to say more accurately – morganatically'.

The sentence also ends in ambiguity ('and so keep each other alive'). Does this reciprocity arise from marriage *per se*, or only from morganatic marriage? Woolf goes on to observe that some sights 'fade and perish and disappear because they failed to find the right mate'. This suggests that marriage *per se* is not sufficient – an appropriately incongruous partner is necessary; but whether 'the right mate' can only be found in a morganatic relationship is not made clear. Woolf predominantly concerns herself with the morganatic. Queen Victoria is her main example of a successfully married 'sight'. Every partner selected from the 'heterogeneous collection of objects', each example of 'alien matter' with which Her Majesty 'has become stuck about', is cast in a role of servility: 'a soldier . . . stooping', the camel, 'the kitchen chair', and the 'distinguished old gentleman waving his hat'. One might argue that *of course* all these are examples of servility, because the sight which prompts them is a queen, and it is almost inevitable that a monarch should only conjure forth morganatic partners in metaphor. Perhaps it is precisely because it gives such a clear-cut model of power relations that Woolf uses it. The initial instruction to the eye and the mind is seen, then, as a sort of royal summons to bring forth the lowly: every subject needs an object through which to establish sovereignty. This tone is reflected in the remark rounding off the opening paragraph of 'The Sun and the Fish': 'On our deathbeds we shall see nothing more majestic than a cat on a wall or an old woman in a sun-bonnet.' (*CDB* 193)

Compare this game with Woolf's observations on the nature of language in 'Craftsmanship' where she talks of words as having minds of their own – 'Our consciousness is their privacy; our darkness is their light' (*DM* 132) – and attributes to them other human qualities:

> [Words are] the wildest, freest, most irresponsible, most unteachable of all things. Of course, you can catch them and sort them and place them in

alphabetical order in dictionaries. But words do not live in dictionaries; they live in the mind . . . they are much less bound by ceremony and convention than we are. Royal words mate with commoners. English words marry French words, German words, Indian words, Negro Words, if they have a fancy. Indeed, the less we enquire into the past of our dear Mother English the better it will be for that Lady's reputation. For she has gone-a-roving, a-roving fair maid.

(DM 130–131)

The example of Queen Victoria is significant not only because it suggests a *hierarchized* opposition, but also because it appears to be an example of a gender opposition in which woman is positioned as master rather than slave.

If '"the" couple man/woman', as Cixous suggests, inheres in all other 'couples' or 'dual *hierarchized* oppositions',[12] we might question the effectiveness of inserting woman in the place of man: the couple Queen Victoria/Camel is in this sense just another example of man/woman. The Queen here is a token man, and the gender implications already written into subject/object relations are reinforced rather than challenged. Man in this opposition may mean both male individual and humanity. Thus the couple may also be expressed as mankind/woman.

This particular articulation of the 'law' of binary opposition is addressed in the leading article of the *Time and Tide* in which 'The Sun and the Fish' was first published. 'Human Beings – and Females' concludes: 'There can be nothing more dangerous to the whole structure of society than this attempt of the reactionaries to train women from their earliest years for a subordinate position and to divide the community into two groups: human beings – and females.'[13] Woolf's 'amusing game', then, in engaging with such oppositions, has particular resonance for the feminist context in which it first appears; and when this context is acknowledged the feminist import of her essay becomes more explicit. Careful comparison between diary entry and essay, I suggest, will also reveal Woolf's feminist interpretation of the eclipse.

'A Sketch of the Past'

Woolf seems to have learned her game early in life: it resembles the method of reaching 'a philosophy' she claims in 'A Sketch of the Past' (1939), where she delineates a 'constant idea of mine' (*MB* 72) along with other observations which must give us pause for thought. 'A Sketch of the Past' shares with 'The Sun and the Fish', in the first place, a similar project – the exploration of memory. Woolf's game is initiated by her recollection of an 'astonishing moment', just as her 'philosophy' comes from three 'exceptional moments' in her childhood: (i) a fight with her brother Thoby, during which: 'I felt: why hurt another person? I dropped my hand instantly, and stood there, and let him beat me. I remember the feeling. It was a feeling of hopeless sadness.'; (ii) in a garden: 'I was looking at the flower bed by the front door; "That is the whole", I said. I was looking at a plant with a spread of leaves; and it seemed suddenly plain that the flower itself was a part of the earth; that a ring enclosed what was the flower; and that was the real flower; part earth; part flower.'; (iii) on overhearing of a suicide: 'The next thing I remember is being in the garden at night and walking on the path by the apple tree. It seemed to me that the apple tree was connected with the horror of Mr Valpy's suicide. I could not pass it. I stood there looking at the grey-green creases of the bark – it was a moonlit night – in a trance of horror. I seemed to be dragged down, hopelessly, into some pit of absolute despair from which I could not escape. My body seemed paralysed.' (*MB* 71)

Each instance involves the individual subject in relation to the (physical, bodily, material, natural) object world. Each 'exceptional moment', as in her game in 'The Sun and the Fish', is recalled with its own 'alien matter': Thoby's fists, the flower bed, the apple tree. There is an element of 'shock' involved, not unlike the surprise element in the game: 'I often tell them over, or rather they come to the surface unexpectedly.' (*MB* 71). In 'A Sketch of the Past' Woolf realises something new: 'Two of these moments ended in a state of despair. The other ended, on the contrary, in a state of satisfaction.' The game, similarly, is sometimes successful, sometimes not. Perhaps the flower-bed resembles the case of Queen Victoria, whereas the fight with Thoby, and the suicide case, are as unsuccessful as the Taj Mahal.

The instance of the flower bed has special relevance. Woolf discovers 'the real flower' is only 'whole' when it is seen with its ground – with what surrounds it – and, that as a whole, it is 'part earth; part flower'. This resembles the example of Queen Victoria: both flower and queen are 'stuck about with . . . alien matter', and in this condition flourish; that is, they move the observer to mental stimulation and satisfaction. Woolf's 'discovery' about the flower is pertinent to understanding her game: the fact that she mentally returned to reflect on ('turn over and explore') this experience made 'a profound difference': one 'between despair and satisfaction' which 'arose from the fact that I was quite unable to deal with the pain of discovering that people hurt each other; that a man I had seen had killed himself. The sense of horror held me powerless. But in the case of the flower I found a reason; and thus was able to deal with the sensation. I was not powerless.' (*MB* 71–72) For Woolf where reason overcomes sensation, satisfaction results; but where reason fails and sensation dominates, she finds despair. She abhors the submission of mind to body (subject to object) but seems to derive great intellectual pleasure from the triumph of reason: 'I was conscious – if only at a distance – that I should in time explain it.' (*MB* 72)

Her sense of reaffirmed human greatness at the 'astonishing moment' of the eclipse is echoed in her consideration of recollecting these 'exceptional moments' which 'are now always welcome; after the first surprise, I always feel instantly that they are particularly valuable. And so I go on to suppose that the shock-receiving capacity is what makes me a writer. I hazard the explanation that a shock is at once in my case followed by the desire to explain it.' (*MB* 72) Reason makes possible an overcoming of this earth-bound position, but is not entirely independent of it. If reason 'blunts the sledge-hammer force of the blow' of sensation (*MB* 72), it also whets its own blade in the exchange.

This process is 'particularly valuable' to Woolf's creative and imaginative powers: she claims it actually makes her a writer. Her celebration of the powers of imaginative and communicative reason here marks her out as a rational rather than a mystical writer. In the passage immediately following this one, words such as 'revelation' and 'rapture' might be taken out of context to endorse a mystical or religious interpretation, but in context, their effect is quite different, having much in common with Conrad's sense of worldly 'mysteries and marvels'. Impressing a more sophisticated response to her moments of shock than her childhood assumption that she had suffered 'simply a blow from an enemy hidden behind the cotton wool of daily life' (*MB* 72), she describes 'a revelation of some order; it is a token of some real thing behind appearances; and I make it real by putting it into words'. But Woolf does not adhere to a principle of discovering one final cause to things in explaining her methods:

> It is the rapture I get when in writing I seem to be discovering what belongs to what; making a scene come right; making a character come together. From this I reach what I might call a philosophy; at any rate it is a constant idea of mine; that behind the cotton wool is hidden a pattern; that we – I mean all human beings – are connected with this; that the whole world is a work of art; that we are parts of the work of art. *Hamlet* or a Beethoven quartet is the truth about this vast mass that we call the world. But there is no Shakespeare, there is no Beethoven; certainly and emphatically there is no God; we are the words; we are the music; we are the thing itself. And I see this when I have a shock.
>
> (*MB* 72)

This sets apart Woolf's ideas on subject/object relations from traditional romantic ones, where the individual subjectivity of the (male) author is thought to be simultaneously outside and immanent in his work in imitation of the creator's relationship to the world.[14] Woolf positions herself as part of a community of subjects, accessible through language but with no transcendent position outside it; and this also marks her departure from the impersonality recommended by fellow modernists such as Joyce and Eliot. Woolf's writing 'rapture' may resemble Roland Barthes' 'pleasure of the text', and her declaration that 'there is no Shakespeare . . . there is no God' may anticipate his 'death of the author'; but her collective, contextually sensitive, model of subjectivity is at odds with post-structuralist views of subjectivity as a site of endless difference and multiple, unresolved paradoxes and contradictions.

Woolf seems to suggest a sense of community when she says 'we are parts of the work of art' or 'we are the music'; she places subjects within, rather than outside, language. For her the individual subject is woven into the group, not isolated but identified, I suggest, 'in terms of intersubjective contexts of meaning'.[15] Woolf's 'pattern' is specifically connected to an 'intuition of mine' developing from the flower-bed incident:

> If I were painting myself I should have to find some – rod, shall I say – something that would stand for the conception. It proves that one's life is not confined to one's body and what one says and does; one is living all the time in relation to certain background rods or conceptions. Mine is that there is a pattern hid behind the cotton wool. And this conception affects me every day. . . . I feel that by writing I am doing what is far more necessary than anything else.
>
> (MB 72–73)

The 'background rods' of Woolf's painting analogy resemble the terms of the painter, Cézanne's dictum: 'treat nature by the cylinder, the sphere, the cone'.[16] "Compare also Lily Briscoe's discovery: 'She saw the colour burning on a framework of steel; the light of a butterfly's wing lying upon the arches of a cathedral.' (TL 78) This relationship between framework and colour is important: it becomes clear in 'The Sun and the Fish' that colour does not lie on, so much as comprise, the structure. Similarly, Woolf's argument about 'background rods' takes a self-reflexive turn: she seems to inscribe her conceptual model at its every level. Her 'intuition' refers to her idea that there is a pattern behind things, and in telling us the origin of this idea, she suggests that it comes from the pattern itself ('it seems given to me, not made by me' (MB 72)). She repeats this tactic when she claims that 'one is living all the time in relation to certain background rods or conceptions', and then defines her own particular rod or conception as precisely this ('Mine is that there is a pattern behind the cotton wool.')! There is no position outside this state of affairs: we are implicated at every level. There is no act of writing or speaking transcending this condition.

Woolf's insistence that 'we are the words' suggests she understands language to be socially constructed and present only in its material utterances. The individual cannot ultimately be separated from the social (or 'whole'). Similarly, for Bakhtin, language has a 'social origin'. Woolf's observation, 'we are the words', corresponds to Bakhtin's 'the word is a social event';[17] and the figure of the flower in its bed may be taken to be the individual instance growing out of the communal (and plural) earth, or the particular word out of the pattern or background rods. Unlike the 'amusing game' where she draws attention to the hierarchized structure of the 'couple', Woolf does not identify hierarchy in her model of the flower and its bed. If the issue of gender is introduced, furthermore, we might ask (with Cixous) of both Woolf's pieces 'Where is she?' If we read man/woman into flower/earth, as in queen/alien matter, is there anything in Woolf's writing to resist or subvert the implied hierarchy of man/ woman?

In 'A Sketch of the Past' Woolf's 'I' is positioned with 'we' – that is, 'we . . . the words . . . the music'. The act of writing is thus for her communal: the individual writer participates in the collective of language. She places in contrast to this model the traditional, masculine trio of authors – Shakespeare, Beethoven and God, exemplifying the now defunct notion of authorial detachment. The question of gender might be clarified by the distinction between morganatic and non-morganatic versions of the couple flower/earth: morganatically it is read as man/woman, master/slave. Perhaps non-morganatically it may be read as the non-hierarchized couple subject/subjects, resembling Habermas's intersubjectivity.

Flower/earth may be read not only as a metaphor or allegory of speech and language, but also as a model of metaphor itself – a metaphor of metaphor in fact. We might consider subject/object as tenor/vehicle, where the subject or tenor (signified) is grounded in the object or vehicle (signifier). In the couple Queen Victoria/camel or Queen Victoria/stooping soldier, the morganatic relationship between subject and object is equivalent to the servile relationship of vehicle to tenor in metaphor. Woolf says that the 'real flower' (the tenor) is 'part earth; part flower' (the vehicle). This is not morganatic: the flower is partly earth – the tenor is partly the vehicle. I will be considering Woolf's gendering of metaphors in what follows.

Woolf's eponymous couple, sun/fish, may be interpreted morganatically and non-morganatically. As subject/object (morganatic) it is in the company of hierarchized couples such as mind/body, spirit/flesh, man/woman. The model subject/subjects, on the other hand, brings out the singular and plural signification of 'the fish', suggesting the couple sun/fish as an appropriate model of individual/social. Sun/shade, a possible alternative couple and perhaps the more expected, does not as readily carry such a dimension. The collective may even perhaps receive more emphasis than the individual in 'The Sun and the Fish' where 'I', as we shall see, is only elliptically registered.

5   The gathering crowd

Following her exordium on Queen Victoria, Woolf applies the rules of her 'amusing game' to the eclipse. This chapter considers how Woolf's narrative organises and genders the landscape, people, sky, and sun prior to the eclipse. The next two explore the gender politics of light, shade and colour in what follows.

> So, on this dark winter's morning, when the real world has faded, let us see what the eye can do for us. Show me the eclipse, we say to the eye; let us see that strange spectacle again. And we see at once – but the mind's eye is only by courtesy an eye; it is a nerve which hears and smells, which transmits heat and cold, which is attached to the brain and rouses the mind to discriminate and speculate – it is only for brevity's sake that we say that we "see" at once a railway station at night.
>
> (*CDB* 193–194)

A sense of collectivity is apparent in Woolf's shifts between 'we', 'us' and 'me' (but not 'I'). The title suggests sun/fish, and the exordium queen/heterogeneous collection; now the visual gives way to multiple sensual and reflective experiences and to the implied couple eclipse/railway-station-at-night. This sequence suggests the plural reading of 'fish'; and the fish half of the couple eclipse/station does carry the suggestion of darkness ('at night') we might expect as a contrary to the sun. The railway station is a connection point for many people:

> A crowd is gathered at the barrier; but how curious a crowd! Mackintoshes are slung over their arms; in their hands they carry little cases. They have a provisional, extemporized look. They have that moving and disturbing unity which comes from the consciousness that they (but here it would be more proper to say "we") have a purpose in common. Never was there a stranger purpose than that which brought us together that June night in Euston Railway Station. We were come to see the dawn.
>
> (*CDB* 194)

The passage begins by describing the crowd objectively in the present tense ('A crowd is gathered'), and ends by describing it subjectively in the past ('We were come . . .'). The narrative technique is cinematic: first we're given a broad, distant and objective view of a station at night, and then a closer view of a crowd, and as the description becomes more detailed and the observation closer, the less confident the narrative objectivity becomes. The transition from outside observation of the crowd to inside experience is marked by the statement: 'They have a provisional, extemporized look', which signals a change of perspective: this way of looking is not going to last. In the next sentence the crowd's status moves from object to subject – 'they' to 'we'. This shift occurs during a description of common experience, more appropriately expressed subjectively than objectively – '(but here it would be more proper to say "we")'. Here the tense shifts from present (or present historic) to past: no longer 'extemporized' in an objectified continuous present, the crowd is recollected as a subjective historical experience.

The crowd's sense of unity is described as 'moving and disturbing' in this transitional sentence, giving a sense of double perspective (the crowd is aware of itself as object and subject), which is reinforced by the larger narrative framework: the essay begins with the impersonal 'one' ('One says to the eye Athens'). It shifts to the subjective 'we': 'Show me the eclipse, we say to the eye'. This sentence demonstrates the individual instance of a common plural experience, evident not only in the play between 'me' and 'we' but also in the pun 'eye'/I. The instruction to the individual self comes from a pluralized subjectivity: the individual speaks from the plural/social subjective 'we' to itself as singular object – 'me'.

The description of the crowd starts with the authorial 'we' seeing a railway station and then a crowd, which turns from 'they' to 'we'. Thus the authorial 'we', which both signals impersonal narrator and conjoins writer and reader, deepens to an experiential 'we' recalling a past common experience. Nowhere, apart from the pun on 'eye', has the first person singular appeared: this is a notable departure from the diary account of the eclipse, where a private, individual self does call itself 'I'. In fact, nowhere at all in 'The Sun and the Fish' is this 'I' discernible.

In her play between objective and subjective experience, Woolf demonstrates the paradox of subjectivity with a plural rather than singular model of the subject. The figure of the crowd raises questions about subjectivity and plurality: is the crowd composed of many different subjects, or is it one homogeneous subject? A hierarchized model of subjectivity, in which one subject subsumes all others (as objects), results in the crowd as one amorphous subject: individual-subject/herd-object. A model of differentiated subjectivity changes subject/object to intersubjective relations within the crowd. I will argue that in Woolf's handling, later in the essay, of light as the traditional metaphor of subjectivity, she uses colour as an indication of plural subjectivity, and she decentres the notion of one light by the creation of multiple points of enlightenment.

'The Sun and the Fish' does not follow Woolf's diary entry in its account of personal companions or particular events on the train journey; instead it emphasizes that the train (more appropriately 'our' train) is one of several:

> Trains like ours were starting all over England at that very moment to see the dawn. All noses were pointing north. When for a moment we halted in the depths of the country, there were the pale yellow lights of motor cars also pointing north. There was no sleep, no fixity in England that night. All were on the roads; all were travelling north. All were thinking of the dawn. As the night wore on, the sky, which was the object of so many million thoughts, assumed greater substance and prominence than usual. The consciousness of the whitish soft canopy above us increased in weight as the hours passed.
>
> (*CDB* 194)

This plurality of trains and cars in some ways suggests a plurality of subjects, yet their common purpose seems to unite them as one large subject; and if the 'pale lights of the motor cars' are registers of these many points of consciousness, they seem to be moving towards subsuming in the larger light of dawn ('All were thinking of the dawn') as if it were one large consciousness. Compare this with Mr Ramsay's thoughts on the tradition of enlightenment: 'His own little light would shine, not very brightly, for a year or two, and would then be merged in some bigger light, and that in a bigger light still.' (*TL* 59) The power of this unifying telos of light is contrasted with its traditional foil – the chaotic darkness of night ('There was . . . no fixity in England that night'). Here Woolf also inserts a sense of national destiny into the common purpose of witnessing the dawn, but this does not suggest the essay itself promotes patriotism or nationalistic pride; for it is clear that everything associated with the security of this dawn light is to be thrown into question by the eclipse.

The effect of the common consciousness upon its main object, the sky, is startling: as attention to it increases it seems to become more and more reified ('assumed greater substance'). More subtly, this palpableness is transferred to consciousness itself. The last sentence of the passage merits careful attention ('The consciousness of the whitish soft canopy above us increased in weight as the hours passed'): the cloud canopy does not gain weight, but 'the consciousness of' it does. The construction is ambiguous enough to see a transference of consciousness from people to the clouds themselves. The cloud is both the subject and object of consciousness, and its fluctuating status between solidity and air, between evanescence and palpableness, reflects a fluctuating subjectivity. Woolf explains that usual subject/object relations have indeed been altered:

> When in chill early morning we were turned out on a Yorkshire roadside, our senses had orientated themselves differently from usual. We were no longer in the same relation to people, houses, and trees; we were related to the whole

world. We had come, not to lodge in the bedroom of an inn; we were come
for a few hours of disembodied intercourse with the sky.

(*CDB* 194)

It seems that subject/object relations have been abandoned altogether ('we
were no longer in relation to people, houses, and trees'), in favour of purely
subjective ones ('disembodied intercourse with the sky'). On approaching the
observation site, 'we' forget material surroundings, mundane relationships,
bodies, and the object world. The subjects of Woolf's story no longer need
define themselves against an object world because they are about to commune
with the ultimate (symbol of) subjectivity. In terms of metaphor construction,
it is as if as tenors they no longer require their usual earthly vehicles – 'people,
houses, and trees' – because they are about to define themselves somewhat
differently in relation to the sky.

'People, houses, and trees' are fundamental metaphors; and they are metaphors of metaphor. 'House' suggests the standard figure of metaphor:[1] the
subject as tenant of the object, the house as space to be occupied. In this sense
they are always and already feminine: 'Woman', it is worth noting, is traditionally read as house or room – a space or gap to be filled, and may be the
archetypal vehicle of personification. Woolf's search for 'a room of one's own'
may be seen as the feminist search for a metaphor which does not, by the very
nature of its construction, exclude the feminine. 'Tree', furthermore, like
'Woman', suggests a naturalized (and naturalizing) metaphor disguising its own
artificial construction. 'We had come, not to lodge in the bedroom of an inn'
makes somewhat melodramatic reference to the happy neglect of sleeping
arrangements: normal, bodily requirements are flouted for the night's vigil
before the dawn is greeted. By avoiding the commodified, economic exchange
of residence at an inn, they also perhaps, in another sense, avoid entering into
the usual power relations of metaphor: 'lodge' contrasts sharply with 'intercourse'. The sublime experience they anticipate, then, is not to be in the bedroom, but with the heavens. The tone here is not entirely serious – both edgy
and slightly camp.

The hyperbolic diction seems to parody the religious connotations of this
implied sublime communication between people and sky, but in no sense less-
ens the air of strange excitement. They are after all, anticipating a momentous event in the heavens. It is of interest as to whether or not the relationship
between people and sky is to be seen as ultimately hierarchized: that is, whether
or not the sky is more than literally *higher* than the people. If the sky is taken as
the harbinger of a higher consciousness, it subsumes the subjective consciousness of those below. On the other hand, it may turn out to be merely an object
after all, onto which the people project their subjective and collective fantasies.

The possibility of reading this as a transcendental experience, in which human subjectivity is translated into communion with a higher noumenal order, is undercut. Given the tenets of the 'amusing game' introducing Woolf's essay, such 'disembodied intercourse' may be viewed ironically as an already thwarted possibility: intercourse, the game infers, can never be disembodied.

Abruptly leaving off from this grandiloquent moment of expectation, the third paragraph of Woolf's essay dramatically shifts in tone to set a new scene. The landscape through which the travellers move to reach their final assembly point is now described. This passage is strongly reminiscent of the diary entry, but also differs from it in significant ways. For example, the essay makes no clear indication of the transfer from train to omnibus or from omnibus to foot, as the diary does; nor does it mention the castle or other features in the landscape recorded in the diary. It does, however, recall the paleness: 'Everything was very pale. The river was pale and the fields, brimming with grasses and tasselled flowers which should have been red, had no colour in them, but lay there whispering and waving round colourless farmhouses.' (*CDB* 194–195) The paleness of the early morning scene is here emphasized even more than in the diary, almost to the point of dogmatism: 'Everything was very pale'. Woolf ascribes this paleness and colourlessness to the river, the fields, the flowers and the farmhouses, just as she does in the diary. But she omits any reference to the lights she notices in the landscape: there is earlier mention of 'the pale yellow lights of motor cars' but these are no longer described as 'burning'. The light 'burning' from the castle window has also disappeared along with the castle itself. In fact, the word 'burn' does not appear at all in the essay version. It is even extinguished from the description of the grasses and tasselled plants with which 'all the fields were aburn' in the diary account. In the essay, the fields are, instead, 'brimming with grasses and tasselled flowers' and they are 'whispering and waving'. 'Brimming' suggests water rather than fire; and 'lay there whispering and wavering' suggests passivity rather than smouldering energy. Like a painter, organizing colour planes, Woolf has homogenized and distilled a complex picture of the landscape into a simple, almost monolithic, paleness. There are no lights or textures to disrupt this anæmic vista, nothing to distract the eye. One tone prevails: 'Everything was very pale'.

There follow subtle differences between diary and essay; and the essay's adaptions to the description of farms glimpsed by the travellers offer significant insight into Woolf's narrative technique. The diary and essay versions follow respectively:

> Pale & grey too were the little uncompromising Yorkshire farms. As we passed one, the farmer, & his wife & sister came out, all tightly & tidily dressed in black, as if they were going to church. At another ugly square farm,

two women were looking out of the upper windows. These had white blinds drawn down half across them.

(D iii 142)

Now the farmhouse door would open, and out would step to join the procession the farmer and his family in their Sunday clothes, neat, dark and silent as if they were going up hill to church; or sometimes women merely leant on the window sills of the upper rooms watching the procession pass with amused contempt, it appeared – they have come such hundreds of miles, and for what? they seemed to say – in complete silence.

(CDB 195)

Woolf generalizes for the essay the singular and specific observations of the diary. For example, in the diary she has a farmer and his wife and sister emerging from 'one' of the 'uncompromising Yorkshire farms'. In the essay this is related as a recurrent event: 'Now the farmhouse door would open, and out would step'. Similarly, in the diary Woolf remembers seeing 'At another . . . farm two women . . . looking out of the upper windows'; and this is transformed into something intermittently glimpsed: 'sometimes women merely leant on the window sills of upper rooms'. These women are particularly interesting. In the diary they are 'looking out', but in the essay they are 'watching the procession pass with amused contempt'. In both accounts they appear in opposition to the farmer and family, and to the visitors, but it is only in the essay that they are explicitly hostile. In the diary the 'white blinds' of their windows contrast with the neat 'black' attire of the farmer's family, but the quaint piety of this family is not openly ridiculed by the women. A similar sort of description of the family – 'as if they were going to church' – is retained in the essay, but the distinctive use of 'black' and 'white' is not.

These differences suggest Woolf has taken out of her landscape all points of light and bright colour which, in the diary, had the effect of punctuating the land with alternative points of illumination (and consciousness) to the light in the sky. In removing them Woolf is tidying up her picture into more uniformly defined areas of light and shade – and paleness. We can no longer be distracted by these points of brightness and energy from our anticipation of the main light above. Even the 'pale lights' of the cars have been schematized into this anticipatory scene.

The anticipation is emphasized in the observation: 'We had an odd sense of keeping an appointment with an actor of such vast proportions that he would come silently and be everywhere.' *(CDB* 195) Just as with the portrayal of the pious locals joining the 'procession' as if it were a religious one, here too is a sense of dressing the occasion in outmoded rhetoric: religious vocabulary is applied to a now rationally understood event. The 'odd sense' comes from the tension between old and new attitudes. The omniscient, omnipresent (and masculine) God of Christianity is mockingly referred to as 'an actor of . . . vast proportions'. The scientific explanation of the solar system informs the 'sense of keeping an appointment', in that the moments of sunrise and eclipse have been scientifically calculated and predicted. The idea of an appointment also suggests an agreement between subjects; but the peculiarity (and humour) of this 'sense' lies with the inherent contradiction in having an appointment (at a particular time in a particular place) with something omniscient, eternal, and omnipresent – or with something whose appearance is as inevitable and insentient as clockwork. There is a similar paradox at work in the wearing of church clothes to witness an event celebrated and anticipated for its scientific significance – its confirmation of rational laws. It is in this ironical context, let us note, that Woolf describes the sun as a male actor of vast proportions.

Comparison of the fourth paragraph's opening passage, in 'The Sun and the Fish', with its corresponding passage in the diary, reveals further evidence of Woolf's revision of the landscape to exclude any mention of points of light in the land. She does, of course, omit other things from the account, such as the incident where 'The driver once got out & put a small stone behind our wheel' (D III 142), but it is her handling of information about light which is of greatest interest.

> We got out, & found ourselves very high, on a moor, boggy, heathery, with butts for grouse shooting. There were grass tracks here & there, & people had already taken up positions. So we joined them, walking out to what seemed the highest point looking out over Richmond. One light burnt down there. Vales & moors stretched, slope after slope, round us. It was like Haworth country. But over Richmond, where the sun was rising, was a soft grey cloud. We could see by a gold spot where the sun was. But it was early yet. We had to wait, stamping to keep warm. Ray had wrapped herself in the blue striped blanket off a double bed. She looked incredibly vast & bedroomish. Saxon looked very old. Leonard kept looking at his watch. Four great red setters came leaping over the moor.
>
> (D III 142–143)

> By the time we were at the meeting place, on a high fell where the hills stretched their limbs out over the flowing brown moorland below, we had put on too – though we were cold and with our feet stood in red bog water were likely to be still colder, though some of us were squatted on mackintoshes among cups and plates, eating, and others were fantastically accoutred and none were at their best – still we had put on a certain dignity. Rather, perhaps, we had put off the little badges and signs of individuality. We were strung out against the sky in outline and had the look of statues standing prominent on the ridge of the world. We were very, very old; we

were men and women of the primeval world come to salute the dawn. So the worshippers at Stonehenge must have looked among tussocks of grass and boulders of rock. Suddenly, from the motor car of some Yorkshire squire, there bounded four large, lean, red dogs, hounds of the ancient world, hunting dogs, they seemed, leaping with their noses close to the ground on the track of boar or deer. Meanwhile the sun was rising. A cloud glowed as a white shade glows when the light is slowly turned up behind it.

(*CDB* 195)

The narrative sequence has been altered considerably: most notably, the comparison to Stonehenge now appears before the sun is seen 'rising'. This complies with Woolf's parenthetical comment in the diary, '(this idea came more vividly with the pale light though;)' (*D* III 143). This difference arises, then, directly out of a narrative instruction in the first text. It makes a considerable difference symbolically to place the piece describing druidic (though she no longer uses the word) sentiments before sunrise rather than after. As we noted of the diary entry, Woolf seems ultimately to be resisting such sentiments, so it makes sense to restore the sequence of thought to a position of pre-enlightenment (that is, the period before sunrise). In the essay, then, the references to Stonehenge grow out of the description of the people on the hillside before dawn, whereas in the diary they occur when Woolf describes those anxious moments when the sun 'had sailed fast into cloud again'. In both cases the sun is not in view. The essay restores the comment to its proper context.

Here the essay's landscape description is more concise than the diary's. It condenses the latter's visual information into a simple coherent (intimately sexual, perhaps) image. Again, Woolf has extinguished the light mentioned in the diary account: the essay does not mention the valley below at this point, and there is no reference to the diary observation that 'One light burnt down there.' Nor is there mention of 'Haworth country'.

The essay, most remarkably, has the land and people merging together, whereas the diary account clearly distinguishes between them (each person is named, and individual activities are recorded). The essay personifies the land ('a high fell where the hills stretched their limbs out over the flowing brown moorland below'), and shows the people to have relinquished 'the little badges and signs of individuality'. The land intimately encloses them. Indeed, their meeting place on a hill, from whose mound limbs stretch, conjures up an image of pubic intimacy, suggestive of the *mons Veneris*. (The reference to the Brontës' 'Haworth country' is perhaps distilled into this feminine mythopœic landscape.)

Woolf's striking use of parentheses reinforces the sense of the land's embrace. Inside the dashes appears an impersonal and generalized account of the human activity; outside, the inclusive 'we' parallels the land in 'put[ting] on a certain dignity'. This generalized set of humanity, with feet in bog water, seems more

closely connected to the land than the individuals in the diary. The personification of the land as sensually feminine encourages the 'red bog water' to be
interpreted as, perhaps, menstrual fluid. The scene has taken on surrealist
dimensions: here are swarms of people tramping the highest point of a terrain
described as if it were an enormous vulva, awaiting the arrival of 'an actor of
such vast proportions that he would come silently and be everywhere'.

There may also be something threatening in this image of feminine expectation, as if the land were thrusting this hill forward as a challenge to the great
actor, the sun. The sheer giganticism makes the human activity irrelevant, and
the land may be seen in a posture, not of submission, but of anticipation. There
may be an air of feminine sexual assertion, then, in the hills' stretching of limbs.
Whatever the details of such an interpretation, however, the feminization of the
landscape makes more explicit the sexual connotations of the earlier description of the sun as masculine. The assigning of the masculine gender to the
sun is, in itself, a significant departure from the diary account. Collapsed into
this description, too, is the sense of the travellers themselves at last stretching
their own limbs after the long journey and organizing themselves for the solemnity of the occasion.

Directly after this, comes the reference to Stonehenge, and the loss of individuality is stressed. The ancient sense of interconnectedness between humanity
and land is emphasized by the graduation of imagery from people to statues
to boulders. In their anticipation of the sun's arrival these people seem to be
devolving back to the 'men and women of the primeval world'. This analogy
seems not entirely serious. As with the clothes of the farmer's family, there is an
awareness that this is parody: 'Rather, perhaps . . . we . . . had the look of . . .
So the worshippers of Stonehenge must have looked'. The intrusion of modern
technology in the form of a motor car jolts us back into the twentieth century.

Whereas the diary states simply that 'Four great red setters came leaping over
the moor', the essay not only has them bounding from a car, but also calls them
'hounds of the ancient world', thus undoing the effects of the car by resurrect-
ing the analogy with ancient times. Woolf's hyperbole ('We were very, very
old; we were men and women come to salute the dawn. . . . Suddenly . . . there
bounded four large, lean, red dogs, hounds of the ancient world') suggests a
gleeful camping up of the experience rather more than a sombre evocation of
ancient customs. The dogs are associated with both the ancient world and a
feudalism which has not altogether died out. Their noses lead us back to the
dominant image in this passage – 'the ground'. The squire in his motor-car
reminds us that the patriarchy of land-based feudalism survives into the modern era of capitalism.

The arrival of the squire's dogs, in the essay, is immediately followed by the
rising of the sun. The dogs seem to be a symbolic composition of the hounds

of hell and the four horsemen of the Apocalypse – after whose appearance, according to the Revelation, 'the sun became black as sackcloth of hair'.[2] In the diary, the dogs are mentioned twice: first, after the activities of Woolf's companions are described, where there follow some bizarre comments about other animals ('There were sheep feeding behind us. Vita had tried to buy a guinea pig – Quentin advised a savage – so she observed the animals from time to time.' (*D* III 143)); and second, when the clouds momentarily obscure the sun, and Woolf contrasts the indifference of the sheep ('they showed no fear') and of the 'setters racing round' with the dignity of the people, who are then likened to druids. These various bestial images are distilled, in the essay, into the single image of the squire's dogs running and hunting, and generally dominating the land. Their actions herald the arrival of the sun, and anticipate its dominion over the land. A sense of hierarchy is implied here: at the top is the sun (or God), below which is the squire, then his dogs, and at the bottom is the land, described in terms suggestive of feminine sexuality. The sun is the absolute subject, the land the absolute object. '"The" couple man/woman' inheres in the opposition sun/land: the sun has already been referred to as 'he', and the land as feminine.

Woolf's revision of her diary account enforces a strict design. In the essay, in compliance with the schematization of sky and land, all references to independent sources of light on the land have disappeared. The diary shows that Woolf was certainly struck by the presence of these lights and by the 'burning' quality of the land's colours. She refers again to these images at the moment of the eclipse: 'Down in the valley it was an extraordinary scrumble of red & black; there was the one light burning.' Yet this compelling vision is missing from the essay. Non-solar light and bright colours do, nevertheless, resurface at the end of the essay, but in entirely different contexts, as we shall see.

The diary describes the sun as a 'gold spot' behind 'soft grey cloud', and the essay recounts this as: 'A cloud glowed as a white shade glows when the light is turned up behind it.' The cloud is emphasized as a veil over the sun. Woolf then draws attention, in the essay, to the sunlight as the source of colour for the landscape: 'Golden wedge-shaped streamers fell from it and marked the trees in the valley green and the villages blue brown.' (*CDB* 195) From behind a screen of cloud the sun dispenses colour – and life. Interestingly, the diary does not mention the trees at all. This is an unusual and important instance of Woolf's addition to, rather than simplification of, the landscape described in her diary.

The essay follows the diary in contrasting the sky behind the observers with the sky in front of them, and develops the image of the sun as a 'gold spot' showing its power to burn through its halo of cloud:

In the sky behind us there swam white islands in pale blue lakes. The sky was open and free there, but in front of us a soft snowbank had massed itself. Yet, as we looked, we saw it proving worn and thin in patches. The gold momentarily increased, melting the whiteness to a fiery gauze, and this grew frailer and frailer till, for one instant, we saw the sun in full splendour. Then there was a pause, a moment of suspense, like that which precedes a race. The starter held his watch in his hand, counting the seconds. Now they were off.

(CDB 195–96)

No reference is made to the red and black cloud or to the light in the valley, which in the diary might be taken as counterpoints to the light and cloud above. The tone of the remaining colour – 'blue' (of the sky behind) – has been subdued: it is now 'pale blue'. Woolf has also inverted the description of the cloud in the sky behind: in the diary she describes 'blue spaces in the cloud' which in the essay become 'white islands in pale blue lakes'. This suggests that the blue areas are surrounded by cloud. The paleness of this blue also suggests less of a contrast with the cloud than in the diary. This again homogenizes the imagery – this time to highlight the conflict between sun and cloud. When the sky is described in the essay as 'open and free', this does not imply that the sky is altogether free of cloud, but rather that there is free *movement* of cloud – the operative word being 'swam'.

The sense of looseness and freedom is contrasted with the static and impenetrable nature of the cloud amassed in front of the observers and veiling the sun. The opposition between sun and cloud is communicated by a sense of agency lent to them: the cloud 'mass[es] itself' to block the sun, and the sun retaliates by 'melting' away the cloud to a state of frailty. This develops into the terminology of open competition between them ('Now they were off'). The starter's watch and the race between sun and cloud are, of course, tricks of narrative which effectively dramatize the spectators' anxiety and excitement at the approaching moment of the eclipse, but they also have wider significance. That the starter's watch is held in a man's hand, for example, serves as reminder of the precise, scientific measurement of the event by a, predominantly male, corps of astronomers. The event is framed, then, within the terms of masculine reason and scientific enquiry.

6 The chasing of the sun and the victory of the colours

The race

The account of the race between sun, cloud and clock, in the essay's fifth paragraph, seems inspired by Marvell: 'Thus, though we cannot make our sun/ Stand still, yet we will make him run.'[1] Woolf describes the sun as if 'he' were being hunted down like an animal for sport, and in this respect, the story seems to develop a mythopœic resonance. The hunting connotations of the 'Yorkshire squire' and his 'ancient world . . . dogs' are continued:

> The sun had to race through the clouds and to reach the goal, which was a thin transparency to the right, before the sacred seconds were up. He started. The clouds flung every obstacle in his way. They clung, they impeded. He dashed through them. He could be felt, flashing and flying when he was invisible. His speed was tremendous. Here he was out and bright; now he was under and lost. But always one felt him flying and thrusting through the murk to his goal. For one second he emerged and showed himself to us through our glasses, a hollowed sun, a crescent sun. Finally, he went under for his last effort. Now he was completely blotted out. The moments passed. Watches were held in hand after hand. The sacred twenty-four seconds were begun. Unless he could win through before the last one was over, he was lost. Still one felt him tearing and racing behind the clouds to win free; but the clouds held him. They spread; they thickened; they slackened; they muffled his speed. Of the twenty-four seconds only five remained, and still he was obscured. And, as the fatal seconds passed, and we realized that the sun was being defeated, had now, indeed lost the race, all the colour began to go from the moor.
>
> (*CDB* 196)

The intense repetition of 'he', 'him', and 'his', leaves no doubt that the sun is, here, masculine. The excessive underlining of the sun's maleness prompts us to look for something we might read as female. Ancient mythology supplies a variety of possibilities, but first we might note the sexually charged violence inherent in Woolf's description of the sun's demise, as well as the less than impartial involvement of the observers: 'he could be felt . . . always one felt him flying and thrusting . . . one felt him tearing and racing'. The lurid sensationalism is rather peculiar in a description of clouds moving across the sun. The observers seem to be *in at the kill*, to follow the hunting metaphor. The verb 'felt' provides the hinge of the ambiguity here: on the one hand, it means merely that those watching can detect the change of temperature as the clouds move across and away from the sun; on the other hand, this physical sensation involves the observers allegorically in the hunt – they actually feel 'him' struggle.

Mythological chase and renewal

Woolf seems to share in her eclipse narrative Whitehead's predilection for classical mythopœic analogies. The cult of the 'Kings of the Wood', described by James George Frazer, may provide ancient precedent to her description of the sun's flight. They, too, 'die a violent death' but they may also

> escape from it for a time by their bodily strength and agility; for in several of these northern customs the flight and pursuit of the king is a prominent part of the ceremony, and in one case at least if the king can outrun his pursuers he retains his life and his office for another year. . . . The life of the god-man is prolonged on the condition of his shewing, in a severe physical contest of fight or flight, that his bodily strength is not decayed, and that, therefore, the violent death, which sooner or later is inevitable, may for the present be postponed.[2]

The parallels between the pursuit of the king and the pursuit of the sun suggest Woolf invests the 'sacred twenty-four seconds' of her chase with a mythopœic significance, allowing us to read the whole event of the solar eclipse as a ritual testing and reaffirmation of masculine sovereignty and subjectivity. The sun's recovery, then, would parallel the reassertion of the masculine. Given such an interpretation, perhaps we might read Woolf's insertion into the landscape of 'the trees in the valley green' as a presage of the 'Sacred Wood'. This has some interesting implications for our readings of the opposition between masculine and feminine set up in the story so far; and we might wonder whether Woolf's account of the eclipse ultimately leaves everything back in place, thus reaffirming masculine sovereignty. For the moments leading up to the eclipse, the conventional story pattern is played out. Two stories from classical mythology, also with some bearing upon this passage, demonstrate the gender opposition inherent in this tale of the sun's flight. Actaeon and Orpheus both die the victims of horrific acts of feminine vengeance, and both their fates resemble the cults described by Frazer.

Actaeon is 'a sacred King of the pre-Hellenic stag cult, torn to pieces at the end of his reign of fifty months, namely a Great Year; his co-king or tanist, reigning for the remainder'; and Orpheus is a 'sacred king [who] was struck by a thunderbolt – that is, killed with a double-axe – in an oak grove at the summer-solstice, and then dismembered by the Mænads of the bull cult, like Zagreus [Dionysus] . . . or of the stag cult, like Actaeon.'³ Actaeon's offence was against Artemis/Diana, the Triple Moon-goddess, sister of Apollo, whom he accidentally surprised naked in her ritual bath, while he was out hunting. She changed him into a stag, and he was torn to pieces by his own hunting hounds. Ovid supplies the gory details:

> Well, indeed, might he wish to be absent, but he is here; and well might he wish to see, not to feel, the fierce doings of his own hounds. They throng him on every side and, plunging their muzzles in his flesh, mangle their master under the deceiving form of the deer. Nor, as they say, till he had been done to death by many wounds, was the wrath of the quiver-bearing goddess appeased.⁴

Woolf's description of the clouds flocking the sun is suggestive of a pack of hounds overcoming some poor victim ('They spread; they thickened; they slackened; they muffled his speed'); but whereas Ovid communicates the victim's experiences quite closely and sympathetically ('well might he wish to see, not to feel'), Woolf relates the pursuers' feelings ('He could be felt' . . .), perhaps suggesting a certain relish in the sun's defeat, a perverse thrill in the chase: we may detect some feminine pleasure in the sun's demise after all.

Orpheus's offence was against Dionysus whom he neglected in favour of devotion to Apollo. He was pursued and torn to pieces by the Thracian women (Mænads or Bacchantae), and his singing head floated out to Lesbos.

> [The Mænads] turned bloody hands against Orpheus and flocked around like birds when they see the bird of night wandering in the daylight; and as when in the amphitheatre in the early morning of the spectacle the doomed stag is the prey of dogs. . . . These savage women caught up and, first tearing in pieces the oxen who threatened them with their horns, they rushed back to slay the bard; and, as he stretched out his suppliant hands, uttering words then, but never before, unheeded, and moving them not a whit by his voice, the impious women struck him down.⁵

This story positions the feminine in even closer association with the bestial and the bodily. The male hero is not the victim merely of a goddess's wrath which causes his transformation into a beast and his death by pursuing beasts, but he actually suffers, untransformed, almost the same fate, this time torn apart by women. Woolf's insistence upon the maleness of the sun in the context of such a chase, may suggest readings which identify as female his pursuers. Yet, it seems, at no point does Woolf's story explicitly refer to anything as 'she' in opposition to this 'he'. There are, however, feminine images of opposition subtly embedded in the narrative: the 'amused contempt' of the women at the farm windows, and the feminine qualities ascribed to the land.

An Orphic reading of the demise of the sun in Woolf's text supplies an interpretation of the sun as symbolic of the soul, or divine intellect, fleeing the constraints of the body, commonly regarded as evil. Her feminine images may suggest dark, chthonic cults, the Dionysian in pursuit of the Apollonian. The couple man/woman within the opposition light/dark is maintained here just as firmly. Yet to celebrate feminine qualities here as positive is not to escape the dominant hierarchy, for as Lloyd warns any 'strengths and virtues' ascribed to the feminine 'are strengths that derive from exclusion'.[6]

The renewal of masculine sovereignty, through its endurance of violent assault by feminine forces, is surely not to be the outcome of Woolf's eclipse story. Woolf, in 'Modern Fiction', makes parodic and subversive use of this imagery in a metaphor for fiction: 'if we can imagine the art of fiction come alive and standing in our midst, she would undoubtedly bid us break her and bully her, as well as honour and love her, for so her youth is renewed and her sovereignty assured.' (*CR* 195) The recommendation of shocking violence towards a female figure personifying certain values is also adopted by Woolf against her target, 'the Angel in the House':

> I turned upon her and caught her by the throat. I did my best to kill her. . . . Had I not killed her she would have killed me. She would have plucked the heart out of my writing. For, as I found, directly I put pen to paper, you cannot review even a novel without having a mind of your own, without expressing what you think to be the truth about human relations, morality, sex. And all these questions, according to the Angel in the House, cannot be dealt with freely and openly by women . . .[7]

Clearly, Woolf is not recommending violence for the sake of vigorous renewal, although the Angel in the House does not go away so easily: 'She died hard. Her fictitious nature was of great assistance to her. It is far harder to kill a phantom than a reality. She was always creeping back when I thought I had despatched her.' (*DM* 153) It is also clear that both figures (fiction and the Angel) are not real. Woolf, at the same time as recommending the renewal of fiction by the violent disruption of tradition, manages both to attack the notion of the feminine as personifying vehicle; and to assert a feminine sovereignty by inverting the gender associations of mythic renewal by violence.

Women and darkness

Given the parallels to an Actaeon or Orpheus-like death in Woolf's eclipse story, it is worth noting how Classical Greek culture understood such oppositions, and how they inform the stories that Woolf seems to echo. 'Male-ordered' Greek societies 'assigned to women ritual presidency over the transitional experiences, dying and birth, which are perceived as passages into and out of darkness'; and so linked women with sacred concepts of pollution (*'hagnos* or *hagios*, "sacred", is cognate with *agos*, "pollution"'): 'women's supposed aptness for handling the more polluting and "darker" aspects of divinity is interdependent on their biological and cultural associations with what comes into and what comes out of darkness, whether the darkness be that of the underworld or of the female body.'[8]

Woolf's reference to the 'sacred seconds' before the eclipse might also suggest this ancient sense of sacred darkness. Frazer tells us of the popular belief that during an eclipse the air is infected, poisoned. 'An eclipse is particularly poisonous', apparently, 'when it happens on a Wednesday' – the day of Woolf's eclipse![9]

> A Cambodian maiden at puberty is said to "enter into the shade". . . .
> But this state of seclusion is discontinued during eclipses; at such times she goes forth and pays her devotions to the monster who is supposed to cause eclipses by catching the heavenly bodies between his teeth. This permission to . . . appear abroad during an eclipse seems to shew how literally the injunction is interpreted which forbids maidens entering on womanhood to look upon the sun.[10]

We may surmise, then, strong cultural traditions in the almost institutionalized ascendancy of feminine and bestial forces at times of eclipse. Darkness and chaos, however temporary, are the province of women, and women must be carefully controlled. The Mænadism of classical literature may also inform Woolf's eclipse. Euripides' *Bacchae* explores 'male Athenian fantasies' about 'women escaping from confinement into the wilds', and

> combines a picture of women who are "out of their minds" with a picture of women out of their proper place within home and city; and it links both to the tearing apart of an individual king, the collapse of a royal palace, and the exile and fragmentation of the founding royal family (*Bacchae*, 633, 1350–63). It establishes women's potentially peaceful physical relation with savage nature through their reproductive functions – the mænads suckle the young of wild animals – but shows male order, and an individual male, destroyed through this relationship, and through the women's relationship with a god who "drives them out of the house in madness" (*Bacchae*, 33).

Similarly, the threat women pose to a male sense of order is shown by Aeschylus' 'mænads tearing apart Orpheus, . . . the archetypal author of order (in that music, in the Greek tradition, was an image of balance and order) and wielder of human power to tame animal nature: women here tear to pieces a man who makes, as Pentheus attempts to maintain, an image of order.'[11]

Woolf and the classical sun

Woolf was familiar with the *Bacchae*, as her reading notes show (*BERG* 13, *RN* 1.19), and with much of classical Greek literature. In 'On Not Knowing Greek' she contrasts the English landscape and its 'impossible' climate with the 'warmth and sunshine' of the Greek: 'If we try to think of Sophocles here, we must annihilate the smoke and the damp and the thick wet mists.' (*CR* 40–41) The sunshine is integral to the drama, as Woolf understands it: 'They were speaking to an enormous audience rayed round them on one of those brilliant southern days when the sun is so hot and yet the air so exciting.' (*CR* 42) She speaks of the directness, the 'sharpness and compression' (*CR* 45) of these plays performed under the naked glare of the sun. The English landscape and weather may be very different, but nevertheless English culture has its roots in the Greek: 'the stable, the permanent, the original human being is to be found there.' (*CR* 44)

Woolf uses the differences in climate as an analogy for the loss of literary directness; it is as if the 'thick wet mists' of England have clouded over the Greeks' sun. Centuries of lesser imitations have obscured the splendour of the originals and turned them into 'the greatest bores and the most demoralising companions in the world. The plays of Addison, Voltaire, and a host of others are there to prove it.' (*CR* 45) In order to feel the benefit of the sun, we must 'encounter them in the Greek', for a 'fragment of their speech broken off would, we feel, colour oceans and oceans of the respectable drama. Here we meet them before their emotions have been worn into uniformity. Here we listen to the nightingale whose song echoes through English literature singing in her own Greek tongue.' In the Greek 'we see the hairy, tawny bodies' of Orpheus and his followers 'at play in the sunlight among the trees, not posed gracefully on granite plinths in the pale corridors of the British Museum.' (*CR* 45)

Woolf read Greek for two and a half years in preparation for this essay (*RN* 101), and even made her own translation of Aeschylus' *Agamemnon* (*BERG* 13, *RN* 3; *D* II 215); so by the time of the eclipse she had certainly basked in the direct heat of the classical literary sun, and was indeed capable of reading (and writing) such analogies into the landscape. 'It is to the Greeks that we turn', Woolf concludes, 'when we are sick of the vagueness, of the confusion, of the Christianity and its consolations, of our own age.' (*CR* 59) The story informing the *Bacchae* warns of the fatal danger of encountering unmediated the heat of heavenly light (and, indeed, of attempting *disembodied* intercourse). It is the story of the mother of Dionysus, Semele, consumed by Zeus' flames in conceiving their son.[12]

Robert Yelverton Tyrrell, whose 1892 edition of Euripides' *Bacchae* Woolf worked from (*BERG* 13, *RN* 1.19), makes some observations of interest to our discussion of rationalism and mysticism in Woolf's work. The play, he notes is reputed to represent an intellectual volte-face (or 'Palinode') for Euripides, 'a recantation of the advanced views found in his earlier plays. It is supposed that, feeling the approach of old age, he here preaches the worship of those gods whom he had despised in his prime, and defends those superstitions which he had in his youth assailed.'[13] This is of particular relevance to the 'vast obeisance' of Woolf's diary account of the eclipse, and to the rather different version she gives in the essay. Woolf, as noted above, seems at times to verge on the mystical in her diary description yet always pulls back to a rationalistic account; and in the essay she plays off the outmoded religious vocabulary of the locals' dress, for example, against the language of scientific calculation and expectation. From this we might gather that she concurs with Conrad in asserting a rationalism capable of embracing experiences of a 'mystical' nature, and that her writing shows the tension to which this embrace is occasionally stretched and tested. Tyrrell counters the palinodic interpretations of Euripides, arguing that on both rationalism and religion *The Bacchae* is consistent with Euripides' other and earlier plays.

> We have not in the Bacchae any change in the point of view from which Euripides regards the old gods of the heathen mythology. . . . Dionysus is not only the god of wine, but a higher personification of passion in religion, and joy in life; and the Hippolytus as well as the Bacchae teaches that we should not neglect these sources of joy, enthuisiasm [*sic*], and passion.[14]

Plato's *Symposium* offers a similarly positive interpretation of the passions and actually connects them with the life of the intellect: 'He who, ascending from these earthly things under the influence of true love', Diotima informs Socrates, 'begins to perceive that beauty, is not far from the end. And the true order of going, or being led by another, to the things of love, is to begin from the beauties of earth and mount upwards for the sake of that other beauty.'[15] In *Philebus* Socrates asks 'Is there not an absurdity in arguing that there is nothing good or noble in the body, or in anything else, but that good is in the soul only . . . ?'[16] Such a model of reason opens up possibilities for criticism of male rationality as dangerously lacking a bodily dimension. The assignment of the bodily to the 'feminine', we might conclude, is a symptom of this false reason. Lloyd demonstrates the paths through philosophy this strand of thought has taken: the 'divided-soul model, when it is later brought into conjunction with male-female symbolism, produces much more complex relationships between femininity and Reason than the alignments of femaleness and matter, male-ness and Reason.' The 'genderization of the ideals [of rationality]', however, has ensured the exclusion of the feminine from 'past ideals of Reason as the sovereign human character trait.'[17]

The *Bacchae*, like Euripides' other plays, 'reprobates . . . *rationalism*', and condemns 'overwiseness, and "too great refinements."' Woolf herself, having noted the 'very odd argument' at *Bacchae* line 310, puzzles at her translation: '"The wisdom to keep the heart and soul from over-subtle wits. That which the less enlightened crowd approves and practices I will accept." What does this mean? Is he laughing at the love of wine?' (*BERG* 13, *RN* 1.19) 'In truth', Tyrrell acknowledges, 'the Bacchic worship may be described as the negation of rationality, and as passionate sympathy with nature. . . . and its condemna-tion of overwiseness, may serve as a fair statement of the moral purport of the play.'[18] This is not to suggest that the play itself, therefore, constitutes a total rejection of rationalism.

Euripides' rationalism lies in his undertaking 'to raise and deepen popular views';[19] Woolf's writing shows a similar project in her continuous engagement with, adjustment and adaptation of common views. Without concurring with patriarchy, she appropriates its vocabulary for her feminist counter-argument. So in the context of the eclipse, she does not banish druidical interpretations altogether, as a militant rationalist or scientist might, but acknowledges and adapts them to her own model of rationalism. The Mænads, it must be noted, represent a difficult challenge to this model. If feminism is to reclaim reason, it must come to terms with the legacy of a masculine rationality, transcending and excluding an always (and already) feminized principle of bodily 'enthui-siasm'. In her story of the eclipse, Woolf responds to this challenge with soph-isticated manipulation of light, dark, and colour.

If the mortal flesh of woman is overcome, in the story of Semele, by a mascu-line and divine light, then the story of the Bacchae and the occurrence of the solar eclipse suggest the opposite state of affairs. According to Frazer, eclipses are attributed in some cultures to a monster biting or attacking the sun; and 'when the sun and moon were in eclipse, the Tahitians supposed that the lumin-aries were in the act of copulation.'[20] In such interpretations the shadow oblit-erating the sun represents the physical and sexual overcoming by something feminine and bestial, of the masculine, metaphysical, spiritual, or intellectual.

The colours

'The Sun and the Fish' has so far described not the actual eclipse, but the obfuscation of the sun by clouds, and the beginning of the eclipse as discerned behind the cloud cover. At some point, the eclipsing shadow of the moon, the umbra, takes over from the clouds in the pursuit of the sun (but the moon itself is not mentioned). It is as if the clouds have finally caught 'him' so that the shadow might finish 'him' off. The shadow has a much more dramatic effect than the clouds. It, too, is obscured by the cloud cover, yet its effects upon the landscape are visible. Most notable is the draining away of colour, suggesting the loss of the victim's lifeblood at the moment of the kill. But if the sun is the victim, the land itself appears to be the corpse:

> . . . all the colour began to go from the moor. The blue turned to purple; the white became livid as at the approach of a violent but windless storm. Pink faces went green, and it became colder than ever. This was the defeat of the sun, then, and this was all, so we thought, turning in disappointment from the dull cloud blanket in front of us to the moors behind. They were livid, they were purple; but suddenly one became aware that something more was about to happen; something unexpected, awful, unavoidable. The shadow growing darker and darker over the moor was like the heeling over of a boat, which instead of righting itself at the critical moment, turns a little further and then a little further on its side; and suddenly capsizes. So the light turned and heeled over and went out. This was the end. The flesh and blood of the world was dead; only the skeleton was left. It hung beneath us, a frail shell; brown; dead; withered.
>
> (*CDB* 196–197)

The most startling difference between this and the diary account is the range of colours mentioned. The diary describes the fading of colour when the eclipse begins, and the only colours mentioned are the blue of the sky behind the observers, and the 'scrumble of red & black' of the clouds and the valley. In the essay, however, Woolf introduces a very different palette: 'The blue turned purple; the white became livid. . . . Pink faces went green . . . the moors were purple'. First we have blue, white, and pink; and then these colours turn to purple, (a 'livid') white, and green. Purple, white, and green, then, are the colours Woolf selects to accompany 'the defeat of the sun'.

Woolf's manipulation of these colours seems to me a feminist gesture, since purple, white and green have special significance for feminists, and most certainly for feminists of Woolf's time.

> The best known suffrage colours are the purple, white and green of the WSPU [the Women's Social and Political Union]. . . . White was for purity, green for hope and purple for dignity. . . . Purple was sometimes given as 'loyalty' or 'courage' and green as 'youth' or 'regeneration'.[21]

These colours were linked with the militant Women's Social and Political Union in particular and 'the cause' in general. By no means the only colours of feminism, they were by far the most famous. The colours were first thought of by Emmeline Pethick-Lawrence in preparation for the 'Woman's Sunday' rally of 21 June 1908. They 'were not selected until the middle of May, but according to Sylvia Pankhurst had "achieved a nation-wide familiarity before the month was out" '.[22] By the 21st they were marked indelibly and politically on the public mind: to see them was to be reminded of the WSPU and its campaign; they were its tricolour, its regimental colours.' The 1908 Chelsea WSPU banner (Plate 1) displays the suffrage colours in opposition to the Union Jack: the purple, white and green become an alternative rallying point to the red, white and blue (perhaps echoed in Woolf's change from blue, white and pink). In keeping with this psuedo-militarism, Joan of Arc, armour-clad and sporting the purple white and green, was adopted as the patron saint of the suffragettes (Plate 2).

'In all ages it has been woman's part to make the banners, if not to carry them,' Mary Lowndes explains, in 'On Banners and Banner-Making' (1910). But this traditionally feminine art, 'the divers colours of needle work', once woven 'in honour and support of [woman's] favourite fighting hero,' has been revived, not to sanction male warfare, but 'for the first time in history to illumine woman's own adventure.' Although 'political colours' are not new, 'now with the new century has come to fruition a new thing, and colour has a fresh significance. What is the new thing? Political societies started by women, managed by women and sustained by women.'[23] Significantly by 1910, then, feminism and colourism are powerfully connected. (Part Two of my study focuses on these connections of 1910, which may be seen here as a 'waver' upon the moment of 1927.)

Pethick-Lawrence describes the intended impact and particular symbolism of the colours. She proclaims the purple, white and green as 'a new language of which the words are so simple that their meaning can be understood by the most uninstructed and most idle of passers-by in the street.'[24] It is precisely this 'new language' of feminist colours that Woolf seems to articulate here in her revised account of the eclipse, and to take up elsewhere in her work; and this feminist language of colours, I will be suggesting, she locks onto a literary sense of Post-Impressionist colourism.

> Purple as everyone knows is the royal colour. It stands for the royal blood
> that flows in the veins of every suffragette, the instinct of freedom and
> dignity . . . white stands for purity in private and public life . . . green is
> the colour of hope and the emblem of spring.[25]

The meaning of the colours was not fixed, and shifted according to context: 'Purple was sometimes glossed as "loyalty" or "courage" in the press, and green as "youth" or "regeneration". So long as the concepts were positive the exact niceties of the symbolism were less important than the decorative impact of the colours and their effect in unifying the cause.' Lisa Tickner rightly stresses the general sense of the positive and unifying effects of these colours. Pethick-Lawrence also defined the green as 'the "green fire" of a new spring tide'[26] which has significance for Woolf's special aesthetic attention in 'The Sun and the Fish'. This fire stands as an alternative source of enlightenment to that of the sun: a fire of the land, of the body, an orgiastic fire, even. We might read Woolf's diary account of 'the fields aburn with June grasses' with this in mind. It is important to emphasize the sense of 'regeneration' which all these colours are said to bring, and the idea that with them feminists were repainting, reinventing, and restructuring the world anew.

A recent exhibition,[27] celebrating the enormous popularity of these colours, demonstrates their massive impact on the business world, which 'quickly became aware of the purchasing power of middle-class suffragettes', and produced a wide range of merchandise bearing the colours: 'the suffragettes . . . turned fashion and consumerism to brilliant political advantage'.[28] The exhibition confirms the lasting impact of the purple, white and green on public consciousness; and it may not be unreasonable to suppose that when 'The Sun and the Fish' appeared in 1928, in the year of the full enfranchisement of women, the suffragette colours would not have been forgotten.

Woolf's (perhaps playful) introduction of potentially suffrage colours at the moment of eclipse suggests a feminist interpretation of the event.[29] The sun's masculine subjectivity may now be defined against the militant feminism of the suffrage tricolour, where previously 'he' was read in opposition to a subordinate feminine/feminized landscape. We may note an historical precedent to this idea in the 'Women's Coronation Procession' of 1911 where suffragists engaged in a colourful 'counter-hegemonic' pageantry in contrast to official celebrations of renewed male sovereignty.[30] Whether or not the colours are specifically suffragist, they may still suggest a prismatic feminist intervention: Woolf engages a feminist colourism to 'enlighten' a traditional masculine solar trope.

The victory over the sun does not incur the deconstruction of the opposition light/dark (the terms are not endlessly transgressed). The victorious element is not the darkness, or the shadow, which Woolf still retains as ominous, but the colours, which are actually refracted light. The shadow, when it comes, is still 'something unexpected, awful, unavoidable', and the light's extinction is still seen as 'the end'. The colours' insertion at this moment in Woolf's eclipse story may not be accidental, but deliberate and precise, especially if we consider the feminist context of its first publication in the feminist magazine *Time and Tide* (February 1928). As a playful gesture to the editor, Woolf's inclusion of the colours may still be taken seriously. (Consider too Woolf's fondness for purple ink.)

Interestingly, Lady Rhondda, the founder and editor of *Time and Tide*, crops up in Woolf's diary of 1922:

> Lady R. who is a good able superficial woman, had psychologised her
> divorce proceedings all the time, which was boring Molly said; & Lady R.
> is a feminist, & Molly is not. But the Lady Rs. ought to be feminists, I said;
> & you must encourage them, for if the rich women will do it we neednt;
> & its the feminists who will drain off this black blood of bitterness which
> is poisoning us all.

(D II 167)

These views on the role of feminists are pertinent to Woolf's feminist account of the eclipse. She adapts for a feminist project traditional notions of women's special relationship with darkness and pollution, using the imagery of a sinister menstrual flow: feminists are to 'drain off this black blood of bitterness which is poisoning us all.' Significantly, Woolf marks a passage in Aeschylus concerning the earth's pollution by the draining of vengeful gore after Clytemnestra's slaying of her husband Agamemnon (*BERG* 13, M19). Lady Rhondda, on the other hand, identifies in her Hogarth Press essay, her eponymous 'leisured women' as the universal source of poison: 'It is the women in the home, the leisured and semi-leisured women, who constitute a positive danger, who do, in fact, act as a focus of poison to the whole of society.'[31] These views coincide with those made popular by Thorstein Veblen, who identifies the pernicious role capitalism has marked out for woman as both her husband's 'drudge and chattel – the producer of goods for him to consume', and 'the ceremonial consumer of goods which he produces'. But, he says, 'she still quite unmistakenly remains his chattel in theory; for the habitual rendering of vicarious leisure and consumption is the abiding mark of the unfree servant.'[32] Even women who are 'a focus of poison' and guilty of complicity with patriarchy, then, are still its victims.

It is not clear whether Woolf's 'us all' speaks of all society, or all women, not just feminists. We can read this imagery, nevertheless, into Woolf's account of the eclipse, where the 'scrumble of black & red' has been drawn off and replaced by the suffrage tricolour. This also fits with the myths about poisonous air at times of eclipse, noted above. There is an analogy, then, between this image Woolf associates with Rhondda, and the image of colour draining from the cloud and moor in the essay written by Woolf for Rhondda's magazine. Feminism, we may conclude, is something which purges 'black blood', and therefore is to be regarded, in view of its positive and bright colours, as a source of enlightenment. This reading may be upheld by the subsequent horror, in the essay, at the arrival of the engulfing shadow. Woolf's recommendation to 'encourage . . . the rich women' as active feminists suggests a strategy of political agitation from the top of the social scale down and it echoes Rhondda's own agenda, noted earlier, to influence the political élite, 'the inner group, the key-stone people who ultimately directed [the] multitude'. This approach is alarm-ing since it implies leaving intact the structure of the *status quo* and leaving unchallenged all other social injustices apart from those to women. But as a temporary measure, Woolf implies, it is temptingly expedient. This idea of attacking patriarchy at its highest level fits with the story of the eclipse, where the sun may be read as the pinnacle emblem of patriarchy, *the* metaphor of male reason and subjectivity. To disarm patriarchy at the top, then, is to elimin-ate it (and perhaps, therefore, the *status quo*) entirely.

The suffragette tricolour may provide a link to another feminist, Ray Strachey, one of Woolf's fellow-witnesses at the eclipse. We might read her presence as abstracted into this feminist reference, given that Woolf erases all references to the individuals comprising the common 'we' observing the eclipse. Such a connection would suggest strong feminist allegiances already at the scene, and not just the retrospective imposition of a feminist slant. In so far as the tricolour has come to stand for feminism and women's suffrage in general, this connection stands; but if specific reference is being made to the WSPU and Lady Rhondda's brand of feminism, then Ray Strachey may not fit so readily with such associations.

Two observations by Strachey illustrate this point. The first is her descrip-tion of the violent tactics favoured by militant activists. Strachey herself was a law-abiding suffragist so her account is not altogether sympathetic.

> The plan of committing technical assaults was accordingly adopted, and Mrs Pankhurst herself led the way by striking Inspector Jarvis upon the face at the door of the House of Commons. Her victim perfectly understood why she did this, and admitted it as he arrested her; but from the Press a howl of indignation arose. Screaming, scratching, biting, kicking and yelling were attributed to the militants, and a flood of generalities about the nature of the female sex filled leading articles, where for the most part it was now maintained that women had proved themselves to be for ever unfitted to vote. The militants paid no attention to this, and a policy of stone-throwing followed, in which shop fronts in Regent Street, as well as public buildings, were attacked.[33]

The militants are shown cheerfully to court their reputation as Mænads, whereas the suffragists see such actions as self-defeating and as playing into the hands of the enemy. 'It seemed to many people' continues Strachey, 'that the militants made a sort of inverted appeal to the privileges of sex. . . . They felt that the suffragettes nicely symbolised the absurdity of the whole ideal, and each manifestation of incomplete rowdyism gave them fresh joy.' Such behaviour, it seems, merely complies with chauvinist stereotypes of wild Bacchanalian women. But on the other hand, it kept the cause right in the centre of the public arena.

Strachey's other observation concerns the suffrage demonstrations, beginning with the 'Mud March' of February 1907, which was 'so called because of the mud, slush and fog through which 3000 women trudged from Hyde Park Corner to Exeter Hall.'[34] Strachey emphasizes the marvellous spectacle of these marches.

> These demonstrations owed their picturesque and dignified quality to the skilled work of the Artists' League for Women's Suffrage, which had been organised by Mary Lowndes, a member of the Committee of the London Society. Under the direction of this League, banners and emblems of real beauty were made for the societies all over the country, and when these were skilfully marshalled together in London the effect was something quite new in political demonstrations.[35]

She reminds us of the tremendous visual impact of the suffrage colours on public politics, and also of the central role played by artists in these demonstrations. Strachey credits them, as the main architects of the events, with impressive organizational and creative skills. This context provides an important key to understanding Woolf's interest in painting techniques and the visual arts. We may no longer accept the aesthetic to be a realm removed from politics. When Woolf talks of repainting, as she does in both diary and essay accounts, we may now see a precedent for this creative act in the work of the Artists' League for Women's Suffrage.

Diane Filby Gillespie makes the rare (for Woolf criticism) connection between 'the suffrage movement and the avant-garde artists, both of whom challenged the status quo and increasingly aroused public indignation.' She does not, however, refer to the suffrage artists themselves or to their creations. Instead she concentrates on the suffrage movement's acts of destruction:

> The violent acts of the more militant suffragists, which included the hacking of paintings, coincided with more frequent displays of avant-garde art. The Vorticist writers and painters asked, condescendingly, that the women discriminate in their acts of violence so that they did not "destroy a / Good Picture by Accident," but they commended the militants for their bravery and vitality.[36]

This offers a limited perspective. The suffrage banners, the work of the Suffrage Atelier and the Artists' League for Women's Suffrage, testify to the fact that the feminist activists were involved in the arts not just as iconoclasts, destroying patriarchal art, but also as creators of a positive new feminist aesthetic.

The Mud March itself, however, does not provide a straightforward link between Woolf's tricolour and Ray Strachey. It was 'the first open-air demonstration the *non-militants* had ever held';[37] therefore the banners described by Strachey did not carry the purple, white, and green of the WSPU (not thought of until the following year). The predominant colours on the Mud March were the red and white of the NUWSS. By 1909 these, 'the colours of the greatest society – the law-abiding, non party society',[38] were also transformed into a tricolour – red, white and green. But this was not the only alternative to the purple, white and green. Every shade of suffragist (and even anti-suffragist) opinion had its own set of colours. For example:

> The colours of the Artists' Suffrage League were blue and silver; of the Suffrage Atelier, blue, orange and black; of the Women's Conservative Union, blue, white and gold; of the Actresses' Franchise League, pink and green; of the Writers' Suffrage League, black, white and gold; of the Church League, white and gold; and of Sylvia Pankhurst's East London Federation, purple, white, green and red. The colours of the National League for Opposing Women's Suffrage were white, pink and black.[39]

The suffrage movement was well aware, furthermore, and indeed made use of, the traditional gender associations of the imagery of light and shade, which this new language of colour subverts. The Suffrage Atelier Broadsheet (1913), for example, shows a poster design implementing traditional chiaroscuro. The left side of the picture shows a man seated in a chair, labelled 'government', illuminated by a lamp held by another man. Around its halo is written 'suffrage'. The right side of the picture shows a group of desolate women, labelled 'sweated labour', lurking in the shadow cast by the men's light, behind the seat of government. The light of patriarchy keeps women in darkness, outside the luminous realm of citizenship. Beneath the picture is the legend: 'IN THE SHADOW'.[40]

The suffrage cartoon, 'The Anti-Suffrage Ostrich' (Plate 3), on the other hand, takes over the image of the sun as symbol of women's suffrage. In the foreground is an ostrich with its head buried in the ground marked 'ignorance' and 'stupidity'. Behind it is the sun rising with the words 'women's freedom' emblazoned on it. The caption reads: 'The sun is *not* rising'. Woolf's colonization of the sun with suffrage colours is very much in keeping with this image. It is in fact a common motif in suffrage iconography: the sense of a new dawn with the rise of women's rights fits perfectly. Ernestine Mills's postcard of 1910, 'The New Mrs Partington' (Plate 4), for example, lampoons this leading anti-suffragist who 'hopelessly tries to sweep back the advancing tide of the demand by Liberal women, medical women, taxpayers, etc. for the vote: "Somehow the tide keeps rising!"' The sun rising over this suffragette ocean is emblazoned with 'votes for women'.

Given Ray Strachey's hostility to the suffragettes, and given the rainbow of alternative suffrage colours, it would perhaps be a mistake to connect her name specifically with the purple, white and green of the WSPU. On the other hand, since these colours were the best known and most instantly recognizable, they may also transcend their immediate associations with militant suffragettes like Lady Rhondda, to embrace all shades of suffragism. We might now read Woolf's story of the eclipse as a feminist allegory; but at the same time Woolf's use of these colours must be carefully considered. I am positing an avant-garde feminist colourism at work in Woolf's revision of solar tropes. This new, colourist language, as we have seen, opens up a spectrum of possible interpretations from the narrow political significance of specific colours to a broader sense of feminist prismatics.

It may make sense to read the tricolour, since it appears at the point of the sun's violent defeat, as specifically referring to the militant tendency. This renders pertinent Woolf's comment on the function of Lady Rhondda's brand of feminism as a necessary (but not permanent) detoxicant. Once upper class militant feminism has purged society of 'this black blood of bitterness', the way is clear for other forms of feminism to flourish. Ray Strachey's position is not neglected or countered in 'The Sun and the Fish'; it is still in attendance, but the moment of triumph over the 'sun' seems to belong primarily to the suffragettes.

7 Elegiacs: capsizing light and returning colour

The moment of triumph, however, was for many feminists hollow. Woolf's account registers a sense of anti-climax that also came with the franchise: 'This was the defeat of the sun, then, and this was all, so we thought, turning in disappointment from the dull cloud blanket in front of us to the moors behind.' (*CDB* 196) The final achievement of the franchise was, indeed, for many women, of little importance compared to the gains they had already made during the period of the Great War: 'entry into what had been seen before as male centres of power.'[1] Citizenship, then, had already been seized by women by the time it was actually granted them. Woolf records exactly these sentiments when she marks the historic moment in her diary on Friday 11 January 1918: 'Another sedentary day, which must however be entered for the sake of recording that the Lords have passed the Suffrage Bill. I dont feel much more important – perhaps slightly so. Its like a knighthood; might be useful to impress people one despises. But there are other aspects of it naturally.' (*D* 1 104) Her remarks about Lady Rhondda, however, come four years after this historic moment, suggesting that Woolf did not see the feminist battle as won, not only because full enfranchisement was yet to happen. The twenties was a period when women were being urged to relinquish their recent gains in the public sphere and return to domestic duties. It was still a man's world. The sun was still masculine.

Priapic light

Indeed, in some literary circles the sun was positively priapic, as revealed in another piece of fiction to emerge in 1928.

> "Let me see you!"
>   He dropped the shirt and stood still, looking towards her. The sun through the low window sent a beam that lit up his thighs and slim belly, and the erect phallus rising darkish and hot-looking from the little cloud of vivid gold-red hair. She was startled and afraid.[2]

D.H. Lawrence's achievement in *Lady Chatterley's Lover*, we might say, is to invest the Apollonian sun of the intellect, the transcendental spirit, with the Dionysian sexual body. He inscribes the object in the subject. While such a manœuvre may be interpreted as liberational (though not for women), here it seems merely libertine. Kate Millett memorably sums up his anti-feminist handiwork as 'a quasi-religious tract recounting the salvation of one modern woman . . . through the offices of the author's personal cult, 'the mystery of the phallus."'

> This passage, a revelation of the sacrament itself, is properly the novel's
> very holy of holies – a transfiguration scene with atmospheric clouds and
> lightning, and a pentecostal sunbeam (the sun is phallic to Lawrence's
> apprehension) illuminating the ascension of the deity 'thick and arching'
> before the reverent eyes of the faithful.[3]

Lawrence, it seems, is not content with the chiaroscuro of Genesis which divides light from dark, man from woman, spirit from body, subject from object; he must appropriate the object, the body, the darkness for the masculine too. 'Lawrence concentrates people back again in the body,' Woolf notes '– that's why he's so monotonous.' His 'triumph of the body' she finds linked 'with a sex theory, which is the most restricting of all – the most savage and binding. Very vivid – very physical – very humourless and stark – but not to me interesting.' (*BERG* 13, *RN* 1.21)

Elsewhere, Lawrence is anxious to defend the body from the ravages of the Renaissance light of reason:

> Since the Renaissance there has been the striving for the Light, and the
> escape from the Flesh, from the Body, the Object. . . . It is light, actual
> sunlight or the luminous quality of day which has infused more and more
> into the defined body, fusing away the outline, absolving the concrete reality,
> making a marriage, an embrace between the two things, light and object.

Lawrence does see the body, however, as that 'which connects us directly to the female', whereas 'the pure male is himself almost an abstraction, almost bodyless.'[4] 'The erect phallus rising darkish' is a Nietzschean gesture of bodily imperialism, encompassing both ends of the spectrum, light and dark, and asserting the physical. The woman is displaced altogether, a 'startled' onlooker to a Narcissus, the masculine subject reflecting on the masculine object. This suggests the immanent masculinity in both sides of traditional male-designated binary oppositions.

The intensely physical, masculine resonance to the image of the sun, might prompt feminism to banish it altogether from the vocabulary of 'the new language'. Woolf's strategy in 'The Sun and the Fish', after the moment of eclipse, is indeed to banish the word, yet she retains positive associations for 'the light'. After 'the defeat of the sun' is announced, the account of the eclipse does not use the word 'sun' again (nor, therefore, its masculine pun), although it does almost appear in the entirely different context of the essay's final paragraph.

Woolf next describes the disappearance and re-emergence of 'the light', which is at no point signalled by the masculine pronoun. This change of vocabulary is highly noticeable: up to the eclipse the sun is persistently personified as male; afterwards 'the light' is not overtly gendered. If Woolf's strategy were a feminine version of Lawrence's, this would be the moment at which to inscribe 'the sun' with the valorized female body, instead of the male. She does not do this. Even the suffragette tricolour is not permanent, for 'suddenly one became aware that something more was about to happen; something unexpected, awful, unavoidable.' (*CDB* 196)

What happens next is the capsizing in tandem of light and dark: 'The shadow growing darker and darker over the moor was like the heeling over of a boat, which, instead of righting itself at the critical moment, turns a little further and then a little further on its side; and suddenly capsizes. So the light turned and heeled over and went out.' Here shadow and light are inextricably linked. The defeat of the sun and the appearance of the tricolour have initiated a chain reaction. The essay communicates the diary's brief statement, 'the light sank & sank', by the dramatic simile of a sinking boat. Woolf's note on Pentheus' 'death scene' reflects a similar eeriness: 'How the tree was bent down, down, down. then the silence.' (*BERG* 13, *RN* 1.19)

Her insertion of the boat image right at the moment of the eclipse, speaks significantly both to the recent artistic 'spectacle' of the suffrage movement, and to the literary tradition of pastoral elegy.

Handicapped

In February 1909, the Artists' Suffrage League held a competition for 'the best design for a poster, suitable for elections.'[5] Duncan Grant (who first met Virginia Stephen with Vanessa and Clive Bell in 1907, and later lived with Vanessa), was joint-winner with his entry, 'Handicapped' (Plate 5), 'one of the most successful and striking of suffrage designs'. This poster may also provide a gloss to the image of the boat in Woolf's eclipse sequence. It depicts, above the legend 'HANDICAPPED', a sturdy young woman (in purple skirt) rowing a boat in a rough sea; behind her on the horizon is the Palace of Westminster; above her, gliding along the crest of a towering wave is a young man languishing in a sailing boat, powered by wind-inflated sails on whose canvas is boldly written 'VOTES'.

> "A man in a *sailing* boat (the sail represents the Vote). A woman with only *oars* – out in the sea *of Labour*." A caption to underline the moral – "Britons why handicap the weaker vessel" – was to run below, but must have seemed redundant and was never used.[6]

If Woolf's eclipse narrative makes use of the suffrage tricolour, perhaps it may also refer to this famous suffrage allegory. Whether the connection is deliberate or not, Grant's poster provides helpful evidence of the kind of metaphorical currency in feminist and suffrage circles. It may make sense of Woolf's boating simile by suggesting that once universal suffrage is achieved, after the defeat of the patriarchal sun, *both* vessels (man's and woman's) sink because both are now inappropriate expressions of the new power and gender relations. But before we allow them to go under, it is important to understand in greater detail how these relations are delineated in Grant's poster.

The poster offers an analysis of gender and power structures. Not only does the image of two separate boats indicate the discrimination between the sexes (the man has something denied to the woman); but it also demonstrates that while the man has merely to guide his boat, the woman has first to generate the power for hers. His sails harness the natural power of the wind, whereas she powers her boat by her own labour: the woman is labourer, the man overlord. This patriarchal model regards women as natural resources (an invisible energy source like the wind) rather than as fellow citizens. Grant's allegory, then, although it represents man and woman in different boats, also suggests that the woman is in a sense carrying the man. The redundant caption may have cast her ironically as the 'weaker vessel', but in the final version of the poster she is without doubt a figure of strength, about to overcome her own exploitation.

The boat's vehicular qualities make it a metaphor of metaphor itself. We may interpret the man as tenor of his (feminine) vehicle, whereas the woman is associated with the vehicular power of hers, and is therefore in a sense both tenor and vehicle. There is then an air of feminist heroism in the strength and direction of this 'Grace Darling type' woman, as the *Common Cause* called her. The main purpose of the woman's determined labour with the oars is, of course, the achievement of citizenship – her destination is Parliament. She seems an awe-inspiring paragon of virtuous hard work and self-sufficiency. The man, on the other hand, somewhat decadently relies on the service of others. This implies that, although the woman requires the assistance of a sail like his (the vote), she may not necessarily behave like him when she gets it. His yacht (together with his implied aristocratic way of life) is being overtaken by the steady toil of a labouring woman. Her labour gives her the right to vote. This may be understood as a war of class as well as gender, a point underlined by the other winning suffrage poster, 'Votes for Workers', by W.F. Winters.[7]

Light capsizing

The capsizing of the light is 'something unexpected, awful, unavoidable', whereas 'the defeat of the sun' itself is not explicitly lamented, and, in fact, seems rather disappointing. The welcome, but anti-climactic, defeat of the sun results in the horrific sinking of the light. The loss of light brings the moment of death: 'This was the end. The flesh and blood of the world was dead; only the skeleton was left. It hung beneath us, a frail shell; brown; dead; withered.' Although, in isolation, this bears conventional interpretations of the parallel demise of sun and earth as the death of both spirit and flesh, careful analysis of Woolf's imagery, in its specific context, suggests she may offer a new set of oppositions. Whereas before the eclipse, the sun was in opposition to the land, following traditional images of the mind/body split, after it, the light is actually identified as 'flesh and blood' itself and is contrasted instead with 'the skeleton'. Instead of taking the death of the 'flesh and blood of the world', then, as a *consequence* of the loss of light, it is possible to read it as a statement of equivalence: the light *is* 'flesh and blood'.

Light here is living, palpable material; no longer regarded as a remote force acting upon the land, it seems integral to earthly existence – part of it. There is an image from Apollinaire that also expresses this new bodily interpretation of light: 'La fenêtre s'ouvre comme une orange/ Le beau fruit de la lumière' ['The window opens like an orange/ The beautiful fruit of light'].[8] Woolf similarly gives the light a sturdiness and structural, organic, quality, which one might have expected to belong to the skeleton. The skeleton, however, is 'a frail shell; brown; dead; withered.' The loss of light has resulted in the dehydration of the world; it has been drained of essential fluids. It is as if Apollinaire's orange has 'withered' and died. Again, this confirms the palpableness of Woolf's light. Light and colour, not skeletal lines, apparently give form. Woolf's description of the recovery of light after the eclipse also emphasizes its physical vigour.

> Then, with some trifling movement, this profound obeisance of the light, this stooping down and abasement of all splendour was over. Lightly, on the other side of the world, up it rose; it sprang up as if the one movement, after a second's tremendous pause, completed the other, and the light which had died here rose again elsewhere. Never was there such a sense of rejuvenescence and recovery. All the convalescences and respites of life seemed rolled into one.
>
> (*CDB* 197)

This moment has a different emphasis in the diary where, first, the colours' re-emergence, heralds the return of the light: 'the cloud took colour on itself again, only a sparky aetherial colour & so the light came back'. In the essay, this sequence is reversed; the light's return precedes the description of colour, suggesting a parody of the Christian resurrection. This passage from 'an eccentric essay', Mark Hussey suggests, 'demonstrates the enormous scope the eclipse had in Woolf's imagination as she appropriates Christian terminology for cosmic significance'.[9] This is to miss some of its subtleties. Although terms such as 'rose again', 'rejuvenescence and recovery' support such a reading, it is undercut by Woolf's references to the elastic qualities of light. The light does not actually die: it experiences 'profound obeisance . . . stooping down and abasement' from which condition it springs back. It has been compressed but never extinguished. Its resurrection is physical and mechanical, not spiritual or otherworldly. Significantly, the word 'aetherial', present in the diary account, is missing from the lexis of the essay.

Black Friday

The Christian resonance is heightened by the context of the solar eclipse itself, which is traditionally offered as explanation of the sky's darkening at the moment of Christ's death on the cross. Good Friday is, for this reason, sometimes called 'Black Friday'. But this phrase was itself appropriated by the suffrage movement in 1910, when a demonstration ended in the violent assault upon most of its participants at the hands of the police. On 18 November 1910 (the first Post-Impressionist Exhibition had opened ten days earlier on 8 November), suffragettes massed to demonstrate at Westminster against the loss of the Conciliation Bill (proposing the enfranchisement of a narrow category of women) because of the crisis in Parliament, and the imminent fall of the Asquith government.

They were met with unprecedented violence and indecent assault. Apparently 'reluctant to make arrests', the police 'used instead a variety of means to force the women back: women were kicked, their arms were twisted, their noses were punched, their breasts were gripped, and knees were thrust between their legs. After six hours of struggle, 115 women and four men had been arrested. On the following day, the charges against most of those arrested were withdrawn.'[10] H.N. Brailsford and Dr Jessie Murray who collected depositions from many of the victims, conclude: 'The action of which the most frequent complaint is made is variously described as twisting round, pinching, screwing, nipping or wringing the breast. This was often done in the most public way so as to inflict the utmost humiliation. Not only was it an offence against decency; it caused in many cases intense pain. . . . The language used by some of the police while performing this action proves that it was consciously sensual.' A testimony by a 'young woman' suggests that this suffrage demonstration was remembered not for the colours of the suffrage banners, but for the colours of bruised flesh: 'I was also pummelled on the chest, and my breast was clutched by one constable from the front. As a consequence, three days later I had to receive medical attention . . . as my breasts were much discoloured and very painful.'[11]

Ada Wright recalls 'the humiliation' she underwent in being 'continually tripped up by the police and thrown to the ground . . . the next morning I found I had been photographed lying on the ground where I had been flung, and the photograph occupied the front page of the *Daily Mirror*. As soon as this became known to the Government, an order to have the picture suppressed was sent to the office of the newspaper, but they could not suppress the copies which had been sold. There were headlines: BLACK FRIDAY.'[12] As well as its origins in the story of Christ, 'Black Friday', then, also has a specifically feminist significance for the context in which Woolf first published 'The Sun and the Fish'.

Elegy

Woolf retains for the essay the term 'obeisance', but removes the diary entry's connotations of this as a personal, individual experience. The essay asserts the universal magnificence of light as 'all splendour'. This seems to support my earlier reading of the diary's use of 'obeisance' as an intertext with *The Prelude*, since Woolf appears to have added another key word from the passage quoted: 'splendour'. Wordsworth's 'auxiliar light', we remember, 'on the setting sun/ Bestowed new splendour.' This may be a reference to Christ, but Woolf signals as illusory any sense of this spectacle as a unifying symbol of rebirth, Christian or otherwise: 'All the convalescences and respites of life *seemed* rolled into one.'

There is a strong elegiac tone to this section of 'The Sun and the Fish', most evident at this moment when the mourning for the lost light is transformed into joy at its reappearance. This complies with the sense of consolation that Christian elegies in particular approach 'when the elegist suddenly realizes that death in this world is the entry to a higher life.'[13]

> Weep no more, woeful shepherds, weep no more,
> For Lycidas, your sorrow, is not dead,
> Sunk though he be beneath the watery floor;
> So sinks the day-star in the ocean bed,
> And yet anon repairs his drooping head,
> And tricks his beams, and with new-spangled ore
> Flames in the forehead of the morning sky:
> So Lycidas sunk low, but mounted high,

Through the dear might of him that walked the waves;
Where other groves and other streams along,
With nectar pure his oozy locks he laves,
And hears the unexpressive nuptial song
In the blest kingdoms meek of joy and love.
. . . Now, Lycidas, the shepherds weep no more;
Henceforth thou art the Genius of the shore,
In thy large recompense, and shalt be good
To all that wander in that perilous flood.[14]

Woolf, from childhood on, was certainly familiar with Milton's poetry. Her father, Leslie Stephen, frequently recited it to his children.[15] Rachel Vinrace, we recall, falls fatally ill listening to a reading of Milton's *Comus*, in spite of Terence Hewet's claims that Milton can 'withstand the power of the sun.' (*VO* 398) In an early story, it is observed that there is 'a soul of beauty that rises unchristened over the words of Milton as it rises over the Bay of Marathon yonder.'[16] This suggests other discourses apart from the dominant Christian one may be recovered from his work. Woolf, furthermore, relates that when she was 'waved back' from an Oxbridge college library, one of the manuscripts she hoped to examine was Milton's *Lycidas* (*AROO* 11). This is an account in microcosm of women's exclusion from the canon and from literary debate. A woman, well versed in the male tradition, who has a sound acquaintance with *Lycidas*, the linchpin of English elegy, and who wants to find out more, is denied access to the poem's manuscript by the academic patriarchy. Woolf later records: 'discussing [with Yeats and De La Mare] what poems we could come back to unsated, I said Lycidas.' (*D* III 330)

It is well known that Woolf came to consider her novels as elegies (*D* III 34), yet critical attention to this term has not prompted rigorous or sustained pastoral-elegiac readings of her work. Most critics have been content, instead, to allow loose definitions of elegy and rather vague personal and biographical interpretations to dominate. It is as if no more can be expected of Woolf. Her essays and fiction, however, show her to be well acquainted with the tradition of pastoral elegy and to be capable of both subtle and spectacular management of it. Pastoral elegy, moreover, is a highly appropriate genre in which to work out a new poetics, and is, therefore, ripe for feminist occupation. At the time of the eclipse, Woolf had just published *To the Lighthouse*, the novel whose formulation first prompted her to think explicitly in terms of elegy (*D* III 18–19).

Woolf directly links elegy with a solar eclipse in 'Sympathy' (1919). The narrator (mistakenly, it transpires) enters an elegiac reverie upon reading in a newspaper of the death of a friend's husband. Her first reaction is to imagine an encounter with the widow in a pastoral setting, but she soon tires of the fantasy:

But it's all fancy. I'm not in the room with her, nor out in the wood. I'm here in London, standing by the window, holding *The Times*. But how death has changed everything! – as, in an eclipse of the sun, the colours go out, and the trees look thin as paper and livid while the shadow passes. The chill little breeze is perceptible and the roar of the traffic sounds across a gulf. Then, a moment later, distances are bridged, sounds merged; and as I look the trees though still pale, become sentinel and guardian; the sky arranges its tender background; and all remote as if exalted to the summit of a mountain in the dawn. Death has done it; death lies behind the leaves and houses and the smoke, wavering up, composing them into something still in its tranquillity before it has taken on any of the disguises of life.

(*CSF* 109–110)

Here again, the solar eclipse is symbolic of the death of a male subject; and the loss of colour from the landscape is in keeping with Woolf 's description in 'The Sun and the Fish'. There is also a sense of elegiac recovery in the story, since in its final twist, the narrator realises she has mistaken her friend's father-in-law for her husband who is not dead after all: 'O don't tell me he lives still! O why did you deceive me?' (*CSF* 111). There is, then, no sense of celebration at Humphry's recovery. In fact, a cancelled passage in the draft betrays the narrator's great disappointment: 'Do you mean to tell me that Humphry is alive after all . . . and I've wasted all this; death never was behind the tree; and I'm to dine with you, with years and years in which to ask questions about the furniture. Humphry you ought to have died!' (*CSF* 299) In *The Waves* Woolf also links the death of the subject ('the world seen without a self') with the image of the solar eclipse; and this will be explored in my final chapter.

Significantly, the setting sun, personified as male, is Milton's simile for the demise of Lycidas, and its reappearance at dawn signifies his rebirth in heaven. Christ's resurrection is also implicit, not only because of the pun on 'sun', but also because of his agency in Lycidas's recovery: 'Through the dear might of him that walked the waves.' The reference to walking on water is a reverse image of the sun's sinking 'in the ocean bed'. The closing lines of the poem connect the sun, not only with the dead Lycidas, and again with the figure of Christ, but also with 'the uncouth swain' who has brought us the lament.

> And now the sun had stretched out all the hills,
> And now was dropped into the western bay;
> At last he rose, and twitched his mantle blue:
> Tomorrow to fresh woods, and pastures new.[17]

The subject of the sentence, 'At last he rose', seems to include Lycidas, Christ, and 'the uncouth swain', as well as the sun. On setting, 'he' has dominion over the land: 'the sun had stretched out all the hills'. This may imply both that the sun stretched himself out over the hills, and that the sun actually stretched out the hills. Either way, in compliance with the fixed oppositions of patriarchy, if the sun is masculine, we might assume the subordinate femininity of the hills. Woolf's earlier description of the meeting place, 'where the hills stretched their limbs out over the flowing moorland', may also echo Milton.

Woolf's story, I suggest, departs from this Christian model of elegiac consolation, but it does appear to fit with many other aspects of pastoral elegy. Not overtly about the death of a shepherd or poet, it, nevertheless, relates the untimely, if momentary, death of the sun and its light, which we may connect to 'primitive laments for the death of Thammuz, Adonis, or other vegetational deities who died in autumn to be reborn in the spring'. The convention that 'all nature joins in mourning' has connotations of Orpheus's death in particular, perhaps signalled in the land's draining of colour in Woolf's story. The convention of 'a procession of appropriate mourners'[18] may be echoed in Woolf's sombre procession of onlookers. These similarities suggest elegiac qualities in Woolf's eclipse scene. The movement of eclipse from light to darkness to light again, itself may describe the mood shift inherent in the structure of pastoral elegy. The phases of darkness and light fit the progression from untimely loss (light to dark) to lyric consolation in the after life (dark to light).

Woolf's sense of lyric consolation, however, comes not from the realization that 'death in this world is entry to a higher life' (transcendence of the material); but from a stunning and unique 'sense of rejuvenescence and recovery' in the world itself, which has been invigorated rather than transcended. This is also an important departure from the narratives examined earlier, showing parallels between the death of the sun and the death of 'the King of the Wood'. Whereas these myths suggest that his pursuit and even defeat (since revival follows) serve to reassert and strengthen the power of the king, Woolf's story, on the contrary, has the victim (the sun) remain defeated, returning only in transfigured form (as the light) to rejuvenate and integrate with the (landscape) elements associated with his pursuers. 'His' sovereignty, then, is not reasserted, but subsumed into feminine elements.

This is where the intervention of the suffragette tricolour is important. It coincides with the emergence of a new, bodily sense of light as 'beautiful fruit'. Woolf is here refiguring the metaphor of the sun and light, previously the province of a transcendent, self-reflexive masculine sovereignty, for feminism. It is transformed by militant feminist action into a metaphor for integrated and pluralized subjectivity. Woolf's innovation here, furthermore, fits with the transformational tradition of pastoral elegy itself. Elegy often concerns more than mere commemoration of the dead: 'It is no accident that Milton brings

into *Lycidas* the archetypal poet-minstrel, Orpheus. The death of the poet cannot but bring to mind the poetic purpose and the future death of that other
poet who is now writing.'[19]

Moving beyond such intimations, elegy not only presents itself as 'a sort of
laboratory' where 'amatory or political problems' are studied, but it may also
include a study of 'poetic art in general and as it is, or will be, practised by the
spokesman himself.'[20] Pastoral elegy traditionally gives space for one poet, in
mourning the death of another, to pronounce not only on public and private
affairs, but also on art. Woolf's feminist adjustments to this convention, and
her departures from its masculine norms, are still within the transformational
province of the genre. It is not that there have never been women elegists, for,
indeed, there is a strong tradition of mothers' elegies on dead children; but there
seems to be no woman's equivalent in the canon to the elegies of Milton, Gray,
Shelley, Arnold, and Tennyson. 'The Sun and the Fish' may be engaging, then,
in a kind of feminist elegiacs.

Lycidas, furthermore, provides an interesting gloss on the 'boat' simile at the
heart of Woolf's eclipse story which recalls the poem's most enigmatic lines:

> It was that fatal and perfidious bark,
> Built in the eclipse, and rigged with curses dark,
> That sunk so low that sacred head of thine.[21]

To refer Woolf's 'boat' to Milton's 'perfidious bark', however, is perhaps
to toss it out of the frying pan and into the fire, since three centuries of schol-
arship have failed to find critical consensus on the meaning of the latter.
Edward King, the man mourned in Milton's elegy, perished at sea; so these
lines suggest primarily that his death is due, not to the natural cause of the
storm, but to the ill fortune of his boat because it was 'built in the eclipse'.
Virgil, Shakespeare, and Milton himself, for example, furnish us with many
precedents to the idea of eclipses as bad omens.[22]

Many commentators have exercised their imaginations as to how, in fact, the
boat might feasibly be 'built in the eclipse'. In contrast to the literalism of some
interpretations,[23] there is a figurative one which seems appropriate to Woolf's
reference: 'Literally the line suggests that King's ship was foredoomed to sink
by malign, supernatural influences. Figuratively, there is perhaps an oblique
allusion in *bark* to King's natural body, and in *eclipse* and *curses*, to the Fall
and its consequences – the chief consequence being the subjection (which
King's death illustrates) of the realm of nature to change and death.'[24] The most
fruitful interpretations, for Woolf's allusion, lie at this figurative level: M. Lloyd
'takes man as "the mortal bark" who since Adam's fall has been under the curse
of sin and mortality';[25] and this might be considered for its gender implications with regard to Woolf's feminist adaption of the reference.

It is Eve – the woman – who, as the 'weaker vessel', is blamed for succumbing to the serpent Satan, and who represents the sins of the flesh. She is, therefore, as the vehicle which conveys humanity into the finite world, most closely linked to mortality. If the 'perfidious bark' is feminine, it may be in direct opposition to the (masculine) sun whose eclipse provides the occasion for her construction. The story of the eclipse at the crucifixion bears out this reading. The death of the eternal God made mortal implies the momentary loss of the permanent light. The resurrection, and the return of the sun, confirm the light as eternal.

Woolf's account reverses this pattern: her 'boat' is not 'built' but sinks 'in the eclipse', and with it may sink the notions of original sin and its attendant 'perfidious' gender implications. The (masculine) sun does not reappear after the eclipse; and the light which is reborn is not eternal. The sinking of the boat signals, not the removal of mortality from the earth, but its introduction as a quality extending to the light of the sun itself. For Woolf, then, 'the beautiful fruit of light' is not everlasting. It is fragile.

> Yet, at first, so light and frail and strange the colour was, sprinkled rainbow-like in a hoop of colour, that it seemed as if the earth could never live decked out in such frail tints. It hung beneath us, like a cage, like a hoop, like a globe of glass. It might be blown out; it might be stove in. But steadily and surely our relief broadened and our confidence established itself as the great paintbrush washed in woods dark on the valley, and massed hills blue above them. The world became more and more solid; it became populous; it became a place where an infinite number of farmhouses, of villages, of railway lines have lodgement; until the whole fabric of civilisation was modelled and moulded. But still the memory endured that the earth we stand on is made of colour; colour can be blown out; then we stand on a dead leaf; and we who tread the earth securely now have seen it dead.
>
> (*CDB* 197)

The recovery of the light is followed by the re-emergence of colour. As we noted, this sequence is an orderly version of the diary account where the return of the colour is described before the return of light. Whereas the diary describes the colour's emergence as sporadic (it is first seen on the cloud, and then 'astonishingly lightly & quickly & beautifully in the valley & over the hills'), the essay has a more graceful progression of colour emanating in a circular movement. This resembles Woolf's 'luminous halo'. It is 'sprinkled' in 'a hoop of colour', expressions which suggest its delicacy and its strength respectively. The diary's 'glittering & aetheriality' is not repeated. 'Glittering' perhaps does not fit with the surer sense of colour as a hoop (for however 'frail' its 'tints', it has structure). 'Aetheriality' does not fit because it seems to signal an otherworldly, transcendent quality, eliminated from the essay account.

The colours' delicate bubble-like quality transforms into a more solid prospect 'as the great paint-brush washed in woods dark on the valley, and massed hills blue above them.' This is the equivalent of Milton's 'fresh woods and pastures new'. Woolf remarks in her diary that they were 'all new colours . . . here blue, & there brown'. The essay mentions the 'rainbow-like . . . hoop of colour' but only specifies the 'blue' of the hills. The blue of the sky before the eclipse has reappeared afterwards as the colour of the 'massed hills'. The earth has taken on the qualities of the heavens. As the 'great paint-brush' creates the world anew, Woolf lists the emergence of 'farmhouses . . . villages . . . railway lines'. She does not talk now of rebirth or re-emergence, but of the world of things being fabricated for the first time ('became solid . . . have lodgement . . . was modelled and moulded').

The paradoxical hyperbole of 'an infinite number' suggests the earth now contains those qualities previously assigned to the after-life. It conjures the idea of the infinite potential inherent in the mundane; of the material as the seat of imagination. 'Lodgement' has an air of the temporary: on a larger scale things may change drastically but humanity relies on a very delicately balanced state of affairs, poised above 'a cage . . . a hoop . . . a globe of glass'. This is reminiscent of the cage that became the final resting place of the Sibyl of Cumæ who in being granted by Apollo eternal life, forgot to ask also for eternal youth, as the epigraph to *The Waste Land* records.[26]

Woolf's boast in the diary, at the culmination of the eclipse, 'Our greatness had been apparent too', is missing from the essay. Instead, she chooses to end the latter's description of the eclipse with a eulogy to solid colour: 'But still the memory endured that the earth we stand on is made of colour.' In my final chapter I will discuss Woolf's later, and differently encoded, version of this passage in *The Waves* where Bernard asks 'How then, does the light return to the world after the eclipse of the sun?' (*W* 313)

I do not seek to reduce Woolf's final celebration of material colour in this section of 'The Sun and the Fish', or indeed the essay itself, to one narrow aspect of suffragism. I have tried to show how the piece also goes beyond this. Woolf's avant-garde colourism simultaneously seems to offer a celebration of the material and historical moment: the glorious, if sometimes fearful, non-transcendence of this life. But that moment, we are reminded, may also be of special historical significance for women. The manipulation of gender-related vocabulary traced in the essay up to now would seem to support this point. The 'whole fabric of civilization' has been 'modelled and moulded' by women's coming to sovereignty. The landscape, the order of things, the naturalized status quo, have all been shown to be (not 'natural', but) constructed. This order has been eclipsed, and a new world created. But, as Woolf's warning testifies, this is no time to take the world for granted.

8 The death of the sun and the return of the fish

This chapter considers the last part of Woolf's essay where she turns from the solar to the contrary state of the piscine. Although her introductory explanation of 'the amusing game' should prepare us for this jolt into the heterogenous, the reader, nevertheless, still experiences a jolt. This is a turning point, too, in my argument. Part Two, similarly, may suggest a jolt into the heterogenous: the world of the 1927 eclipse will give way to that of 1910 and Post-Impressionism. But just as the moment of 1927 has been shown to 'waver' with the past concerns of 1910, so the moment of 1910 may be seen to 'tremble and quiver' with the future concerns of 1927. Since what will dominate in Part Two is an investigation of light and colour in Woolf's handling of Post-Impressionist aesthetics, it may perhaps seem wiser to ignore the piscine element of 'The Sun and the Fish' and make off now with the apparent feminist appropriation of solar narrative, but this would be not only to miss half the benefit of Woolf's game, but also to ignore its rules: we cannot understand the solar without also addressing the piscine. But first we must consider some of broader implications of the death of the sun. From this will emerge a discussion of worms, pythons and sea-monsters, leading finally to Woolf's fish.

Degeneration

To eclipse solar light, reclaiming its imagery for feminism, is one thing, but it is quite another to have it permanently dead. The death of the sun was a dread prospect, haunting the minds of the nineteenth century; and theories of entropy, devolution, and cultural decline held currency in the first decades of the twentieth. Max Nordau's *Degeneration*, for example, was highly influential on reactionary aesthetic opinion. 'Degenerates,' he declares, 'are not always criminals, prostitutes, anarchists, and pronounced lunatics; they are often authors and artists.' The latter share 'the same mental characteristics' and 'somatic features' as the former 'anthropological family, who satisfy their unhealthy impulses with the knife of the assassin or the bomb of the dynamiter, instead of with pen and pencil.'[1] Nordau's proto-fascist thesis on art and degeneration,[2] as we will see, influenced early detractors of Post-Impressionism in Britain. Theories of degeneration, furthermore, were gendered. For example, Oswald

Spengler, whose theories were popular in the 1920s (Woolf speaks of Spengler with apparent familiarity in May 1929 (*D* III 224; *L* IV 56)), links the decline of civilization to the rise in women's liberation, the use of contraceptives, and women's neglect of familial and domestic duties.

> The primary woman, the peasant woman, is *mother*. The whole vocation towards which she has yearned from childhood is included in that one word. But now emerges the Ibsen woman, the comrade, the heroine of a whole megalopolitan literature from Northern drama to Parisian novel. Instead of children, she has soul-conflicts; marriage is a craft-art for the achievement of 'mutual understanding'. It is all the same whether the case against children is the American lady's who would not miss a season for anything, or the Parisienne's who fears that her lover would leave her, or an Ibsen heroine's who 'belongs to herself' – they all belong to themselves and they are all unfruitful.[3]

Spengler's description of the ensuing destruction of 'civilization' shows the process occurring from the top of the social and political hierarchy downwards:

> The whole pyramid of cultural man vanishes. It crumbles from the summit, first the world-cities, then the provincial forms, and finally the land itself, whose best blood has incontinently poured into the towns, merely to bolster them awhile. At last, only the primitive blood remains, alive, but robbed of its strongest and most promising elements.[4]

This is a negative interpretation of the feminist strategies recommended by Lady Rhondda, approved by Woolf and inscribed into her account of the solar eclipse. The land draining of blood is also in keeping with this account.

For Spengler, woman is outside life, a cosmic force; and man, 'the master', is active in life; whereas men are animal-like, 'emancipated from . . . servitude', women are 'plant-like' and '*cultureless*'. The feminine, something to be consumed and excreted by 'animal and human species', is passively in the sway of the solar: 'flowers at the eventide . . . one after the other, they close in the setting sun.'[5] The subhuman feminine is governed by the solar. The death of the sun (the decline of civilization) is effected by the feminine's refusal to comply with this vision, by woman's decision to 'belong to herself'. Progressive feminism, then, is linked to solar decline.

'Many Victorians,' observes Gillian Beer, 'including Darwin himself, were disturbed by the apparent contradiction between the "progressive" implications of evolutionary theory and the emphasis in the physics of Helmholtz and Thomson on the ageing of the sun, which would eventually make the world too cold for life.'[6] The sun in this context was typically personified as masculine[7] in accordance with the dominant 'Müllerian monomania'. The mythographer Max Müller was thoroughly obsessed with solar mythology ('so much of the old mythology, the daily talk, of the Aryans, was solar: – what else could it have been?').[8] His observations have bearing on Woolf's eclipse descriptions: the sun for him symbolizes masculine sovereignty. 'The character of *Yama* [from the Rig-Veda],' for example, 'might well have been suggested by the setting sun, personified as the leader of the human race, as himself mortal, yet as king, as the ruler of the departed, as worshipped with the fathers, similar to the immortality enjoyed by the gods themselves.'[9] The sun is the pinnacle image of transcendent patriarchal authority. Solar rhythm ('the whole solar drama') – the repeated cycle of darkness and light – is for Müller the foundation of all mythology. The regularity of solar movement, 'immortal, i.e. unfading, as compared with the feeble and decaying race of man', is precisely what gives it primacy for Müller, who is less impressed by the irregular and unpredictable movements of the clouds, the 'subjects' or 'enemies' of the 'immortal bright beings'. He explains 'the battle that takes place between the dark clouds and the bright sun, which for a time is covered by them, is but an irregular repetition of that more momentous struggle which takes place every day between the darkness of the night and the refreshing light of the morning.'

Müller's preference for solar regularity leads him to side with 'the solar theory' of mythology, against 'the meteoric theory' which 'looks upon clouds and storms and other convulsive aspects of nature as causing the deepest and most lasting impression on the minds of those early observers who had ceased to wonder at the regular movements of the heavenly bodies.'[10] Woolf's account of the eclipse, although concerned with regular movements of heavenly bodies, falls in with meteoric theories in its depiction of the sun's flight from the clouds. Müller dismisses rival proto-Zoroastrian interpretations of the (male) sun ' "embrac[ing] the goddess, the cloud" ':

> I cannot imagine that men, standing on a level with our shepherds, should have conversed among themselves of a dark storm-cloud soaring in space, and producing by a marriage with light, or with the sun, the first human beings, or should have called the blue sky the son of the cloud because the sky appears when the storm-cloud has been either embraced or destroyed by the sun.[11]

Just as he favours steady, predictable solar rhythms above the inconstancy of meteoric conditions, Müller likewise sees human nature as unchanging: the 'men' of ancient times he envisions 'standing on a level with our shepherds'. The human subject is always and already masculine for Müller. He promotes a set, unchanging, masculine hegemony against the threatening chaos of a feminine meteorology. Beer suggests that Müller's 'solar mythography was so powerful because it gave expression to covert dreads then current,'[12] namely the death of the sun and the end of the world. He offers a reassuring vision of the solar. If the imminent decline of civilization, symbolized by solar death, is linked to the rise of feminism, the discreet gender associations in Müller's rhetoric seem to reassure the patriarchal status quo, just as Woolf's later manipulation of his terms seems to unsettle it.

In her nightmare vision of the world without the sun, Frances Power Cobbe, describes a sense of horror very like Woolf's at the moment of solar eclipse:

> It was totally dark, but I was sure that I was in the midst of an immense crowd. We were all gazing upward into the murky sky and a sense of some fearful calamity was over us, so that no one spoke aloud. Suddenly overhead appeared through a rift in the black heavens, a branch of stars which I recognised as the belt and sword of Orion. Then went forth a cry of despair from all our hearts! We knew, though no one said, that these stars proved it was not a cloud or mist which, as we had somehow believed, was causing the darkness. No; the air was clear; it was high noon, and *the sun had not risen!* That was the tremendous reason why we beheld the skies. The sun would never rise again![13]

This event, an uncanny presage of the scene of Woolf's solar eclipse, cannot be as reassuringly explained by science. Yet there are less obvious parallels to draw: the glimpse of the stars allowed by the sun's absence reminds us that other points of enlightenment are now available. Cobbe's rhetoric suggests a horror at the loss of the unifying solar light, perhaps representative of Christianity, and the further horror of recognizing the starlight of Orion's belt, perhaps symbolic of an unwanted return to the pagan pre-Christian universe. The 1927 solar eclipse, we recall, allowed scientists to make calculations about the stars made visible at the moment of total eclipse; but as Cobbe's dream illustrates, such an event could only be interpreted negatively by the Victorians. Their fears about solar death dovetail with anxieties about a world bereft of the certitudes of Christianity, where the old order is crumbling, and patriarchy is under threat. In Woolf's fiction, however, to glimpse the stars is usually a positive (perhaps feminist) experience: for example, Katherine Hilbery's secret nocturnal life as a mathematician.

> It was only at night, indeed, that she felt secure enough from surprise to concentrate her mind to the utmost.
> Perhaps the unwomanly nature of the science made her instinctively wish to conceal her love of it. But the more profound reason was that in her mind mathematics was directly opposed to literature. She would not have cared to confess how infinitely she preferred the exactitude, the star-like impersonality, of figures to the confusion, agitation, and vagueness of the finest prose.

> *(N&D* 40)

During the conventionally chaotic darkness of night she pursues (traditionally 'unwomanly') rationality and precision, which are further reclaimed as feminine provinces by the invocation of the planets – not as literary, amatory, mystic forces, but as mathematically chartable points of reference in the night sky. Katherine's joy in things rational is used subversively throughout *Night and Day*, and most effectively in love scenes as, for example, when Denham ('a person who feels') proposes:

> she was no more listening to it than she was counting the paving-stones at her feet. She was feeling happier than she had felt in her life. If Denham could have seen how visibly books of algebraic symbols, pages all speckled with dots and dashes and twisted bars, came before her eyes as they trod the Embankment, his secret joy in her attention might have been dispersed . . . all the time she was in fancy looking up through a telescope at white shadow-cleft disks which were other worlds, until she felt herself possessed of two bodies, one walking by the river with Denham, the other concentrated to a silver globe aloft in the fine blue space above the scum of vapours that was covering the visible world. She looked at the sky once, and saw that no star was keen enough to pierce the flight of watery clouds now coursing rapidly before the west wind.
>
> (*N&D* 316–17)

Katherine is conscious of the night sky, while Denham is associated with the more mundane 'paving stones at her feet'. The clouds of this world obscure her vision of other worlds; and if 'the scum of vapours' suggests Müller's conventional, feminine imagery, we are implicitly reminded that daylight, and, by association, the solar light of masculinity, prevents these other worlds being visible at all. Woolf celebrates the sun-free night sky for its liberating and rational potential for women. She shows the 'dark country' of feminine experience to be luminous, rational, and chartable. If the light of the man's world is regarded as obscuring Katherine's true self, then it is certainly with irony that one reads of Denham's sudden realization 'that he had never seen her in the daylight before'. (*N&D* 246)

The contrasting Victorian gloom at the prospect of solar death was not entirely undissipated: 'The discovery of radioactivity relieved anxieties about the imminent death of the sun – but the happy end of that story was to prove the start of another more terrifying one with which we are all-too familiar.' Yet if the discovery of radioactivity offers a mixed blessing, Darwin's renewed interest in 'the least Apollonian of creatures', the earthworm, is put forward by Beer as an (unconscious) 'counter to the solar myth', and one which enjoyed 'immense and immediate popularity'.[14] It is of significance, too, in Woolf's refigured solar economy.

Worm, python, dragon, fish

Darwin's worm, I want to suggest, is related (via mythic permutations) to Woolf's fish. 'Worms have played a more important part in the history of the world than most persons would at first suppose' claims Darwin:

> When we behold a wide, turf-covered expanse, we should remember that its smoothness, on which much of its beauty depends, is mainly due to all the inequalities having been slowly levelled by worms. . . . It may be doubted whether there are many other animals which have played so important a part in the history of the world, as have these lowly creatures.

Worms are even responsible for levelling the toppled stones of the ancient site of solar worship itself, Stonehenge: "some of the outer Druidical stones are now prostrate, having fallen at a remote but unknown period; and these have become buried to a moderate depth in the ground. They are surrounded by sloping borders of turf, on which recent [worm] castings were seen."[15]

Beer alerts us to Leslie Stephen's wry remarks on Darwin's 'kindly feelings for worms',[16] and refers to Andrew Lang's explanation of the 'function of Darwin's worm' as in keeping with the Apollonian sungod's association with the mouse.[17] This 'conjunction of the lowest and highest', Beer suggests, 'may have the function of warding off threats to stability by a fictional alliance of most and least powerful . . . "All sentient beings are doomed to complete annihilation after such long-continued slow progress", [Darwin] wrote of the cooling sun. But the obscure worm allows him an image, at once matter-of-fact and newly dignified, for the unchanging Saturnian world hidden away from the controversies of physics . . .'[18] Woolf's piscine counter to the dying sun, I suggest, draws on, not the conjunction, but the opposition, of highest and lowest; for the 'obscure worm' may not be Apollo's ally after all, but, like the fish, a version of his traditional enemy.

'Apollo's enemy was the great dragon Python, whom he had to fight and kill before he could establish his temple and oracle at Delphi,' begins Joseph Fontenrose's guide to the many permutations of the Apollo/Python myth (from Perseus and Andromeda, for example, to St. George and the Dragon). Significantly, the python was female in the earliest accounts of this conflict. For example, the Homeric Hymn to Apollo tells how the god 'fought a she-dragon (*drakaina*) beside a spring and killed her with an arrow from his bow'; and 'it is likely', Fontenrose deduces, 'that Apollo encountered her while he was at work on the foundations not more than a few hundred yards from her spring.'[19]

The acclaimed source of Western lyric poetry, then, is founded on the destruction of this she-dragon, who represents an autonomous femininity, alien to that approved by (and approving of) patriarchy.

> She was a monstrous creature, huge and savage, guilty of terrible violence against the people and the flocks of the land. To meet her meant death to any man. She had, moreover, been nurse to Typhaon, Hera's monstrous child, whom the queen of the gods had borne in anger at Zeus, because he had brought forth Athena from his head, and had had no need of her, his wedded wife. Deciding to equal Zeus's feat by producing a child without male help, Hera succeeded, but the child she bore was the monstrous Typhaon, like neither to gods nor to mortal men. She turned him over to the Delphinian drakaina, an evil to evil.[20]

Hera and the she-dragon represent a reviled and redundant femininity in the new patriarchal economy. Athena, on the other hand, we remember, made the crucial judgement in favour of patrilineal primacy when she sanctioned Orestes' vengeance on his mother, Clytemnestra (who dreams she swallows a snake, and is called a 'dragon' in Aeschylus), for the murder of her husband, and his father, Agamemnon. Athena puts this above Clytemnestra's avenging the sacrifice by Agamemnon of her daughter, Iphigenia. 'For the thing he did to the blossom born of me and him; my long wept Iphigenia,' Woolf herself translates, 'justice is done upon him!' (*BERG* 13 *RN* 3) But motherless Athena, born from Zeus' head, has no loyalty to these feminine bonds.

In the Homeric Hymn, 'our first notice of the etymology that derives the place name Pytho from the rotting of the serpent's corpse', we find the 'female serpent is given no name', but 'is called Delphyne in later literature. Nor was she the guardian of Ge's or Themis's oracular shrine, since the Hymn knows of no shrine at Delphi before Apollo founded his.' The previously feminine associations of Apollo's shrine are here erased so that Apollo appears to found a shrine for the first time, not displace one he opposes. In later accounts the serpent/dragon is sometimes described as male.[21] 'When the snake of Pytho, feminine of course, at first, as guardian of Gaia, had to be killed,' notes Jane Harrison, 'he became a male serpent, a foeman worthy of Apollo's steel.' She explains the transition whereby Apollo comes to stand 'for light and reason' in terms of 'the passage from Earth to Sun by way of Moon, from Gaia to Phoibos by way of Phoibe.'[22] Apollo is conqueror of his sacred feminine origins. According to a note to Aeschylus which Woolf follows, he is 'the invader and appropriator of that sanctuary and there is even some evidence that anciently the feminine [Phoebe], as well as [Phoebus], was used at Delphi.'[23] Woolf seems to be aware, then, of a lost, and luminous, feminine source of poetry, one displaced into the demonized figure of the dragon.

If the dominant tradition of poetry is constructed on the grave of the feminine, women writers may find problems negotiating a form founded on their own displacement and destruction. The act of inscription, of illumination, may be simultaneously an act of (self-) erasure and occlusion. One solution is to resurrect the drakaina as a positive source for women's writing. Woolf may playfully be making modified allusion to this in *Mrs Dalloway* where she describes 'the voice of no age or sex, the voice of an ancient spring spouting from the earth' which is yet the voice of 'the battered woman':

> As the ancient song bubbled up opposite Regent's Park Tube Station, still the earth seemed green and flowery; still, though it issued from so rude a mouth, a mere hole in the earth, muddy too, matted with root fibres and tangled grasses, still the old bubbling burbling song, soaking through the knotted roots of infinite ages, and skeletons and treasure, streamed away in rivulets over the pavement and all along the Marylebone Road, and down towards Euston, fertilising, leaving a damp stain.
>
> (*Mrs D* 123, 124)

Not only may this rude mouth connote the pre-Apollonian Pythian spring or shrine, a source of feminine inspiration; but its imagery might also bear connections with the modern suffrage movement. The muddy trail of the woman's voice weaving through London streets may suggest the famous 'Mud March', and other suffrage marches we looked at earlier. One suffrage marching song, 'March of the Women' (1911), was composed by Ethel Smyth, whose close friendship with Woolf began in 1930.

Darwin's worm, I am suggesting, seems to have more in common with Apollo's ancient enemy, the python, than with his weak ally, the mouse.[24] The Victorians' discovery of the sun's mortality, suggests in mythological terms the reversal of Apollo's victory over the Python. There is to be no transcendence to a higher Apollonian state, but instead a return to the earth, to the corporeal worms. Darwin's elevation of the earthworm, then, might be read as 'a counter to solar myth' because it constitutes the rehabilitation (and domestication) of the Python as a collective force for social good. It is no longer occluded by enlightened civilization, but embraced. A version of Darwin's earthworm which brings out its original associations with the feminine would be useful to feminism, suggestive perhaps of the constituency of women (and) workers undermining the foundations of (solar) patriarchy in the late nineteenth and early twentieth centuries. I will be investigating Woolf's fish as a version of this Python-worm; for in some versions of the myth, this she-dragon opponent of Apollo is a fish, fish-goddess, sea-serpent or sea-monster. Euronyme, for example, 'a form of Ge' was 'a fish in her lower body'.[25] 'The Sun and the

Fish', then, may suggest and subvert Apollo and the Python. I will approach the fish section via two other short pieces by Woolf: a later story and an earlier review.

Suns and fishes

Woolf opposes manly sun and womanly fish in 'The Shooting Party' (1938), a story about the household of a 'Squire' who busies himself with the sport of pheasant-shooting 'out on the King's Ride'. He strongly resembles the Yorkshire Squire in (the earlier) 'The Sun and the Fish'. Inside his house, his sister observes the play of sunlight:

> And then on it went, the sun's feeble but impartial finger, and lay upon the coat of arms over the fireplace – gently illumined the shield; the pendant grapes; the mermaid; and the spears. Miss Antonia looked up as the light strengthened. Vast lands, so they said, the old people had owned – her forefathers – the Rashleighs. Over there. Up the Amazon. Freebooters. Voyagers. Sacks of emeralds. Nosing round the islands. Taking captives. Maidens. There she was, all scales from the tail to the waist. Miss Antonia grinned. Down struck the finger of the sun and her eye went with it. Now it rested on a silver frame; on a photograph; on an egg-shaped baldish head; on a lip that stuck out under the moustache; and the name "Edward" written with a flourish beneath.
> "The King . . ." Miss Antonia muttered.
>
> (*CSF* 255)

The sunlight offers patriarchal blessing upon the shield's testimony to the plundering imperialism of the Squire's ancestors. As in 'The Moment: Summer's Night', this moment of illumination seems to sanction the oppression of the feminine. The mermaid (half-woman, half-fish) is amongst the representations of the vanquished, and the booty, expropriated in conquests of the Americas. The portrait of King Edward sanctions the scene. Miss Antonia seems to be a complicit victim of this order, which, it transpires, is itself hardly secure. The house is falling to pieces. Miss Antonia and the ancient Miss Rashleigh toast the demise of the men:

> "It was a day like this, d'you remember?" said old Miss Rashleigh, fingering her glass. "They brought him home . . . a bullet through his heart. A bramble, so they said. Tripped. Caught his foot. . . ." She chuckled as she sipped her wine.
> "And John . . ." said Miss Antonia. "The mare, they said, put her foot in a hole. Died in the field. The hunt rode over him. He came home, too, on a shutter. . . ." They sipped again.

> "Remember Lily?" said old Miss Rashleigh. "A bad'un." She shook her
> head.
> "Riding with a scarlet tassel on her cane. . . ."
> "Rotten at the heart!" cried Miss Antonia. "Remember the Colonel's letter?
> 'Your son rode as if he had twenty devils in him – charged at the head of his
> men.' . . . Then one white devil – ah hah!" She sipped again.
> "The men of our house . . ." began Miss Rashleigh. She raised her glass.
> She held it high, as if she toasted the mermaid carved in plaster on the
> fireplace. She paused. The guns were barking. Something cracked in the
> woodwork. Or was it a rat running behind the plaster?
>
> (*CSF* 258; Woolf's ellipses)

The men's downfall begins with a bramble, then a mare, then a woman,
which suggests the feminine principle progressing from vegetation to animal
to (almost) human. The mermaid, the siren luring men to their death, symbolizes this sense of transition (from fish to woman). The hunting dogs, however, are not associated with the feminine, but with the weaponry of the male
hunter: 'The guns were barking.' The Squire himself is earlier described as
having a 'hang-dog, purple-stained face'. (*CSF* 255) He returns irate:

> With one lash he curled to the ground the vase of chrysanthemums.
> Another caught old Miss Rashleigh on the cheek. The old woman staggered
> backwards. She fell against the mantelpiece. Her stick striking wildly, struck
> the shield above the fireplace. She fell with a thud upon the ashes. The shield
> of the Rashleighs crashed from the wall. Under the mermaid, under the
> spears, she lay buried.
>
> (*CSF* 260)

His violence towards his sister brings down the whole house. The story of a
man brought down by women suggests an allegory of the abdication crisis, in
which the king's relationship with, and subsequent, morganatic marriage to,
an American divorcee (the return of the vanquished Americas perhaps) results
in his relinquishment of sovereignty: 'The wind lashed the panes of glass; shots
volleyed in the Park and a tree fell. And then King Edward in the silver frame
slid, toppled and fell too.' (*CSF* 260)

Edward VIII's abdication (December 1936) is played out in the allegorical
terms explored in Woolf's eclipse narrative; the images of sun and mermaid
dominate. Woolf develops the sun/fish opposition in 'The Shooting Party'
to examine the crisis of masculine sovereignty surrounding the abdication, a
crisis anticipated in 'The Sun and the Fish' where, having tailored her account
of the solar eclipse to fit a feminist appropriation of the solar for a celebration
of women's sovereignty, she completes her overhaul of patriarchal imagery with
a feminist revival of the fish.

The Aquarium

'But the eye has not done with us yet.' So Woolf opens the final paragraph of 'The Sun and the Fish', where she turns from matters solar to the contrary state of the piscine. In addressing the fish, then, Woolf focuses on the other primary (but negative) element in the founding binary opposition of patriarchy. As with the darkness (with which it is associated), the opportunity arises to redeem this negative and assert it as positive: that is, to valorize the python. But, again, Woolf seems to resist the straightforward implementation of such a strategy.

> In pursuit of some logic of its own, which we cannot follow immediately, [the eye] now presents us with a picture, or generalized impression rather, of London on a hot summer day, when, to judge by the sense of concussion and confusion, the London season is at its height. It takes us a moment to realize, first, the fact that we are in some public gardens, next, from the asphalt and paper bags thrown about, that they must be the Zoological Gardens, and then without further preparation we are presented with a complete and perfect effigy of two lizards.
>
> (*CDB* 198)

Woolf zooms in on this scene as on the railway station earlier in the essay. She returns us from the moors of Yorkshire, to the tamed (asphalted and littered) greenery of metropolitan gardens. This is the site of the other half of the morganatic marriage between sun and fish. We are introduced first to two lizards, then in what follows, to some fish, and finally to human beings and bankers! Before following Woolf's eye further, we might look at an earlier description of the same scene.

Woolf describes for *Nation & Athenaeum* 'the new aquarium at the London Zoological Gardens, opened to the public on Monday, 7 April 1924':

> Aesthetically speaking, the new aquarium is undoubtedly the most impressive of all the houses at the zoo. Red fish, blue fish, nightmare fish, dapper fish, fish lean as gimlets, fish round and white as soup plates, ceaselessly gyrate in oblong frames of greenish light in the hushed and darkened apartment hollowed out beneath the Mappin terraces. Scientifically, no doubt, the place is a paradise for the ichthyologist; but the poet might equally celebrate the strange beauty of the broad-leaved water plants trembling in the current, or the sinister procession of self-centred sea-beasts forever circling and seeking perhaps some minute prey, perhaps some explanation of a universe which evidently appears to them of inscrutable mystery. Now they knock the glass with their noses; now they shoot dartlike to the surface; now eddy slowly contemplatively down to the sandy bottom. Some are delicately fringed with a fin that vibrates like an electric fan and propels them on; others wear a mail boldly splashed with a design by a Japanese artist. That crude human egotism

> which supposes that Nature has wrought her best for those who walk
> the earth is rebuked at the aquarium. Nature seems to have cared more
> to tint and adorn the fishes who live unseen at the depths of the sea than
> to ornament our old, familiar friends, the goat, the hog, the sparrow, and
> the horse.
>
> (*E* III 404–405)

Woolf celebrates the exotic colours of the fish newly brought into the human realm. This previously 'unseen' alien life, brought to the surface from 'the depths of the sea', puts the 'familiar' world of creatures to shame with its exquisite beauty. As her first words indicate, Woolf presents the scene from an aesthetic point of view; claiming it from scientific interest for the attention of the poet, she finds the fish 'boldly splashed with a design by a Japanese artist'. Nature, moreover, personified as a woman, is the artist who 'seems to have cared more to tint and adorn the fishes who live unseen at the depths of the sea than to ornament our old, familiar friends'.

Although the fish are an exotic spectacle compared with the norm of 'those who walk the earth', they themselves do not remain merely the object of the human gaze. They are autonomous ('self-centred sea-beasts') and intelligent (they move 'contemplatively'). They not only possess basic instincts ('seeking . . . prey'), they are also philosophically inquisitive ('seeking . . . explanation of a universe'). They have the advantages of technology too: 'a fin . . . like an electric fan . . . a mail boldly splashed'.

Woolf's anthropomorphizing of the fish has a levelling effect for both sides of the aquarium glass. 'Now they knock the glass with their noses' might apply to human spectators as well as fish. Each side sees the other as exotic spectacle, 'inscrutable mystery'. This light-hearted valorization of the fish, who move in status from spectacle to spectator, observed to observer, object to subject, may be ripe for feminist appropriation. Their bright colours, especially, make them suitable for just such an appropriation in the context of 'The Sun and the Fish', where the suffrage tricolour has already intervened in the solar half of the essay. There may be a resonance from this passage already in the essay: 'those who walk the earth' is close to the essay's 'we who tread the earth'. Further, we might take 'crude human egotism' more narrowly to refer to the arrogant male presumption of masculine supremacy. The fish may suggest a countering feminine principle.

Solar ruin and still rapture

Woolf's 'amusing game', however, does not oblige us with such a manœuvre. Having led us to the Zoological Gardens, 'the eye' offers a rather different view.

In the first place, the piscine phase of 'The Sun and the Fish', as we have noted, introduces us not to fish but to 'the perfect effigy of two lizards'. Lizards, however, are still in keeping with the trope of python and dragon.

> After destruction, calm; after ruin, steadfastness – that, perhaps, is the logic of the eye at any rate. One lizard is mounted immobile on the back of another, with only the twinkle of a gold eyelid or the suction of a green flank to show that they are the living flesh, and not made of bronze. All human passion seems furtive and feverish beside this still rapture.
>
> (*CDB* 198)

This 'still rapture' is not the celebration of the flesh we might expect from the fish side of Woolf's essay. Indeed, the first glimpse of the lizards suggests them to be artificial. Woolf explains 'the logic of the eye' in morganatically marrying the 'destruction' and 'ruin' of the sight of the eclipse to the 'calm' and 'steadfastness' of this sight. What could be a more heterogeneous couple than a solar eclipse and a pair of static lizards? Yet the lizards, for all their immobility, appear to be in mating position (if not exactly *flagrante delicto*!). This makes a stark contrast to the tumultuous violence noted in the sexual imagery of the clouds and sun of the eclipse. Whereas this heavenly cavorting is not quite beyond the human experience, the 'still rapture' of the lizards makes 'all human passion seem furtive and feverish'.

She continues: 'Time seems to have stopped and we are in the presence of immortality. The tumult of the world has fallen from us like a crumbling cloud.' (*CDB* 198) The temporal event of the eclipse is contrasted with the timelessness of fleshly generation. 'The tumult of the world' and the 'crumbling cloud' remind us of the emotional upheaval involved in witnessing the eclipse. On the other hand, these phrases may also refer to the world immediately outside the enclosed space of the aquarium where 'the London season is at its height'. The aquarium itself is presented as an arcade of art. The 'effigy' of the lizards suggests this, and also fits with Woolf's way of 'aesthetically speaking' established in her earlier piece. 'Immortality' and the stopping of time, then, are qualities of the aesthetic. The lizards are almost (but not quite) like the figures on Keats's Grecian Urn: a 'Cold Pastoral!'

> Tanks cut in the level blackness enclose squares of immortality, worlds of settled sunshine, where there is neither rain nor cloud. There the inhabitants perform forever evolutions whose intricacy, because it has no reason, seems the more sublime. Blue and silver armies, keeping a perfect distance for all their arrow-like quickness, shoot first this way, then that. The discipline is perfect, the control absolute; reason there is none. The most majestic of human evolutions seems feeble and fluctuating compared with theirs.
>
> (*CDB* 198)

This subaquatic world resembles a military training ground, where troops have been honed to martial perfection. The vocabulary bristles with weaponry, conveying a sinisterly sleek hostility: 'armies . . . arrow-like . . . shoot . . . discipline . . . control'. Gone are the anthropomorphic qualities of reason. These creatures are not contemplative, they are machines of war. There is no trace of rationality: this world 'has no reason . . . reason there is none'. The fish, introduced as 'Blue and silver armies', are seen to occupy the pinnacle of evolutionary progress because, paradoxically, they betray no sign of change or mutation, unlike the 'feeble and fluctuating' 'human evolutions'.

This comparison again pushes human experience into sympathy with the solar phase of the essay. Yet it is in this piscine context that the word 'sun' reappears for the first and only time since the account of the eclipse (after which, we remember, Woolf drops 'sun' in favour of 'light' and 'colour'). It is not the 'sun' itself that appears but 'worlds of settled *sun*shine', for the scene is after all indoors. The light in the enclosures mimics sunshine. These sealed, contained, tanks, 'squares of immortality' have continuous artificial 'sunshine'. They admit 'neither rain nor cloud'. This is very unlike the eclipse scene where the real sun is in conflict with clouds, and is seen to be discontinuous, intermittent, and impermanent.

The natural world in the eclipse scene overwhelms the humans momentarily, and it is a world they tread themselves. In the Zoological Gardens 'Nature' has been packaged and contained as a spectacle for human curiosity. Its lack of reason makes it 'seem the more sublime' yet its constrictions belie sublimity. Comparison of the two states suggests Blake's line: 'The cistern contains; the fountain overflows.'[26] The sight of the eclipse is part of a larger experience: it 'overflows' and changes; the sight of the fish in their tanks shows life dissected, imitated, frozen, diminished and contained. The former corresponds to a romantic view, the latter is classical.

The 'worlds of settled sunshine, where there is neither rain nor cloud' also resemble Müllerian solar theory, possibly suggesting an unchanging masculine hegemony. The fish inhabit an unchanging world of permanent sunshine, bereft of rain and clouds (feminine at the eclipse), but also bereft of reason. It is a pretty dull place:

> Each of these worlds too, which measures perhaps four feet by five, is as perfect in its order as in its method. For forests, they have half a dozen bamboo canes; for mountains, sandhills; in the curves and crinkles of a seashell lie for them all adventure, all romance. The rise of a bubble, negligible elsewhere, is here an event of the highest importance. The silver bead bores its way up a spiral staircase through the water to burst against the sheet of glass, which seems laid flat across the top.
>
> (CDB 198)

'The silver bead *bores*' in more than one way, for this is a life of tedium. There is scorn, tinged with pity, in Woolf's description of this series of tiny, limited worlds, where everything is smaller than life and recorded in dull measurements. It corresponds to the definition of life Woolf scornfully rejects: 'Life is not a series of gig-lamps symmetrically arranged.' We have already commented on the post-eclipse scene's similarity to Woolf's 'luminous halo'. In contrast, these small points of illumination are miniature worlds of small-scale 'adventure and romance'. Any ripple or movement is contained and defeated: nothing 'overflows'.

'The rise of a bubble' is, in the aquarium, 'an event of the highest importance', yet seen from the vantage point of 'elsewhere' – that is, of the world outside the tank, as well as of the eclipse scene – it is 'negligible'. Its progress is soon flattened. This is a perfect, almost stagnant, world, without surplus or excess, where everything exists solipsistically, yet in harmonious function with its environment. There is no conflict, no reason, no progression.

> Nothing exists needlessly. The fish themselves seem to have been shaped deliberately and slipped into the world only to be themselves. They neither work nor weep. In their shape is their reason. For what other purpose except the sufficient one of perfect existence can they have been thus made, some so round, some so thin, some with radiating fins upon their backs, others lined with red electric light, others undulating like white pancakes on a frying pan, some armoured in blue mail, some given prodigious claws, some outrageously fringed with huge whiskers?
>
> (*CDB* 198–99)

The fish, inhabiting a world of dull, meaningless, irrational privilege, constitute a pointless aristocracy in nature: 'They neither work nor weep'. They are born perfect into the world purely to fulfil a 'perfect existence'. Gone are the comparisons to art (that quality seems to have been transferred to their tanks); gone too the references to 'Nature' (feminine or otherwise) as their maker. Unlike the lizards' world, theirs is not one of 'settled sunshine', but of untroubled waters through which they sleekly move. The fish carry their own luminescence: 'radiating fins' suggests both shape and light; and there are 'others lined with red electric light'. Light is not a source outside them, it is internalized by them: they integrate light into flesh.

Described in increasingly more sinister terms, the fish are armed and dangerous ('armoured' or with 'claws'). Finally, they are pompous, verging on the decadent: 'some outrageously fringed with huge whiskers'. At the point when they seem almost to be middle-aged men, we are reminded that, far from it, 'More care has been spent upon [these] half a dozen fish than upon all the races of men.' (*CDB* 199)

Considering the significance of colour in the eclipse section of the essay, we must look carefully at Woolf's handling of colour here. In fact, there appears in this passage a discreet reference to another flag – not at all like the suffrage tricolour. The colours of the Union Jack are discernible in the ordering of the fishes' colours: 'red electric light . . . white pancakes . . . blue mail'. (In Woolf's earlier description the order was 'red fish, blue fish . . . fish round and white'.) Perhaps it is this imagery's incipient British nationalism that makes these fish sound increasingly like the contents of the Empire's finest gentleman's club! When Woolf reminds us of the exclusive care they enjoy, she tempts us to see these fish as the pampered male hegemony, the bellicose imperial bores, who define themselves as an élite, sheltered from and above 'all the [*other*] races of men'. The use of the passive construction ('more care has been spent') leaves the question of agency open. We have seen that 'Nature' is no longer credited with the responsibility of their creation. They are self-made, 'slipped into the world only to be themselves'. They do not earn their keep for they 'neither work nor weep'. Yet Woolf calls them fish not men: they are sinister alien creatures, frightening in their autonomy and solipsism. In the essay's closing statement we are asked to identify with these fish.

> Under our tweed and silk is nothing but a monotony of pink nakedness. Poets are not transparent to the backbone as these fish are. Bankers have no claws. Kings and Queens themselves have neither ruffs nor frills. In short, if we were to be turned naked into an aquarium – but enough.
>
> (*CDB* 199)

Humanity, it seems, has no natural hierarchy. We are not born with the 'badges and signs of individuality', as Woolf says earlier in the essay, however rapidly we acquire them. The symbols of authority and sovereignty ('ruffs' and 'frills') are not biologically given. Like 'our tweed and silk', they are outer trappings, constructed and endowed not by nature but by ourselves. Beneath them is a 'monotony of pink nakedness'. Evidently only one race is discussed here – the dominant one – and one, privileged, class. One reader misses the satirical edge here, choosing instead to interpret the essay as a monument to mysticism: it is an exploration of 'an inner reality' and the 'emotional significance' of 'our sensuous experiences' in which the eclipse scene and the aquarium show how 'human nature has stood apart, after fighting the scurry of human, everyday life, and in dignity has for a moment glimpsed the immutable.'[27] This not only ignores the humour of the essay, but also leaves unexplored its implicit questioning of 'human nature' from a feminist perspective, as well as its feminist context.

Woolf contrasts the dull opacity of human flesh with the transparency and integral luminosity of fish flesh. Humanity has to look outwards for illumination; it has no natural sign of authority. It does not live in a sealed tank, nor in a timeless 'world of settled sunshine'. All our attributes, evaluations, interests, are socially and artificially constructed, and are, therefore, changeable. The declaration, 'Poets are not transparent to the backbone as these fish are. Bankers have no claws', is a surrealistic illustration of this point, and reminds us that poetry too is not naturally, innately given. It also reminds us of one poet – and one poem – in particular. T.S. Eliot, we remember, was a banker. 'The Love Song of J. Alfred Prufrock' (1917) recounts: 'I should have been a pair of ragged claws/ Scuttling across the floors of silent seas.'[28] The Eliotic pose of the subject's desire for (or fate of) oblivion as an object, and the fragmentation of subjectivity is mockingly countered by Woolf. If 'Prufrock' tracks the disintegration of the masculine subject at the time of the Great War, 'The Sun and the Fish', in its aftermath, constructs a new plural feminist model of subjectivity in the ruins of the old. She ridicules the desire to return to the condition women so recently were escaping (and still endured at the time of Eliot's writing): the condition of the object, the spectacle, the insentient, creature of the deep. Having exposed some of its more reactionary implications, she dismisses Eliot's line as ludicrous: '– but enough.'

Woolf ends the essay with a joke, and a magician's wink: 'The eye shuts now. It has shown us a dead world and an immortal fish.' (*CDB* 199) The wink of the eye signals the end of the 'amusing game' as well as accompanying Woolf's legerdemain, and the perpetration of a trick. The wink is also the fleshly, organic, version of the solar eclipse, and the eclipse of the dominant, transcendent, masculine 'I'. The solar element in the essay, traditionally *the* masculine province, has been appropriated, with the assistance of the suffrage tricolour, as a positive feminist trope. The piscine element, traditionally assigned to the feminine, has been adapted to describe the ruling caste of British patriarchy. This latter world is seen to be hopelessly oblivious to the events of a larger scale described in the former, and soon to overtake it. At the same time, its weaponry as well as its pomposity have been assessed. There is surely irony in the final declaration of 'a dead world and an immortal fish'; for we have seen the recovery of the 'dead world', and the deadness of the 'immortal fish'. Woolf seems to have kept the hierarchy of sun/fish in place (with some adjustments), but filleted it of the traditional hierarchy ' "the" couple man/woman'. Light and colour are claimed for woman, man is made piscine. The original Python and Apollo swap gender. Woolf was not the first feminist to perform this trick.

The cover of *The Suffragette* ('The Official Organ of the Women's Social and Political Union'), Friday, October 17, 1913 (Plate 6), sports a picture of Joan of Arc, dressed in armour, standing in a pool of light. She is wearing the band of the WSPU, and is armed with a sword in her right hand and a shield marked 'purity' in her left. St George-like, she loftily confronts a dragon, on whose collar is marked 'INDECENCY'. It is dragged out of the darkness towards her by a bearded man, carrying in his other hand a flag marked 'THE PRESS'. Three pairs of male hands assist in pushing the beast, with its talons raised, towards its target, as if confronting the woman with patriarchy's stereotype of the draconian feminine. This is an allegory of the disgraceful press treatment of the suffrage movement. The legend below reads: 'THE FORCES OF EVIL DENOUNCING THE BEARERS OF LIGHT'. *The Suffragette* defines itself as the organ of enlightenment in a world blackened by the dragon of patriarchy.

Woolf's regendering of the opposition sun/fish is more subtle than this suffrage cartoon's neat, subversive image. It offers a morganatic marriage between sun and fish in which both partners undergo important surgery before they are wed. The sun is eclipsed, no longer seen as an absolute, remote, unchanging symbol; its masculine sovereignty usurped. Instead, Woolf offers a new trope of light and colour, but one that carries with it the ravaged remains of the old. Within the dominant solar discourse of patriarchy, then, are the seeds of its own destruction in the form of emergent, oppositional feminist discourses of colour.

In contrast to this world of intermittent illumination and colour, of change and conflict, Woolf shows us the aquarium: a world of uninterrupted 'sunshine', of fixed identity, of self-contained, limited, flat and *boring* existence. From the perspective of the aquarium, the scene of the eclipse is one of 'destruction' and 'ruin', but this is revealed as the perspective of the ruling patriarchy, whose 'calm . . . steadfastness' and 'immortality' have given way to the increasing pressures of the new prismatic feminism. Woolf builds her new mutable, and mortal, model of feminist subjectivity in the ruins of the old, masculine, solar trope. But this model must be comprehended by means of her 'amusing game' which demonstrates that such a vision is achieved, and survives, only by reference to its contrary. Therefore Woolf morganatically marries her trope of solar ruin to its contrary trope – the undesirably sleek, aquatic perfection of the piscine. Given her early preference for the ruins of Stonehenge over the perfection of Salisbury spire, this comes as no surprise.

PART TWO

Prismatics

9 Post-Impressionism: the explosion of colour

But the coloured canvasses would not wait until dawn. Blue stepped forward and bowed down and sang a melody with the tones from which he had created the damp depths of his ploughed fields, and the stone of his rocks, the height of his skies, and the glitter of his water. Then came Green, carrying the sap of his cypress trees, the silver of his olives, and the silent wealth of his bushes and grass. Then Orange leapt forward in her garment of fire, raising a shout as she passed through the room. Orange was not alone, Carmine and Geranium Red danced with her. They moved like waves of luminous smoke from licking flames, and sometimes they seemed like large winged butterflies with great patterns on their backs. The floor was covered with the red of the tiles in Arles, and in between shone sapphire and emerald. When they had all come to pay their tribute a fanfare sounded, and Yellow, his black-eyed mistress, entered in her Chinese robe of state. Ten women came with her, the fairest of the Empire, garbed in gentler tones of the same yellow, and stood at her side bearing sunflowers.

His beloved made a deep obeisance before the catafalque and the ten women did likewise. And as they bowed, all the sheaves of wheat in the field, all the flowers and the fruit bowed down likewise, and the sun shed his rays on the cottage in Auvers.

Three days afterwards Vincent was buried in the little cemetery between the corn-fields.[1]

So Julius Meier-Graefe closes his biography of Van Gogh, one of the painters, along with Cézanne, Gauguin, and Matisse, to be represented, for the first time in Britain, at Roger Fry's notorious exhibition of 1910, 'Manet and the Post-Impressionists'.[2] Meier-Graefe's was a formative influence on this event. His florid, solar elegy, then, provides a serendipitous, if gaudy, link between our first area of discussion, the eclipse, and our second, Woolf's engagement with Post-Impressionism. Woolf, herself, it seems, was *au fait* with Meier-Graefe's 'standard life of van Gogh' [*sic*] since she mentions it in reviewing a later 'more modest biography' of the artist.[3]

Meier-Graefe envisions Van Gogh's death as that of a pagan sun-god, illuminated in his final hours by the tributes of the gloriously vibrant colours for which his paintings are famous. Personified as exotic women and likened to butterflies, these colours drain from his canvasses to parade before him. Van Gogh's prismatic celebration of sunflowers, wheatfields, the sun itself (*him*self), and of every colour in the spectrum, is reciprocated by this genuflection at his death.

There are parallels between this passage and Woolf's treatment of the solar eclipse, and there may be potential for feminist adaptation in Meier-Graefe's fantastic rhetoric. Feminine colours may turn feminist, as we have seen, and Van Gogh's handmaidens of colour might be liberated or transformed into suffrage activists. Consider the vision in *Orlando* of a landscape (which echoes Woolf's eclipse description) bringing luminous colour to the previously 'dark country' of feminine sexuality.

> After an hour or so – the sun was rapidly sinking, the white clouds had turned red, the hills were violet, the woods purple, the valleys black – a trumpet sounded. Orlando leapt to his feet. The shrill sound came from the valley. It came from a dark spot down there; a spot compact and mapped out; a maze; a town, yet girt with walls; it came from the heart of his own great house in the valley, which, dark before, even as he looked and the single trumpet duplicated and reduplicated itself with other shriller sounds, lost its darkness and became pierced with lights.
>
> (*O* 21)

When day meets night, a man (who later becomes a woman) looks down upon a valley in dying sunlight: as the sun goes down each item seen is described as a darker colour than the last – from 'white clouds' to 'valleys black', in shades of red. When blackness is reached instead of nothingness or amorphous obscurity, a trumpet call heralds a new landscape, in which is discerned a 'dark spot'; and as eyes adjust, darkness becomes 'pierced with lights'. The landscape this (still male) figure surveys represents a positive feminine sexuality in the terms of luminous colour, and so already challenges his male gaze (under which traditionally it would be passive and submissive). The subversiveness of this vision becomes more fully apparent in the ambiguous interpretation of the discovery by this man (who is to become a woman) of 'his own great house in the valley': as a man he might be considered proprietor of the object (feminine) world he surveys, but the phrase also anticipates his forthcoming gender change which puts a different emphasis on his (or her) ownership, suggesting not vanquished but autonomous feminine sexuality.

Like Meier-Graefe's colourful handmaidens, this vision of a liberated feminine sexuality is accompanied by a 'fanfare'. In Woolf's landscape, however, the 'shrill sound' of the 'trumpet', anticipating the fanfare of trumpets awakening Orlando to a new female identity (*O* 126–127), marks not subservient, but autonomous, feminine pleasure. Also different is her celebration of feminine pleasure culminating, after the attentions of various servile men have been noted, in a coded and playful suggestion of orgasm:

> Some were small hurrying lights, as if they burnt in empty banqueting-halls made ready to receive guests who had not come; and others dipped and waved and sank and rose, as if held in the hands of troops of serving men, bending, kneeling, rising, receiving, guarding, and escorting with all dignity indoors a great Princess alighting her chariot. Coaches turned and wheeled in the courtyard. Horses tossed their plumes. The Queen had come.
>
> (O 21)

The mounting sense of excitement in the first, long, sentence, suggested by the rhythmic catalogue of participles denoting arousal ('bending, kneeling, rising . . .'), contrasts with the explosive and climactic effect of the perfect tenses in the statements following ('turned . . . wheeled . . . tossed'). The sexual pun in the final report, 'The Queen had come', is in keeping with the Elizabethan flavour of the scene.

I want to bring out, as a context to Woolf's ideas on colour and writing, the connections made in contemporary reviews of Post-Impressionism between the shocking colours and depiction of women in the paintings, and the shocking colours of the women's suffrage movement. This will entail leaving Woolf herself in the background at one stage, but such an excursus is necessary in our exploration of less orthodox readings of Post-Impressionism.

'All great writers are great colourists'

Woolf saw a number of Van Goghs, of course, at Fry's historic exhibition, which is often cited to explain her enigmatic statement: 'on or about December 1910 human character changed'.[4] Andrew McNeillie, for example, glosses Woolf's date with reference to the Post-Impressionist exhibition and the death of Edward VII (E III 437). But 1910, as I will explore below, saw other events we might acknowledge as relevant. First, Woolf's elaboration on her choice of date is worth consideration, not least because she uses a photological turn of phrase to illustrate it.

1910's shift in human relations, represented in the work of Samuel Butler and Bernard Shaw, Woolf sees symbolized in the figure of 'one's cook'. She explains: 'The Victorian cook lived like a leviathan in the lower depths, formidable, silent, obscure, inscrutable; the Georgian cook is a creature of sunshine and fresh air; in and out of the drawing room, now to borrow the *Daily Herald*, now to ask advice about a hat.' (E III 422) The imagery of a woman servant emerging leviathan-like from the dark depths of the kitchen into sunlight, fits suggestively with the opposition Woolf goes on to manipulate in 'The Sun and the Fish'; and may suggest a shift from women's dark, subliminal, creaturely existence to luminous, colourful liberation. Compare Mrs. McNab's depiction as 'a tropical fish, oaring its way through sun-lanced rocks' (*TL* 206). Woolf's vocabulary is similar to that of Mary Lowndes's 1910 essay on suffrage colourist banner-making: 'now into public life comes trooping the feminine; and with the feminine creature come the banners of past times.'[5]

December 1910 may mean for Woolf, then, material improvement for women workers, and the emergence of women from intellectual darkness into enlightenment, from obscurity into public life. After the creaturely cook, Woolf gives a 'more solemn instance . . . of the power of the human race to change': a revised reading of the *Agamemnon*, in which 'sympathies' (usually reserved for the patriarchal order sanctioned by Athena) may now be 'almost entirely with Clytemnestra' (avenger of her daughter's death). In asking us to 'consider the married life of the Carlyles,' she returns to the theme of women's servitude, perhaps mindful of the suffragette scorn for Thomas Carlyle (resulting in a cleaver attack on his portrait in the National Gallery).[6] He personifies 'the horrible domestic tradition which made it seemly for a woman of genius to spend her time chasing beetles, scouring saucepans, instead of writing books.' Woolf spells out this tradition's hierarchized, gendered, relations as she announces its demise: 'All human relations have shifted – those between masters and servants, husbands and wives, parents and children. And when human relations change there is at the same time a change in religion, conduct, politics and literature. Let us agree to place one of these changes about the year 1910.' (*E* III 422) The dramatic, suffrage events of 1910 and the Post-Impressionist exhibition, 'a shock to most people', according to Woolf,[7] provide political and artistic contexts for such change.

Woolf, furthermore, was aware of possible literary analogies to Post-Impressionism, something Roger Fry himself encouraged (*RF* 180, 183). Arnold Bennett makes such a challenge in his (at the time, almost uniquely) favourable review of 'Manet and the Post-Impressionists',[8] which Woolf in turn reviewed: 'These new pictures, he says, have wearied him of other pictures; is it not possible that some writer will come along and do in words what these men have done in paint?'[9] Woolf takes up Bennett's gauntlet, I suggest, and effects some feminist literary innovations, analogous to Post-Impressionism, and based primarily on the use of colour. Her review of Bennett, as McNeillie notes, 'appeared in the same month as that in which Woolf published her experimental story "The Mark on the Wall" and, probably, shortly before she began to write *Kew Gardens*.' (*E* II 132)

Both these works were illustrated by her sister Vanessa Bell. *Kew Gardens* (1919), furthermore, is a vivid celebration of colour. Colours here are almost the language of flowers, and are closely connected to the wafts of human conversation drifting past the flower beds, the story's main focus.

From the oval-shaped flower-bed there rose perhaps a hundred stalks spreading into heart-shaped or tongue-shaped leaves half way up and unfurling at the tip red or blue or yellow petals marked with spots of colour raised upon the surface; and from the red, blue or yellow gloom of the throat emerged a straight bar, rough with gold dust and slightly clubbed at the end. The petals were voluminous enough to be stirred by the summer breeze, and when they moved, the red, blue and yellow lights passed one over the other, staining an inch of the brown earth beneath with a spot of the most intricate colour. . . . Then the breeze stirred rather more briskly overhead and the colour was flashed into the air above, into the eyes of the men and women who walk in Kew Gardens in July.

(*CSF* 90)

The flowers are like mouths with tongues of colour, which become reference points for the snatches of conversations flitting around them. The story is quilted together with patches of dialogue and description of the natural life. The colours signal multi-vocalness, and human figures are likened to butterflies "who crossed the turf in zig-zag flights from bed to bed." (CSF 90)

Woolf's homage to colour in her essay on Walter Sickert celebrates 'the violent rapture of colour' (*WS* 12) in modern painting, and the correspondence of colours in literature. This is a symposium on colour.

Just as dinner was announced, somebody asked: "But when were picture galleries invented?", a question naturally arising, for the discussion about the value of coloured lights had led somebody to say that in the eyes of the motorist red is not a colour but simply a danger signal. We shall very soon lose our sense of colour, another added, exaggerating, of course. Colours are used so much as signals now that they will very soon suggest action merely.

(*WS* 5–6)

Questions arise concerning the status of art as a separate or integrated realm of life; and the evaluation of colour as an aesthetic, spiritual or sensuous pleasure, or as an active intervention in the world. As in the final part of 'The Sun and the Fish', Woolf turns to the world of creatures for examples of colour as something naturally and fully integrated into existence. This time the creatures are not fish, but insects – forest insects in South America which are 'all eye', which prompts one of the diners to ask: 'Were we once insects like that, too . . . all eye?' (*WS* 7, 8) The response echoes Woolf's eclipse essay:

When I first went into Sickert's show, said one of the diners, I became completely and solely an insect – all eye. I flew from colour to colour, from red to blue, from yellow to green. Colours went spirally through my body lighting a flare as a rocket fell through the night and lit up greens and browns, grass and trees, and there in the grass a white bird. Colour warmed, thrilled, chafed, burnt, soothed, fed and finally exhausted me. For though the life of colour is a glorious life it is a short one. Soon the eye can hold no more; it shuts itself in sleep, and if the man who looks for cactuses had come he would only have seen a shrivelled air-ball on a red plush carpet.

(*WS* 9)

Colours are in one moment as fleeting as a firework display and in another as physically solid and sustaining as food, as physically stimulating as sex. After a short-lived orgy of indulgence in colour, 'the eye can hold no more', and all becomes 'shrivelled'. This reverie as well as developing the insect and flower imagery of *Kew Gardens*, reverberates with the imagery of Woolf's post-eclipse eulogy to colour and to life's precious transience. If 'The Sun and the Fish' closes with the realization of humanity's unintegrated relationship to colour, here Woolf observes: 'Ages ago we left the forest and went into the world, and the eye shrivelled and the heart grew, and the liver and intestines and the tongue and the hands and the feet.' (*WS* 10) Not only has the course of evolution lessened humanity's visual sense, but humanity itself has moved from passive integration in the world of colour to a more active intervention, as the hands and feet testify. Nevertheless, there is an insect-like quality to the movements of thought and voices in this symposium. Colours serve, like flowers, as nourishing points of reference in this collective meditation. Like *A Room of One's Own*, the text is spoken by several subjects, and speech marks are not used consistently to differentiate between them. Woolf uses colour in close connection with her rendering of multi-vocal intersubjective expression.

Towards the close of *Walter Sickert*, Woolf turns to inter-artistic analogies: 'The novelist is always asking how can I bring the sun on to my page?' (*WS* 22) How can words express colour? Woolf formulates a response in terms reminiscent of her 'amusing game': 'It is a very complex business, the mixing and marrying of words that goes on, probably unconsciously in the poet's mind to feed the reader's eye.' But she, then, strongly equates writing with painting: 'All great writers are great colourists, just as they are musicians into the bargain; they always contrive to make their scenes glow and darken and change to the eye. Each of Shakespeare's plays has its dominant colour. And each writer differs of course as a colourist. . . .' (*WS* 23–24)

Although Woolf makes other painterly analogies for writing (draughtsmanship and line drawing), it is colour she emphasizes. On one level she uses colouring as a metaphor for the writer's descriptive powers – the only way to have colour in writing is the secondary one of merely naming, although we are shown its considerable power. On another level, this metaphor extends to Woolf's description of the physical act of writing itself: like painting, writing is a process of marking – to write is to paint with words, to create colour. (Conversely, discussing the work of a caricaturist, Woolf elsewhere describes how 'the very paint on the canvas begins to distil itself into words – sluggish, slow-dropping words that would, if they could, stain the page with colour; not writers' words.')[10] She recommends inter-artistic awareness to critics too, the best of whom used to be 'acutely aware of the mixture of elements, and wrote of literature with music and painting in their minds. Nowadays we are all so specialized that critics keep their brains fixed to the print.' As a result contemporary criticism is 'starved' and 'attenuated and partial' in approach (WS 24). She recommends instead the 'hybrid': some artists 'bore deeper and deeper into the stuff of their own art; others are always making raids into the lands of others. Sickert it may be is among the hybrids, the raiders.' (WS 27)

Gillespie identifies Woolf herself as a 'raider',[11] and the territory she invades most regularly in her work as that of her sister, the painter, Vanessa Bell. In Gillespie's fascinating account of the long and close professional relationship enjoyed by the sisters, Vanessa Bell emerges as the primary influence from the visual arts upon Woolf's literary aesthetic. Gillespie's dense analysis of this relationship assures her aim: 'to shift the emphasis in the ongoing discussion of Virginia Woolf and the visual arts from Roger Fry to Vanessa Bell; to shift the emphasis in the discussions of the sisters from the psychological to the professional and the aesthetic; and, in these contexts, to define and reveal more fully the pervasive role of the visual arts in Woolf's writing.'

Gillespie's discussion of colour is particularly interesting. Persuasively using Woolf's diary entry on the eclipse, the 'hoop of colour' passage from 'The Sun and the Fish', and the corresponding one in The Waves, to illustrate her point that 'Woolf's equation of the world with color is close to the view of modern painters like her sister and like Cézanne',[12] she, nonetheless, misses the possible feminist import of colour in 'The Sun and the Fish'. Although Gillespie in general emphasizes the aesthetic rather than the feminist dimension of Woolf's work (without connecting them), this in itself benefits the debate on Woolf's feminist aesthetics. She has demonstrated the importance of Woolf's professional relationship with her sister, and focused the inter-artistic debate on the practice and ideas of the woman artist closest to Woolf.

From the platform built by Gillespie, I want to examine Bell's development as a colourist, suggesting Woolf's literary understanding of colour and light as a parallel. This colourist aesthetic dovetails in Woolf's work, I propose, with the feminist aesthetic of the suffrage movement to produce a politicized deployment of colour.

Orthodox views of Woolf and Post-Impressionism

Mine is not the orthodox route taken by criticism in discussions of Woolf's debt to the visual arts. Gillespie's is a long overdue acknowledgement of the primacy of Vanessa Bell in this debate,[13] not just because Bell was close to Woolf but also because she was a prominent (British) Post-Impressionist who exhibited in the 1912 show. As a woman colourist she is even more exciting. Orthodox criticism passes over these connections, as until recently it saw Bell's work 'as a pale imitation of'[14] that of her companion artist Duncan Grant. Instead it has favoured the theories of Roger Fry and Clive Bell as major influences on Woolf,[15] a bias that persists even after Gillespie's challenge.[16] My argument does not deny these influences, but reconsiders them contextually from a feminist perspective and in the light of Vanessa Bell's critical reappraisal.

The theory most often applied to Woolf is the theory of significant form, actually formulated first by Clive Bell, but close to Fry's theory of pure form. Woolf's 'close intellectual relation with Fry' and 'their intimate friendship' is typically emphasized: 'his conception of the novel as "a single perfectly organic aesthetic whole", and his readiness to centre this within the comprehensive theory of Significant Form and the nature of perception itself gave Woolf the confidence to convert it all to her own artistic purposes.'[17] Woolf's even closer 'intellectual relation' and 'intimate friendship' with her sister is ignored. Marianna Torgovnick has attempted an analysis of Woolf's professional relationship with Vanessa Bell, but she still discerns Roger Fry as 'the thinker who most shaped her views'.[18] Bridget Elliott and Jo-Ann Wallace have recently examined the professionalism of the sisters (as 'anomalous woman modernists') and their position within Bloomsbury,[19] but their aesthetic practice is more often homogenized and subsumed under the rubric of the 'Bloomsbury aesthetic', itself largely assembled from the theories of Fry and Clive Bell. For this reason, in looking at the feminine sources of Woolf's visual aesthetic and their precedents, we must travel the more beaten track as well as chart a newer one. It is the path Fry turns from in his early formulations of Post-Impressionism that Woolf, in sympathy with the work of her sister, seems to follow.

The Gunpowder Plot

The 'Art-Quake of 1910' was 'no gradual infiltration, but – bang! an assault along the whole academic front of art.'[20] This riotous and shocking explosion of colour happened appropriately enough on 5 November.

> A date more favourable . . . for revealing the existence of a wide-spread plot to destroy the whole fabric of European painting could hardly have been better

1 'Chelsea' Banner, painted cotton banner of Chelsea WSPU, designed by Herman Ross, 1908.

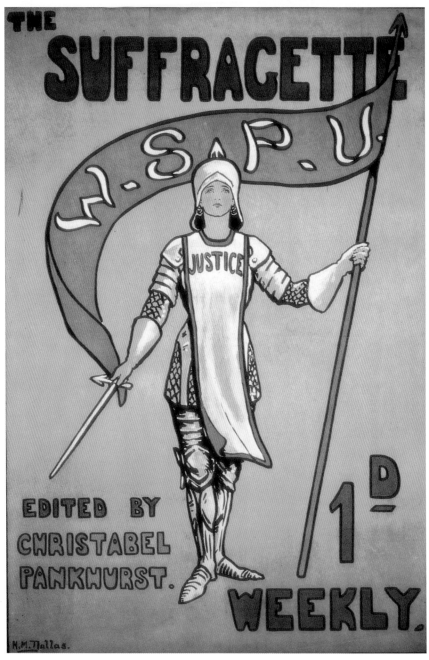

2   'The Suffragette' Poster, advertising *The Suffragette* newspaper, designed by Hilda Dallas in 1911.

3 Anti-Suffrage Ostrich, Cartoon.

above

4 'The New Mrs Partington'
Postcard, *c.* 1910.

right

5 'Handicapped!' Poster: the
joint winner of the Artists'
Suffrage League poster
competition in 1909;
designed by Duncan
Grant.

THE FORCES OF EVIL DENOUNCING
THE BEARERS OF LIGHT.

6 *The Suffragette* 17 October 1913. Page 1.

above

7   Vanessa Bell,
    Studland Beach,
    1912.

right

8   Vanessa Bell,
    Abstract, 1914.

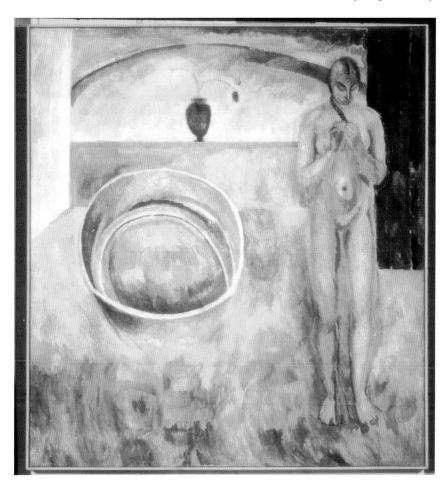

9   Vanessa Bell, *The Tub*, 1917.

10   Vanessa Bell, *A Conversation*, 1913–1916.

chosen. On Saturday accordingly the Press was invited to the Grafton Gallery – an admirable substitute for the vaults of Westminster – where the new Guido Fawkes, his colleagues, and alleged predecessors are exhibiting their gunpowder. Mr. Roger Fry, I regret to say, has acted the part of Catesby, while a glance at the names of the honorary committee reveal that more than one member of the Upper House is implicated. It is the way of modern conspiracies; we all join them sooner or later. To-day, which is the private view, it will be decided whether the anticipated explosion is going to take place.[21]

Before we identify and test the artists' gunpowder, to which Robert Ross (in keeping with most early reviews of the show) acrimoniously refers, it is worth noting the wider context in which his rhetoric detonates. From the distance of eighty odd years since the exhibition, it is easy enough to appreciate in a general sense the wit in the impresario's choice of date;[22] but it was not necessarily the *festive* associations of the date that would come most prominently to mind in November 1910. At this time people sensed a very real danger of the commemorated event itself being repeated: the government, if not indeed blown up, was in fact to fall (forcing a second narrowly survived election). This contemporary aspect should not escape our notice. In London 1910, George Dangerfield reminds us, the old order was '*Dying!* . . . There was talk of wild young people in London, . . . of night clubs; of negroid dances. People gazed in horror at the paintings of Gauguin, and listened with delighted alarm to the barbaric measures of Stravinsky.'[23] All this, and political upheaval too:

> A constitutional crisis over the power of the House of Lords developed, and in the winter of 1910 Asquith dissolved Parliament and called for a general election. In November, a few days after the opening of the Post-Impressionist exhibition, the Home Secretary, Winston Churchill, ordered the troops in to break up the strike of Welsh miners at Tonypandy, an action that was to have lasting effects on labour relations in Britain. Throughout that year the suffragette movement gained momentum.[24]

'Black Friday' – when police turned to brutal tactics against women demonstrators – came only days after the art show opened (18 November 1910), as we have noted; and Woolf herself, as it opened, attended the two Albert Hall rallies preceding the march (*L* 1 438). 'Vitality and absolute commitment motivated both the Suffragettes and Post-Impressionism', comments Frances Spalding, noting that reports on growing suffragette violence 'mingled with those on the Post-Impressionists', as ' "Black Friday" set off a programme of window-smashing, picture-slashing, arson and bombs.'[25] Dangerfield having noted, echoing Woolf, that 'the Women's Rebellion – the outrageous Suffragette Movement of 1910–14 – was above all things a movement from darkness into light, and from death into life,' points out that the 'militant suffragettes did not actually become militant until November 1910'. He reminds us of the 'purple bannerettes' carried by the suffragettes, and later 'torn and trampled' by their police assailants on 'Black Friday'.[26] At the time of the Post-Impressionist show, then, the suffrage movement was making a massive impact, as well as an equally colourful spectacle, on the streets. According to William C. Wees, 'between 1910 and 1914, labour strife, the Parliament Act, screaming suffragettes, and artists' 'maltreatment of the human form divine' seemed, to many people, to be parts of a conspiracy to undermine traditional order and decency.'[27]

J.B. Bullen, moreover, indicates that the exhibition, which 'represented an attack on the values of western culture from the ground of art', was received in a climate fearful of imminent decline into anarchy;[28] and furnishes ample evidence that it was initially understood as a symptom of the cultural degeneration already prophesied in the work of Nordau, and later addressed by Spengler.[29] Before looking at the presentation and (in brief) the content of 'Manet and the Post-Impressionists', we can gain an insight by surveying the findings of its outraged and hostile recipients; for long after the exhibition's close, as Woolf recalls, Fry's 'hall table was littered with letters. They were still abusing him.' (*RF* 162–63) The impact of Post-Impressionist art in 1910 is after all very different to its reception today (from the distance of 1939 Woolf herself makes a similar point (*RF* 153)).

Ebenezer Wake Cook, follower of Nordau and enemy of modernism, was one of the most vitriolic detractors of the Post-Impressionists, who, he claims, 'present a case for historical, psychological, and pathological analysis, rather than art criticism.' The aim of the show, 'intentionally made to look like the output of a lunatic asylum', was 'to shock the bourgeoisie' with a *succès de scandale*.[30] Ross detects 'the chicanery of spiritualism, automatic writing, and the narratives of the neuropath', and talks of racial degeneracy and inferiority. Fearing that artists might ' "gauguinise" the European landscape or the Aryan race', he observes that a 'later blossom of an unsavoury stock has not only dispersed with chiaroscuro (one of the achievements of Cézanne, I learn) but has dispensed with painting.'[31] Notions of racial impurity associated in the minds of detractors with the paintings of Gauguin, and the insanity of Van Gogh, then, are seen to accompany the abandonment of traditional representation of light and dark: chiaroscuro.

The source of the evil 'plague', it transpires, is 'Romanticism'. Cook, in a letter to the press, concurs with Ross's diagnosis[32] of Satanism, and remarks significantly on Post-Impressionism's precursors who had 'a mania for painting flesh with mud, making Eve's fair daughters look unwashed; while others painted it in ghastly greys and greens, as if in the last stages of decomposition.'

'These sickening aberrations could never have got a footing' but for the 'anti-patriotic campaign in favour of anarchism and ultimate chaos' by the '"Modernity" critics'.[33] Cook's letter appears in the *Morning Post* the day after 'Black Friday'. Consciously or not, he seems to speak both to the exhibition and headline-making suffrage demonstration, his disgust at the mud-besmirched and ghastly-coloured daughters of Eve applicable to both realms. So, just as the Suffragettes 'were attacked for being unfeminine; Post-Impressionism was seen to assault standards of female beauty.'[34]

When reactionary critics are not deriding the primitivism and insanity they see represented on the walls of the Grafton, they are snorting in disbelief at the most obvious symptom to them of such degeneracy: the 'barbaric'[35] colours. Only those 'not absolutely colour blind' could disagree with their findings. Most furore is aroused where women, perhaps because of their stereotyping as 'Nature', are depicted in exotic and 'unnatural' colours. Matisse's *La Femme aux Yeux Verts*, for example, was one of the most reviled images.[36] An anonymous reviewer typically comments on the paint's capacity to effect 'a violent bilious headache':

> In a typical [Gauguin] hideous brown women, with purple hair and
> vitriolic faces, squat in the midst of a nightmare landscape of drunken palm
> trees, crude green grass, vermilion rocks, and numerous glaringly coloured
> excrescences impossible to identify. . . . Words are powerless to describe an
> epileptic landscape by Henri Matisse, quite without form, its kaleidoscopic
> colour scheme only bearable from the next room.
>
> A revolution to be successful must presumably revolve; but, undeniably
> clever as they often are, the catherine-wheel antics of the Post-Impressionists
> are not likely to wake many responsive chords in British breasts.[37]

The colours' impact is apparently so overpowering that it obscures the subject-matter of the painting: 'vermilion splodges'[38] have taken over. It is unclear, however, whether 'hideous brown women' refers to the distorted palette of the artist or the women's natural skin colour. Such ambiguity allows a strongly racist interpretation to creep in. Wilfred Scawen Blunt admits in his diary (which was later quoted by Woolf (*RF* 156)) to finding the colours themselves attractive, in some cases, but the subjects, where discerned, unsavoury: Gauguin's brightly coloured Tahitian women 'are not works of art at all, unless throwing a handful of mud against a wall may be called one. They are works of idleness and impotent stupidity, a pornographic show.' He responds with racialism and misogyny to the subject matter, and with scorn to the technique. The sensuous depiction of 'brown people' and 'a woman suckling a child'[39] is considered an outrage to decorum.

Woolf herself outraged decorum when she and her sister, Vanessa, 'gauguinised' themselves for the Post-Impressionist Ball where they appeared 'as bare-shouldered bare-legged Gauguin girls, almost – as it seemed to the indignant ladies who swept out in protest – almost naked.'[40] Having earlier 'blacked-up' and cross-dressed as an Abyssinian Prince for the 'Dreadnought Hoax' (the recent public memory of which also contributed to Bloomsbury's notoriety at the time of the exhibition),[41] Woolf seems to have relished the scandal she created as 'a South Sea Savage' (*L* 1 455), gleefully exploiting the sexual/racial politics evoked by brazenly donning the Post-Impressionist colours of 'native' femininity: 'Was I less alarming as a Savage – or as bad as ever?' (*L* 1 455) Such orientalist masquerades, themselves suspect reinscriptions of sexual/racial stereotypes, were nevertheless understood to challenge the racist establishment.

Nordau popularized reactionary views of such 'barbarism' in championing a return to 'The Social Mission of Art' against the predominant 'theory of art for art's sake: *l'art pour l'art*'. But his vision seems more religious than social: 'The art of the future will be . . . a mighty cathedral, . . . the hallowed place wherein mankind will rise again to the childship of God.' Under 'Physiognomies in Painting', Nordau assesses Cézanne, in terms which anticipate the main critical response to Post-Impressionism: Cézanne is a revolutionary member of the 'rabble', already back in his true lowly station; and his art effects a social revolution which pulls everyone down into the gutter.[42]

Fry himself comments on the social and political impact of 'Manet and the Post-Impressionists', confirming its challenge to the 'cultured' upper classes, who 'felt instinctively that their special culture was one of their social assets':

> It was felt that one could only appreciate Amico di Sandro when one
> had acquired a certain considerable mass of erudition and given a great
> deal of time and attention, but to admire a Matisse required only a certain
> sensibility. One could feel fairly sure that one's maid could not rival one in
> the former case, but might by a mere haphazard gift of Providence surpass
> one in the second. So that the accusation of revolutionary anarchism was
> due to a social rather than an aesthetic prejudice.[43]

The idea of 'one's maid' conversing on equal terms about art is anathema to Fry's 'cultured public'. It is reminiscent, however, of Woolf's celebration of the emergence of the leviathan cook into the polite sunlit company of the drawing room. Significantly, both Fry and Woolf identify the figure of a woman-worker as the principal threat to the 'cultured' élite. They both reflect Dunlop's and Wees's identification of Post-Impressionism with the radical political climate of the period.

Reviewers' language was 'in keeping with [their] papers' own politics';[44] and negative comparisons between Post-Impressionism and feminism were not unknown.

The *Westminster Gazette* used a husband and wife dialogue as its format. The husband showed no interest in visiting the show, but the wife was determined to fit it in with her 'non-militant' women's meeting and plays by Bernard Shaw and Shakespeare. The woman it portrayed was, moreover, of a particular cast, as her attitudes revealed. She was interested in suffrage and in Shaw, who was associated with the portrayal of radical women and with socialist politics. But, the *Westminster* hinted, it was a limited and perhaps fashionable radicalism. The woman attended a group which did not advocate militant feminist action, and the safety of Shakespeare tempered the socialism of Shaw.[45]

Connections between suffragism and Post-Impressionism could be interpreted in more or less radical ways. But the connection between Shaw and Post-Impressionism is made by Woolf herself shortly after the show had opened.

> I suppose you have been going everywhere – to the Grafton Galleries and the Bernard Shaw play. Now that Clive [Bell] is in the van of aesthetic opinion, I hear a great deal about pictures. I dont think them so good as books. But why all the Duchesses are insulted by the post-impressionists, a modest sample of painters, innocent even of indecency, I cant conceive. However, one mustn't say that they are like other pictures, only better, because that makes everyone angry.
>
> (*L* I 440)

S.K. Tillyard has surveyed the press for other feminist connections with Post-Impressionism: 'underneath the humour these sketches revealed men's shock, anxiety and, perhaps, fear that women were entering an institution that had hitherto been almost exclusively masculine.' But she does not link them to the dramatic and large-scale suffrage upheavals being played out on the streets at the time of the exhibition, nor with the feminist implications in the imminent collapse of government. Instead, she proposes Post-Impressionism's connections with a longer and quieter revolution in women's lives: 'A modicum of social and financial emancipation may have contributed to their presence.' For Tillyard, Post-Impressionism's significance for women lies mainly in its connections with the Arts and Crafts Movement and its roots in the nineteenth century. She does identify in Post-Impressionism, however, a new language for women, whose grounding in the Arts and Crafts Movement, she suggests, put them 'in a position to use the language and aesthetic provided to understand Post-Impressionism for themselves.'[46]

Although Tillyard stresses women's involvement with Post-Impressionism as 'limited' to the role of audience or patron, and shows they were lampooned for flocking 'to the gallery as if it were a fashion house', she, nevertheless, confirms that as a new language for women, this art was understood to threaten patriarchy. Tillyard's interest in women and the Arts and Crafts Movement, however, does not extend to a consideration of its connections with the suffrage artists who played such an important part in the feminist demonstrations during the politically volatile period of the first exhibition. Contrary to Tillyard's assessment, the reason for the disappearance of 'satirical attacks upon women'[47] by the time of the 1912 show, I suggest, is that Post-Impressionism was by then sanitized, in some circles, of its initially potent, political associations.

The neglect of such obviously fruitful connections between women's involvement in the nineteenth century Arts and Crafts Movement and suffrage art in the political context of the early twentieth century, casts doubt on Tillyard's reasoning that Post-Impressionism has more in common with the former than the latter. Art historians, she suggests, have been misled by Dangerfield and his followers who 'overestimated the dangers of social upheaval and the degree of crisis in Edwardian Britain. Bloodshed in the cause of political change was very limited and parliament held on firmly to its executive authority.' This assertion diminishes the impact of the new reign of violence meeting not only the striking miners but the women's movement at that time. Tillyard never mentions the infamous 'Black Friday', an omission that unsettles her conclusion that her 'new historical interpretation' in effect 'ruins the notion of Post-Impressionism as a sign of, or element in, social turbulence.'[48] We might more readily conclude that the immediate impact of Post-Impressionism should be summarized in the broad terms of 'social turbulence'. It is associated in the reviews with romanticism, manifold degeneracy, the revolutionary overthrow of the social and political status quo, suffragism, and riotous colour.

Colour, so offensive to Post-Impressionism's detractors, meets with warm approval in the pages of a feminist journal:

> His glowing patches of colour have a marvellous quality of subdued light, as though, indeed, the rays of the sun were truly veiled and controlled by them as they are by passing through the semi-transparent glass of a thirteenth-century church window. . . . In certain ancient glass a deep flesh-tone of a brown or pinkish brown is used, and this low tone . . . has a marvellous effect in harmonising and subduing colours that might in different company have been violent and even offensive. . . . Gauguin has found the secret in the isles of the Pacific, and, with his wonderful bronze flesh-tones, we find him also in full possession of the glorious glass colours which the old glass-blowers of eight hundred years ago began to make, and which Nature has finished in her own laboratory with water, wind, and the dust of the earth.[49]

The suffrage artist Mary Lowndes does not find Gauguin's colours 'violent' or 'offensive', as do most reviewers, but harmonized and subdued.[50] She enjoys his depiction of women's flesh tones, and her window analogy suggests their transformation of solar light. Perhaps it is not only her interest in stained glass, but also her experience as organizer of suffrage colours, that makes Lowndes sympathetic to Gauguin's palette. Indeed, her analogy with glass-blowing might be seen to prefigure Woolf's description of post-eclipse colour as a delicate 'globe of glass'.

I have stressed the terms of its early reception before looking at Post-Impressionism as it was first theorized, because I want, in the next chapter, to consider the theories of those who mounted the exhibition, with the nature of its public impact already in mind. Rather than remaining fixed and unchanging, these theories evolved into very different formulations by the time of the second Post-Impressionist exhibition in 1912. By then the tumult surrounding the first exhibition, including its political associations as well as its romantic, colourist reputation, had subsided.[51] Post-Impressionism became the quasi-religion of 'Significant Form', a spiritual experience for the initiated – and was mocked as such by its detractors. Yet in the *Daily Herald* (the newspaper Woolf, as an index of change since 1910, finds the cook borrowing), Christina Walshe declares of the second exhibition: 'The Post-Impressionists are in the company of the Great rebels of the World. In politics the only movements worth considering are Woman Suffrage and Socialism. They are both Post-Impressionist in their desire to scrap old decaying forms and find for themselves a new working ideal.'[52]

I will compare Fry's early formulations on Post-Impressionism with his later theoretical developments, arguing that these, along with Clive Bell's more extreme opinions, are not the most appropriate for investigating Woolf's aesthetic. Woolf, on the contrary, stays with earlier interpretations of Post-Impressionism, developing an interest in colour closely related to the aesthetic practice of her sister Vanessa who exhibited at the second Post-Impressionist exhibition. My argument centres on colour, which Fry and Clive Bell do not reject as an important factor in Post-Impressionism; but they do come to subsume it in the promotion of 'Significant Form', where colour loses the kind of impact and definition commanded in other influential theories about the art. Woolf's literary engagement with Post-Impressionism, I suggest, might be differently read with consideration of colour as independent of significant form.

10 Romantic to Classic: Post-Impressionist theories from 1910 to 1912

'On or about' *November* 1910, Roger Fry invented the term Post-Impressionism to describe the departure from Impressionism by French-based artists ('out of the cul-de-sac into which naturalism had led them'). Cézanne, Gauguin and Van Gogh, the most prominently represented in the exhibition, were all, by 1910, 'long since dead'.[1] A smaller sample of work by Fauves and Cubists, such as Matisse and Picasso, was shown to indicate the continuation of this newly defined school, but 'the whole emphasis was thrown on to the old masters.' The living were not represented by their most recent, avant-garde, achievements; Cubism in fact 'was the most serious omission.'[2] The exhibition, heavily biased 'in favour of "Expressionism",'[3] put forward a strongly romantic aesthetic, 'popul009aris[ing] the notion that artists were romantic geniuses'.[4]

The 1910 exhibition catalogue

According to MacCarthy, who anonymously performed for Fry 'the ticklish job of writing the preface to the catalogue',[5] the Post-Impressionist artist's individual expression is at odds with the naturalistic project of the Impressionists, who 'were interested in analysing the play of light and shadow into a multiplicity of distinct colours; they refined upon what was already illusive in nature.'[6] Impressionism, then, is concerned with pushing analysis of the object world to the limits. The Post-Impressionists use larger, flatter areas of colour in departing from their technique and their naturalism.

The Impressionists' atomistic observation of the natural world might lead us, following Bergsonist criticism, to connect this method with Woolf's recommendation: 'Let us record the atoms as they fall.' Woolf, however, is interested not merely in how the eye physically records the world, but in how consciousness, 'the mind', deals with the information. Her sentence in full reads: 'Let us record the atoms as they fall upon the mind in the order in which they fall, let us trace the pattern, however disconnected and incoherent in appearance, which each sight or incident scores upon the consciousness.' (*CR* 190) This process is similar to the workings of Woolf's 'amusing game': each sight, just as in 'The Sun and the Fish', 'scores upon the consciousness' – that is, starts up a 'pattern', or fits in the mind by finding a mate. This is not a cold objective exercise in observation, but a dynamic subjective interaction with the world: a feat of imagination. The Post-Impressionists 'were not concerned with recording impressions of colour or light' and 'were interested in the discoveries of the Impressionists only so far as these . . . helped them to express emotions which the objects themselves evoked; their attitude towards nature was far more independent, not to say rebellious.'[7] They did not reject light and colour so much, then, as the action of 'recording impressions'. Light and colour become vehicles for the artist's expression of emotions before the object world. 'Derive this abstraction from nature while dreaming before it,' Gauguin instructs, 'and think more of the creation which will result than of nature.'[8] 'Nature' and 'the object world', it is worth noting, are usually gendered feminine.

In insisting 'so much upon the importance of rendering . . . exact impression', Impressionism betrays the object it seeks to capture which 'as transferred to canvas . . . was just so much shimmer and colour. . . . All the emotion and associations' that the object 'may be made to convey in poetry were omitted.'[9] Consider the gender implications here: the Impressionist artist (presumed male), by virtue of his 'exact impression' of the object-world ultimately prevents that world from being 'rendered at all'. His surface, subjective, impressions get in the way of his object to the point of obliterating, or overwhelming it. This intervention may be interpreted in explicitly sexual terms ('phallographic' perhaps), as in the infamous quip by the Impressionist painter, Renoir whose crippled hands prompted a journalist to ask: 'With such hands, how do you paint?' Renoir replied: 'With my prick'.[10]

MacCarthy refers Impressionism's failings to the superior capacity of poetry to convey the 'emotion and associations' of the object. Post-Impressionism exhibits dissatisfaction with this failing in traditional fidelity to nature, of which the Impressionist plein-air technique is a culmination. Post-Impressionists abandon this conscientious tradition in favour of expression and design. The expression of the object's true essence and its emotional and associative evocation in the subject is the proper task of art: 'a good rocking-horse often has more of the true horse about it than an instantaneous photograph of a Derby winner.'[11] Manet's 'revolutionary' achievement is thus the abolishment of the conventional opposition of light and shade in painting: 'He adopted, too, hitherto unknown oppositions of colour. In fact he endeavoured to get rid of chiaroscuro.' At the root of Post-Impressionism, then, is the revolutionary use of 'oppositions of colour' which overturns traditional chiaroscuro. Woolf's use of colour in her eclipse essay, where bright colour displaces the traditional opposition of sunlight and shade, suggests a similar revolutionary project.

The 'architectural effect' achieved by Cézanne, following Manet, appears to be founded on the use of the new oppositional deployment of colour planes: this makes for 'geometrical simplicity', as well as for the schematization of the picture. Again the structural quality of colour and its conscious arrangement, coincide with Woolf's own design practice. Interestingly, MacCarthy's response to Matisse bears little resemblance to that of the early reviewers (their hostility aside), who explode in anger or mirth at Matisse's 'epileptic' and 'Kaleidoscopic' *colour*. But MacCarthy lights upon 'line' and 'rhythm' as the most notable features of this 'primitive', or 'barbaric', art.[12]

Roger Fry's sources

Fry's 'conversion to the cause of modern art'[13] came in 1906 when he saw two Cézannes at the International Society's exhibition.[14] His review shows that Cézanne's art is 'effected without any chiaroscuro – merely by a perfect instinct for the expressive quality of tone values.'[15] Elsewhere he remarks on Cézanne's decorative use of colour, 'the values of . . . which indicate mass':[16] colour is again linked to mass – it is structural. Yet Fry's formative piece, 'An Essay in Aesthetics' (1909), having identified 'the emotional elements of design' as rhythm of line, mass, space, light and shade, and colour, concludes: 'Colour is the only one of our elements which is not of critical or universal importance to life, and its emotional effect is neither so deep nor so clearly determined as the others.'[17] Fry's enthusiasm for colour seems to have lessened.[18] Yet MacCarthy's introduction, as we have seen, heavily emphasizes the deployment of oppositional colour planes and the abandonment of traditional chiaroscuro.

Julius Meier-Graefe

Fry's earliest understanding of the art he was to celebrate as Post-Impressionist is 'much indebted to' the expressionist and romantic theories of Meier-Graefe.[19] The English translation of Meier-Graefe's influential book, *Modern Art*,[20] appeared in 1908; and, according to one critic, 'virtually provided the script for the show at the Grafton Galleries'.[21] But Falkenheim, who summarizes Meier-Graefe's influence in terms of heavy theoretical emphasis on colour,[22] suggests Fry's 'temporary flirtation with German art criticism' was responsible for a 'romantic inclination which is uncharacteristic of [his] fully developed tastes and critical thought'.[23]

'COLOUR AND COMPOSITION', his heading for modern artists, reflects the structural status of colour in Meier-Graefe's theory. Cézanne's painting is characterized by kaleidoscopic 'vigorous contrasts' and line-free 'mosaic of colour'; and Meier-Graefe identifies modern art's route out of Impressionism through the innovatory use of colour by artists such as Monet, Seurat and Signac. He finds elegiac consolation in a vision of Impressionism's luminous colours lingering long enough to kindle new colourist flames: 'the light they gave us was not extinguished until it had revealed the way of the future.'[24]

Meier-Graefe's histrionic accounts of his methods have been fundamental to Van Gogh's reputation as a wild and tormented, paint-hurling expressionist. Yet he sees Van Gogh, not as a purely northern romantic painter, but as the product of that northern tradition meeting with the classicism of the south. In 'Provence, where the sun bathes the earth in pure colour . . . the new country, in which all the conditions were sharply opposed to those of his own nation: flame met flame.'[25] His alchemical terminology is prescient of Woolf's own.[26] He describes Van Gogh's colourism in the mixed terms, not unlike Woolf's, of carnage and sexuality: 'It is gruesome to see him paint – a kind of orgy, in which the colours were splashed about like blood.' Van Gogh is above all a colourist. His paintings evidence 'a colossal combat of colours, that take on an almost objective significance'. The artist's bodily involvement in his art is expressed in this physical emphasis on colour; and, like Cézanne, he constructs in colour, 'having gained a decorative method equal to that of the old mosaicists.'[27]

Gauguin's colourist achievement is the move towards the 'systematic division of large planes of colour'. Pertinent to our understanding of Gauguin's reception at Fry's exhibition, is Meier-Graefe's quotation from Gauguin's own exhibition catalogue of February 1895. Here, Gauguin's barbed exchange with Strindberg concerns the depiction of women in relation to his replacement of old chiaroscuro with the new colour techniques. 'Gauguin's world was not [Strindberg's]. "It is too sunny," he wrote, "for me, the lover of chiaroscuro. And in your Eden dwells an Eve, who is not my ideal – for indeed, I too have a feminine ideal – or two."' Gauguin's response emphasizes the moral implications of Strindberg's chiaroscuro vision.

> "Your civilisation is your disease," he says, "my barbarism is my restoration to health. The Eve of your civilised conception makes us nearly all misogynists. The old Eve, who shocked you in my studio, will perhaps seem less odious to you some day. . . . Only the Eve I have painted can stand naked before us. Yours would always be shameless in this natural state, and if beautiful, the source of pain and evil . . ."[28]

Gauguin's Eve is not defined by the moral oppositions inscribed in Strindberg's chiaroscuro. She stands in full light, expressed in bold oppositional colours. Meier-Graefe sees Gauguin's art itself as a similarly unshaded source of illumination in a chiaroscuro world.

> Everyone is of Strindberg's opinion now, even the boldest of those who owe their culture to literature. They love chiaroscuro, twilight facts, which are

altered by a change of illumination, the meaning of which is inspiring but obscure. When one appears who would break through the gloom and who offers us elements shining in all the undimmed lustre of their nature, they screen their eyes angrily with a hand, and judge by what they believe they see through their fingers. Of course all that remains is the detail so dear to criticism. The beauty has been shut out.[29]

We have seen how suffrage art depicted patriarchal discrimination against women in terms of chiaroscuro (that is, masculine solar light in relation to feminine shadow), which in turn was to be dispelled by luminous suffrage colours. Woolf's leviathan cook may epitomize this feminist move from darkness into light. We may also connect Gauguin's reflections on misogyny and chiaroscuro, with suffrage attacks on patriarchal chiaroscuro. The colourism Meier-Graefe finds a source of modern aesthetic enlightenment, may also be a source of feminist, political enlightenment.

Maurice Denis

To understand how Fry, a man whose 'constantly changing notions' directed the course of Post-Impressionist theories,[30] rejected his early, colour-based, romantic definition of Post-Impressionism, we must turn to another of his early sources: the French artist and critic, Maurice Denis (who exhibited in Fry's 1910 show). In January 1910, Fry's translation of Denis's influential essay on Cézanne appeared in the *Burlington Magazine*. Unlike Meier-Graefe, Denis considers Cézanne a classical painter,[31] 'at once the climax of the classic tradition and the result of the great crisis of liberty and illumination which has rejuvenated modern art. He is the Poussin of Impressionism.'[32] This vague, shifting sense of classic and modern reflects Habermas' observation that 'the relation between "modern" and "classical" has definitely lost a fixed historical reference.'[33] Denis defines Cézanne's classicism specifically 'against expiring naturalism and romanticism'. Even Cézanne's early work, which is considered romantic, Denis sees as the artist's 'assimilation' and transmutation of 'classic tendencies'. In Cézanne's 'second period', he identifies a 'transmutation into classicism', manifest in the use of colour.[34] Where Meier-Graefe emphasizes the emotional significance of colour, Denis stresses the rational ('reasoned colour system'), but they both agree on Cézanne's importance as a colourist.

Yet Denis' 'classicism', however similar in places to Meier-Graefe's 'romanticism', also suggests, in other places, the elevation of form above colour, even where he celebrates Cézanne's inextricable deployment of colour as form. Colour may well be the source of Cézanne's essential achievement of volume, but it can also be seen as a secondary element, a variant on this voluminous form. Denis's terms nevertheless suggest the displacement of chiaroscuro by colour: 'Colourist before everything, as he was, Cézanne resolves this antimony by chromatism – the transposition, that is, of values of black and white into values of colour.' Where modelling was previously achieved by the shading of black and white, Cézanne '*modulat[es]*' in colour planes.[35]

In view of Fry's later emphasis on the classical, and his toning down of the romantic, Denis's essay is often afforded equal, if not greater, importance as an influence. Some problems arise in this debate over the application of the terms classical and romantic: Fry's definition of the classical was very early disputed; Meier-Graefe's romanticism is not straightforwardly defined; and Denis's ideas, moreover, were at first subsumed by Fry into the 'expressionist' framework supplied by Meier-Graefe.

From romantic to classic

The formal, abstract qualities associated with the classical interpretation of Cézanne, were not enhanced by the romantic context provided by Fry. But, 'on the eve of the first exhibition, the expressionist and abstract tendencies in modern art are not held to be irreconcilable': the two critics occasionally overlapping in ideas, 'approach their subjects from totally different angles'. But Fry's 1910 exhibition, Nicolson shows, 'bore out what Meier-Graefe, *not* what Denis, had written'.[36] I emphasize Nicolson's point because it has been underestimated by later critics, and even misquoted by one.[37] Fry's early admixture of the theories of Meier-Graefe and Denis is understandable, given their points of overlap;[38] but in his later rejection of Meier-Graefe's romanticism, Fry focuses on the points of difference in Denis's classicism.

Meier-Graefe uses imagery of striking similarity to Woolf's 'semi-transparent envelope' in describing Denis's own use of 'only pure colour' and 'gradations . . . so delicate, that his planes are like a crystal veiled in gossamer, and reflecting sunbeams. His line is no less delicate; a breath draws it. . . . In this delicate envelope everything that art ever gave of grace to line seems to be united.'[39] Meier-Graefe calls this latter the 'third element between the author and the world, which, even if it be only a veil of transparent threads, causes his expression to be different, better because more universal, than his good will alone could make it.'[40] Woolf again comes close to this description:

> Now my brain I will confess – for I dont like talking about it, floats in blue air; where there are circling clouds, soft sunbeams of elastic gold, and fairy gossamers – things that cant be cut – that must be tenderly enclosed, and expressed in a globe of exquisitely coloured words. At the mere prick of steel

they vanish . . . I will teach no more. "O no more – darkness has vanquished light."[41]

Like Meier-Graefe's 'veil of transparent threads', Woolf's model of consciousness, constructed out of 'a globe of exquisitely coloured words', is tenuous and evanescent, yet strong and binding ('things that cant be cut'). On the other hand, like the post-eclipse world it is fragile, and easily extinguished ('At the mere prick of steel they vanish').

Post-Impressionist theories from 1912

By the second Post-Impressionist exhibition, 'the situation has entirely changed,' for it 'was planned on more systematic lines. Now the emphasis was shifted to the contemporary movement, and of the precursors only Cézanne was retained'.[42] Nicolson does not address the contribution of the British artists: Duncan Grant, Eric Gill, Frederick Etchells, Roger Fry, Adeney, Charles Lamb, 'Mrs [Vanessa] Bell', 'Miss [Jessie] Etchells', Wyndham Lewis, Frederick Spenser Gore, and Stanley Spencer. He is primarily interested in establishing how Fry's selection of the major, continental artists reflects his new interpretation of Post-Impressionism. My focus, however, will turn to Vanessa Bell and her local, London art scene in relation to the Post-Impressionist exhibitions. First we should acknowledge the interpretative context set up by Fry and Clive Bell in the second exhibition, since the concepts and vocabulary they now establish form the orthodox view of Post-Impressionism, and inform the orthodox assessment of both Vanessa Bell and Woolf. I will argue that Vanessa Bell's development as a colourist, and Woolf's response to Post-Impressionism, including, in particular, her understanding of her sister's work, may be at odds with the theories of Fry and Clive Bell.

The most obvious shift in emphasis from the first to second exhibition was from romantic to classic, reflected in the new predominance of Cubism. Nicolson is not surprised 'to find that criticism emerging out of the second show differed radically from that emerging out of the first. Whereas the first had popularised the notion that artists were romantic geniuses, the second gave birth to the much more rigid doctrine of significant form.'[43] This new doctrine emphasizes an emotional understanding of form for its own sake above everything else. The overwhelming concern with colour as a main point of definition in 1910 is largely ignored. The term 'significant form' begins to become almost synonymous with Post-Impressionism. This later interpretation is, generally, considered the more authentic. In the two years between the exhibitions, and, in fact, very soon after the first, Fry, with the assistance of Clive Bell, was moving towards this position.

Falkenheim notes that Fry's change of tack to become the better known 'connoisseur of ordered, "classical" compositions'[44] actually began in 1910 when, in three articles for the *Nation*, he sought to refine and defend his ideas on Post-Impressionism.[45] Falkenheim is in sympathy with Fry's later understanding of Post-Impressionism: 'the romantic bias' of the first exhibition 'offered the British public a distorted notion of what were the objectives of Post-Impressionist artists'. She cites Fry's *Nation* articles as the source of his 'more reasoned and explicit explanations', which were belied by the bias of the first exhibition's selection, and of which the general public remained ignorant: 'few probably read beyond the catalogue introduction.'[46]

Fry's most startling revision is, perhaps, his re-classification of Cézanne, who, 'initially represented as the wild romantic',[47] now shows 'a supremely classic temperament'. Cézanne is now 'the great classic of our time', whereas 'Van Gogh represents as completely the romantic temperament.'[48] 'If Fry had made these distinctions between classical and romantic earlier', Falkenheim speculates, 'and had also drawn on the antecedents for the new art, as he does here with Cézanne, Post-Impressionism might initially have seemed more acceptable to the now generally hostile public.'[49] Since her project is to trace the development of formalist art criticism from Fry's theories, Falkenheim minimizes and casts doubt on his less amenable early formulations. Nevertheless, she demonstrates, in detail, Fry's shift of focus. Not least, Falkenheim explores Fry's development of a more socially ameliorative, less radical, theory of Post-Impressionism. Very soon after Guy Fawkes Night, Fry, it appears, began to defuse his explosives. The romantic colour theory of Meier-Graefe, understood as, potentially, the most powerful explosive, is notably absent from the pages of the second Post-Impressionist exhibition catalogue.

The 1912 exhibition catalogue

> We have ceased to ask "What does this picture represent?" and ask instead, "What does it make us feel?" We expect a work of plastic art to have more in common with a piece of music than with a coloured photograph.[50]

Clive Bell's opening remarks on the theoretical premises of the second exhibition imply that Post-Impressionism, no longer avant-garde or revolutionary, is now established, mainstream art, part of the new status quo. This art is not concerned with depiction, but with the arousal of emotion. Bell explains the 'revolutionary' aspect of Post-Impressionism in these emotional terms. The romantic idea of self-expression is retained but given equal weight with his theory of form. Bell makes quite clear the Post-Impressionist revolution is over: the English artists are capitalizing on the advances already made by the French and 'their master, Cézanne'. Bell's task is to 'discover in the work of these English painters some vestige of the qualities that distinguish Post-Impressionists from the mass.' This choice of phrase suggests that Post-Impressionism is to be associated with an aesthetic élite, implying qualities of privileged refinement rather than revolutionary innovation. Bell calls these qualities 'simplification and plastic design'. In expanding on these terms, he refers for the first time to the concept by which Post-Impressionism has become best remembered: 'significant form'.[51] According to Bell, the Post-Impressionist claims the privileges of a literary artist: 'those facts that any one can discern for himself or discover in a text book he leaves to the makers of Christmas-cards and diagrams. He simplifies, omits details, that is to say, to concentrate on something more important – on the significance of form.'[52] In dismissing the descriptive and diagrammatic, Bell also implies that sentiment, allegory, political or social comment (all, paradoxically, literary qualities), are of no interest to the artist either: form and design *per se*, without specific meaning, have priority. He dismisses the work of traditional English artists as 'merely descriptive' and 'at best, romantic'.

The object becomes incidental to the Post-Impressionist's resolution of it into the formal design of the picture. Bell's mundane example of a coal-scuttle emphasizes the trivial significance of ostensible, subject matter: it is 'an end in itself, as a significant form related on terms of equality with other significant forms. Thus have all great artists regarded objects.'[53] This means that the native women of Gauguin's Tahitian paintings, for example, are no longer to be considered as relevant to an understanding of the art. Reduced to the primitive and decorative in MacCarthy's account, they are to be elided altogether according to Bell's rationale. Bell's 'significant form', intentionally or not, smooths over the cultural and political implications of such images.

Bell in fact emphasizes the universal appeal of the new English Post-Impressionism:

> the art of Mr. Wyndham Lewis, whatever else may be said of it, is certainly not descriptive. Hardly at all does it depend for its effect on association or suggestion. There is no reason why a mind sensitive to form and colour, though it inhabit another solar system, and a body altogether unlike our own, should fail to appreciate it. On the other hand, fully to appreciate some pictures by Mr. Fry or Mr. Duncan Grant it is necessary to be a human being, perhaps, even, an educated European of the twentieth century.[54]

The democratic appeal of Bell's significant form – the notion that humanity or even just sensitivity to form and colour is all one needs to appreciate it – is here vying with an appeal to cultural élitism. In the former case, presumably 'one's maid' would find this art easily accessible, but in the latter, she would first need the privilege of an education in European art.

Bell's vocabulary moves further towards a sense of élitism and imperialism, the more he elaborates. The English Post-Impressionists have purged the nation of romanticism and its 'irrelevant qualities that for two centuries have made our art the laughing-stock of Europe'. Paradoxically, Bell closes in unabashed romantic strains, declaring Post-Impressionism a manifestation 'of a spiritual revolution which proclaims art a religion, and forbids its degradation to the level of a trade'. This art is 'intended neither to please, to flatter, nor to shock, but to express great emotions and to provoke them'.[55] He turns attention away from the material aspects of painting to the transcendent and spiritual, and, although emphasizing formal properties (line, mass, colour), he does not attempt to analyse them specifically. Whereas MacCarthy dwells on such matters, Bell virtually ignores them. His introduction amounts to a mystical declaration of the existence of significant form.

Fry's introduction to the French artists, although not as dogmatic, follows on from Bell's spiritual interpretation. Whereas Bell asserts 'The battle is won' as far as the public acceptance of Post-Impressionism, Fry still feels the need to be understanding of past misinterpretations, but, like Bell, declares the object of Post-Impressionism is 'to express by pictorial and plastic form certain spiritual experiences'.[56] He is anxious to shake off the accusations of degeneracy and incompetence, but, at the same time, he makes Post-Impressionism more palliative to the reactionary tastes of his initially critical audience.

Fry's argument follows Bell's distinction between art that imitates and art that creates, but emphasizes less the emotional and religious significance of Post-Impressionism than the intellectual and contemplative. He also seems to offer, at this point, a more materialist understanding of the art: in calling it a 'new reality', he is suggesting art constitutes an alternative material reality, which is not really like Bell's transcendent spiritualism. However, Fry does also dwell on the 'logical extreme of such a method', which he sees as 'a purely abstract language of form – visual music'. Fry is certainly open to the development of this possibility: 'It is too early to be dogmatic on the point, which can only be decided when our sensibilities to such abstract form have been more practised than they are at present.'[57]

Fry stresses Matisse's 'entirely new use of colour', but does not develop the point. He makes his clearest statement of the change in emphasis from the first exhibition when he asserts that the art on show is not romantic but classic.

> I do not mean by Classic, dull, pedantic, traditional, reserved, or any of those similar things which the word is often made to imply. Still less do I mean by calling them Classic that they paint "Visits to Æsculapius" or "Nero at the Colosseum". I mean that they do not rely for their effect upon associated ideas, as I believe Romantic and Realistic artists invariably do.[58]

Fry, consolidating with Bell, closes his introduction by disassociating the art on show from the notion of 'associated ideas': 'All art depends upon cutting off the practical responses to sensations of ordinary life, thereby setting free a pure and as it were disembodied functioning of the spirit.' An art which cuts off 'practical responses' must exclude, for example, the art of the suffrage movement, which by Fry's definition must be impure. Yet he acknowledges the notion of disassociated spirituality is an almost impossible ideal. Fry's argument allows for the possibility of 'romantic associations', which we might consider the hostile critics of the first exhibition to have lighted upon; but it establishes that these associations are secondary, and passing, compared to the regenerative and eternal aspects of the classic, formal properties of this art. This is behind his oxymoron, the 'disinterestedly passionate state of mind'[59] (recorded by classic art). It is an art free of literary, but also of social, political and historical, associations, and therefore it is 'disinterested'. It is an art of pure emotion.

In spite of his protestations, Fry's 'classic' art remains close to romanticism. To call the 'concentration of feeling' 'classic' does not really dispel this. He does, however, succeed in minimizing the bodily and physical associations of this idea of 'feeling', which he parenthetically reminds us 'by no means implies abandonment'. In doing so he distances himself further from the orgiastic excesses of Meier-Graefe's theories, which, as we have seen, connect the application of colour with the artist's physical, bodily functions; and he reassures his public of the spiritual rather than sensual pleasures of Post-Impressionism. The absence of Gauguin's nudes, and of the romantics, Van Gogh and Rouault,[60] as well as the introduction of cubist abstraction, assists his argument. So, too, does the dwelling on form rather than colour as the most notable aspect of Post-Impressionism.

Boris Von Anrep's introduction to 'The Russian Group'[61] begins with the words 'Russian spiritual culture' and continues with a religious and spiritual interpretation in keeping with the dominant tone of Bell and Fry: Post-Impressionism has become a religion. Nowhere in these three introductory pieces is there emphatic reference to colour, nor is there reference to the abandonment of traditional chiaroscuro. The art is to be summed up in the nebulous term, 'significant form'.

The doctrine of Significant Form

> What quality is shared by all objects that provoke our aesthetic emotions?
> . . . Only one answer seems possible – significant form. In each, lines and colours combined in a particular way, certain forms and relations of forms, stir our aesthetic emotions. These relations and combinations of lines and colours, these aesthetically moving forms, I call "Significant Form".[62]

'Significant Form', according to Clive Bell's *Art*, no longer applies specifically to Post-Impressionism but is 'the one quality common to all works of visual art': from 'the windows at Chartres' to 'Mexican sculpture' to 'the masterpieces of Poussin . . . and Cézanne'. The Post-Impressionists 'concentrate' on this quality above all others. Bell also comments on colour in relation to significant form, suggesting 'the distinction between form and colour' to be 'unreal': 'you cannot conceive a colourless line or a colourless space; neither can you conceive a formless relation of colours. . . . When I speak of significant form, I mean a combination of lines and colours (counting white and black as colours) that moves me aesthetically.' For Bell colour is in fact form, and, therefore, presumably, structural. Yet he persists in maintaining the distinction between 'lines and colours' while claiming their congruity. The power of colour is subsumed in the abstract notion of significant form. As an aspect of pure form, colour is deprived of all meaning except the mystically emotional. The materially different handling of Post-Impressionist colour in comparison to traditional chiaroscuro, furthermore, is lost in Bell's generalizations. It is not his business to address such distinctions. The issue of colour and significant form is problematic, however, in the context of criticism on Woolf and Post-Impressionism, where significant form tends to dominate.

Bell develops the notion of the spiritual dimension of significant form into a full blown religion of art. He closes with a vision of 'aesthetic rapture': 'the religion of art will serve a man better than the religion of humanity. . . . What he loses in philanthropy he may gain in magnanimity; and because his religion does not begin with an injunction to love all men, it will not end, perhaps, in persuading him to hate most of them.'[63] This is the source of the 'transcendent . . . aesthetic' Johnson attributes to Woolf's Bloomsbury-based modernism. Not only is Bell's religion of art alarmingly reminiscent of Nordau's, however, his 'aesthetic rapture' seems to be satirized in the 'still rapture' of Woolf's lizards in 'The Sun and the Fish'. The idea of communing with an unchanging, perfect, aesthetic rapture is rejected, we remember, in favour of the model of art as a ruin, perpetually open to historical and political change, and to new theories 'without end', as Woolf comments on the ruins of Stonehenge. Whereas the 'perfect effigy' is, for Bell, the totality of art, for Woolf, it is a contrary point of definition in her dynamic model.

Bell admits to disagreeing 'profoundly' yet 'amicably' with Fry (but also acknowledges his assistance in refining some ideas in *Art*),[64] a caveat that does little to prevent the common assumption of their unanimity. Indeed, Henry Tonks, in *The Unknown God* (exhibited in 1923), painted them as a double-act performing before an audience of their opponents: 'Fry holds up a dead cat, a symbol of "pure form", while Clive Bell rings a bell announcing the new creed: "Cézannah Cézannah".'[65] D.H. Lawrence likewise saw this as 'almost

Calvin come to art'.[66] The politically explosive associations of the first Post-Impressionist exhibition seem to have long since been displaced by the quasi-religious dogma of significant form.

Tillyard finds a religiosity and redemptiveness in Post-Impressionism in keeping with Fry's Quakerism, and a common link between Post-Impressionism's 'early Modernism' and the Arts and Crafts Movement in terms of the 'religious framework' behind the notion of 'Pure Form': this 'religious language' reflects 'the religiosity of the early socialist organizations of the 1880s and early 1890s.' But Tillyard does not want to connect this socialist heritage with the contemporary radical politics of the Post-Impressionist period.

> The use of Arts and Crafts language, both formal and religious, by Post-Impressionist critics in 1910 carried with it, in consequence, an echo of the heady socialism of twenty years before. It is in this context . . . that the limited "politicisation" of Post-Impressionism in England should be seen. Hostile critics, many of them of an age to remember the 1880s, were responding to the threat of socialism as it had been constituted twenty years previously, not as it presented itself or was perceived in the gradualist, materialist climate of the pre-war years.[67]

Tillyard's argument is weakened by her attributing the same spirit of religious fervour to the 1910 exhibition as is more prominently at work in the 1912 exhibition. She may also stretch credulity in suggesting that, in 1910, the hostile critics of Post-Impressionism were thinking back twenty years, given that the first Post-Impressionist exhibition, as we have seen, opened to the imminent fall of government, the possible demise of the House of Lords, the likelihood of Home Rule for Ireland, and the mounting violence meeting striking miners and militant suffragettes. It seems an understatement to call this climate 'gradualist'. The effect of this preferred connection with nineteenth-century, religiously based socialism, is to de-historicize the 1910 exhibition, and to disassociate it from the radical, materialist politics of its time.

The aesthetic practice Tillyard seeks to identify as a continuation from the Arts and Crafts Movement to Post-Impressionism – 'ideas of purity and limitation' – is identified by her as a primary concern with structure, which 'led to the associated ideas of naked and skeletal form'. Her emphasis on the Modernist translation of 'these ideas into practice' draws on the extremism of Wyndham Lewis's Vorticism and Clive Bell's Significant Form, compared with Fry's less rigorous endorsement of form.[68] It is towards this extreme, nevertheless, that Fry's theories tend at the period of the second exhibition. As for finding in Woolf's work a correlation of this interest in the skeletal, the evidence of 'The Sun and the Fish' suggests only a negative one. Here, as we have seen, the rejuvenating flesh of colour takes precedence over the skeletal.

Tillyard rightly stresses that the more lasting definition of Post-Impressionism arises from the second exhibition and the religion of significant form;[69] but it is apparent that alternative interpretations to this dominant definition are possible. H.G. Wells, in a novel reviewed by Woolf, satirically connects Fry's Quakerism to his establishment of the Omega workshops:[70] 'the reaction of the revolting generation has always been toward colour; the pyrotechnic display of the Omega workshops in London is but the last violent outbreak of the Quaker spirit'. Wells notably connects this spirit, not to the concept of significant form, nor to a sense of the skeletal, but to 'a thirst for chromatic richness behind the lead of William Morris and the Pre-Raphaelites'.[71] He does not, then, refer this project to the influence of the French; but Wells's satire incidentally alerts us to a colourist tradition of sorts within English aesthetics.

Whatever the theorists did to impose the concept of significant form, the practitioners of the new art, and their audience (friends or foes), it appears, held and saw a somewhat different set of priorities. This becomes clearer when the work of the English artists, introduced by Clive Bell under the rubric of significant form, is examined in the context of their local traditions and practices, as well as in relation to the romantic content of the first exhibition. What is of interest here is how the changes in aesthetic practice of the English artists, exhibited in the second exhibition, came about in response to the first. Whereas Fry, with the assistance of Clive Bell, shifted the emphasis of his theory away from colour towards significant form, the artists promoted under this new label were engaging with the colour-based romanticism from which their spokesmen were rapidly distancing themselves.

The English colourist tradition, if it is to be referred to the legacy of Arts and Crafts, emerges transformed in 1910, I suggest, in the feminist public realm where politics and aesthetics meet: suffragist banner-making. In 1910, Lowndes describes this art in terms uncannily similar to those of Post-Impressionist theories: 'A banner is not a literary affair, it is not a placard: leave such to boards and sandwichmen.' Anticipating the flavour of Bell's 1912 observations on 'the makers of Christmas-cards and diagrams', she identifies the non-verbal, political significance of feminist colourism, while at the same time drawing on a discourse of aestheticism:

> A banner is a thing to float in the wind, to flicker in the breeze, to flirt its colours for your pleasure, to half show and half conceal a device you long to unravel; you do not want to read it, you want to worship it. Choose purple and gold for ambition, red for courage, green for long-cherished hopes. If above these glories of colour you write in great letters "Troy Town," that is not now a placard, it is a dedication.[72]

11 The new prismatics: Virginia Woolf, Vanessa Bell and English Post-Impressionism

'One should be a painter,' writes Woolf to her artist sister. 'As a writer, I feel the beauty, which is almost entirely colour, very subtle, very changeable, running over my pen, as if you poured a large jug of champagne over a hairpin.' (*L* VI 233–4) Her love of colour, combined with her fascination for literary analogy, I suggest, fits not so much with ideas of significant form as with iconographic interpretations of Post-Impressionism which I will explore in connection with the work of Vanessa Bell who was for Woolf 'a poet . . . in colour.' (*L* VI 381)

'The Grafton, thank God, is over', exclaims Woolf whose husband was secretary to the second Post-Impressionist exhibition: 'artists are an abominable race. The furious excitement of these people all the winter over their pieces of canvas coloured green and blue, is odious. Roger is now turning them upon chairs and tables: there's to be a shop and a warehouse next month.' (*L* II 15) Colour as index of the new art, not significant form, prompts her causticity. Woolf's response to Bell's *Art* was mixed: 'There are many things I don't agree with, where I understand. But it's great fun.' (*L* II 46) The book may well join 'the confused mass of ethics, mysticism, aestheticism, and Art' Woolf finds to 'have . . . served, for the most part for the serious literary criticism of the movement.'[1]

Six years after the second exhibition, time enough to absorb the teachings of Fry and Bell, Woolf records her impressions on seeing a picture by the messiah of significant form, Cézanne. Without reference to significant form or spirituality, Woolf responds directly to Cézanne's deployment of luminous colour which she finds intoxicating; his apples are themselves endlessly suggestive to her eye: 'What can 6 apples *not* be? I began to wonder. Theres their relationship to each other, & their colour, & their solidity.' Picking up on the artists' discussion of Cézanne's technique, she is impressed by the solidity of image and materiality of the painting, but above all by the colours.

> To Roger & Nessa. . . . [i]t was a question of pure paint or mixed; if pure which colour: emerald or veridian; & then the layering on of the paint. . . . We carried it into to the next room, & Lord! how it showed up the pictures

there, as if you put a real stone among sham ones; the canvas of the others seemed scraped with a thin layer of rather cheap paint. The apples positively got redder & redder & rounder & greener.

(*D* I 140)[2]

Writers, according to Woolf's essay, 'Pictures' (1925), do not attend art exhibitions 'to understand the problems of the painter's art. They are after something that may be helpful to themselves.' (*M* 142) This suggests a consciously literary and independent approach to the art and art theories of her circle. For Woolf, then, Cézanne's silent art has a special literary appeal: 'no painter is more provocative to the literary sense, because his pictures are so audaciously and provocatively content to be paint that the very pigment, they say, seems to challenge us'. Indeed, the 'opal colour' of one picture 'stirs words in us where we had not thought words to exist; suggests forms where we had never seen anything but thin air.' Yet pictures may also move us beyond words: 'As we gaze, words begin to raise their feeble limbs in the pale border of no man's language, to sink down again in despair.' (*M* 142)

In 'Pictures and Portraits' (1920), Woolf describes how 'those used to deal in words seek out the pictures with the least language about them – canvases taciturn and congealed like emerald or aquamarine.' Again, unspeaking colour is paradoxically attractive to the writer. 'Let us wash the roofs of our eyes in colour', Woolf enthuses, 'let us dive till the deep seas close above our heads.' (*E* III 164)

The writer's words, conjured up in the presence of painting, fascinate Woolf, not those of the art critic or the artist, for nothing, she says, empties a gallery of writers more effectively than the latter:

> But writers have said enough. Their consciences are uneasy. No one knows better than they do, they murmur, that this is not the way to look at pictures; that they are irresponsible dragon-flies, mere insects, children wantonly destroying works of art by pulling petal from petal. In short, they had better be off, for here, oaring his way through the waters, mooning, abstract, contemplative, comes a painter, and stuffing their pilferings into their pockets, out they bolt, lest they should be caught at their mischief and made to suffer the most extreme of penalties, the most exquisite of tortures – to be made to look at pictures with a painter.
>
> (*M* 143–4)

If writers are insects, then, according to Woolf's evolving ideas, they must be attracted to colour. We will return to the matter of the painter's fish-like silence, and to Woolf's own pilferings of her sister's paintings, but first we will hear more from the artists and their theorists.

'Colour had meaning in 1910'

For Vanessa Bell, writing to Roger Fry in 1925, the 1910 exhibition was the cause of 'a great deal of excitement about colour . . . which perhaps has rather quieted down now. I suppose it was the result of trying first to change everything into colour.' (*VB* 272) 'It is impossible', she was to recall later, 'that any other single exhibition can ever have had so much effect as did that on the rising generation. . . . That autumn of 1910 is to me a time when everything seemed springing to new life'.[3]

Bell's recollections of the singular impact of colour confirm Simon Watney's view that the reputation of English Post-Impressionists has suffered under the dominant 'critical model' of significant form. This has 'ensured that English Post-Impressionism would, henceforth, be judged as if it were a provincial school of French painting, thus denying any notion of its own autonomy.'[4] In consequence, the work of Gore, Gilman, Sickert, Grant, Vanessa Bell and many others 'was perceived – where it was seen at all – through the conceptual filter which could only legitimate a modern art . . . critically soluble in the ideas and values of Cubism, as seemingly championed by Fry before the revision of his 1912–14 position.'[5] That momentary position of Fry's, closely allied to Bell's 'Significant Form', becomes the dominant measure of modern art.

Although there was a 'constantly evolving quality to Bloomsbury formalism', then, the earlier aesthetics remain dominant in critical accounts because of 'their usefulness to the next generation of Americans' who followed Clement Greenberg's theories.[6] Fry, nevertheless, did move some way from his earlier formulations.[7] His 'partner in developing the second phase of formalist theory was not Clive Bell . . . but Charles Mauron',[8] whose essays addressing 'psychological volume' in art the Hogarth Press published in 1927.[9] Mauron, who translated an early version of 'Time Passes',[10] is invoked by McLaurin as an influence on Woolf's use of colour 'to create psychological volume';[11] but it is not this refinement of Fry's aesthetic that Watney pursues, nor does it differ much from the emotional and somewhat vague approach of significant form. However, Fry's essay, 'Plastic Colour',[12] influenced by Mauron, indicates the technical precedents for Watney's defining element in the work of the English Post-Impressionists: colour.

Before turning to Watney, it is worth noting Fry's discussion of the evolution of colour from decorative to structural use. In Cézanne 'colour has ceased to play a separate *rôle* from drawing' he claims. 'It is an integral part of plastic expression.' Planes are 'defined rather by their colour relations than by their relations in light and dark.'[13] Matisse's 'taste in colour enabled him to arrive at entirely new and surprising oppositions.'[14] Fry sees these two influences taken further in the paintings of the English artist Matthew Smith who relies more strongly on colour than Matisse 'to achieve suggestions of chiaroscuro', while 'pushing to its furthest limits the essentially modern view of the functional as opposed to the ornamental *rôle* played by colour in pictorial design.'[15] Watney claims for English artists, as even Fry is beginning to acknowledge here, a specific quality: it was their deployment of colour that 'most decisively separated the English Post-Impressionist movement from anything which immediately preceded or followed it. Colour had meaning in 1910. It was simultaneously the pre-condition for the iconography of English Post-Impressionism, and part of that iconography itself.'[16] Watney's emphasis upon colour and his suggestion that it 'had meaning in 1910' counters interpretations of colour as significant form. His emphasis on subject matter – iconography – in the painting of English Post-Impressionists derives from the work of Erwin Panofsky. Iconography addresses the 'subject matter or meaning of works of art as opposed to their forms.'[17] Watney investigates the central importance of colour in the iconography of English Post-Impressionism both as its very 'pre-condition' and its substance.

We have already seen that, in the political sphere, 'Colour had meaning in 1910', and that colour may well have held such meanings for Woolf in (and in relation to) 1910, as her later allegorical deployment of suffrage colours in 'The Sun and the Fish' suggests. Watney's reappraisal of English Post-Impressionism complements these findings, and provides an appropriate entrance into an understanding of the prismatic aesthetics of Vanessa Bell which inform Woolf's writing. Bell, he suggests, along with other English artists, 'took from French painting only what could be assimilated to a strong local tonal tradition, namely, colour.'[18] Before coming to Bell, however, it is worth briefly considering with regard to iconography the work and views of Sickert, an important influence on Bell, and whose colourism, as we have seen, Woolf herself formulates in terms of language.

Sickert, one of the first English artists to respond to French Impressionism, dominated English art before and after the first Post-Impressionist exhibition;[19] and, as Woolf's essay shows, his innovations in colour made his reputation. 'Concerned with the all-over pattern of areas of colour, [Sickert] rigorously subordinates the modelling of individual forms to this general pattern. Pictorial space is suggested almost exclusively by colour.'[20] In the work of the French Impressionists, Sickert observed and responded to the new tendency to ignore traditional handling of light and shade: 'For the dark-and-light chiaroscuro of the past was substituted a new prismatic chiaroscuro. An intensified observation of colour was called in, which enabled the painter to get the effect of light and shade without rendering the shade so dark as to be undecorative.'[21] English Post-Impressionism constitutes the continuing engagement with this notion of 'a new prismatic chiaroscuro', and its absorption into the tonal tradition of English, colourist art.

Subject matter, as Watney emphasizes, is here an important factor; he argues against the subordination of Sickert's subject matter to the rubric of significant form (Wendy Baron's approach).[22] Sickert and his fellow painters were interested in portraying the everyday life of ordinary, working people. Their position 'seems to have been much closer to that of Virginia Woolf in the 1930s', Watney appropriately suggests, 'recognising that the necessary radical changes in social structure which she looked forward to, could only be realized at the expense of the very culture within which her own writing had value and meaning, than to men like [Wyndham] Lewis and Clive Bell, who simply plunged headlong into reactionary politics'.[23] We might find parallels in the work of these artists with Woolf's interest in the rise of the lower classes from darkness into light. Consider, for example, Gilman's explorations of character in the portraits of his landlady, Mrs Mounter.[24] Not only does this portraiture of ordinary people mimic Van Gogh's taste in subject matter (the 'romantic' artist dropped for the second Post-Impressionist exhibition), it is also close to Woolf's interest in 'human character'. Woolf, I suggest, in keeping with the English Post-Impressionists under Sickert's influence, records social change in terms of new colours.

Vanessa Bell

> So then let us turn – and where? First, I think, to Vanessa. . . . Are not all Arts her tributaries, all sciences her continents and the globe itself but a painted ball in the enclosure of her arms? But you dwell in the Temple, and I am a worshipper without.
>
> (*L* 1 282)

Bell's development is, in many respects, typical of her generation of British avant-garde artists, in that she moved closer and closer to abstractionism during what is considered the second period of internationalism in British Post-Impressionism (c.1906–1915).[25] Her work culminates in a flirtation with pure abstractionism by the beginning of the Great War and sobers to more naturalistic methods after it.

That there is an antithesis between 'Artist' and 'Woman' in the established canon of art history has long been acknowledged,[26] and certainly did not escape the attention of the Stephen sisters. Both were mainly educated at home by their father, whereas their brothers attended official establishments of education. Vanessa, however, was given drawing lessons by Sir Arthur Cope, and between 1901 and 1904 was permitted to attend the Royal Academy schools. Here she was instructed in painting by J.S. Sargent whose lessons were chiefly about tone. He insists upon thick paint and makes one try to get the right tone at once. Apparently the drawing is to be got entirely by painting thickly the different tones, which doesn't sound very clear. He generally tells me that my things are too grey. The one thing he is down upon is when he thinks anyone is trying for an effect regardless of truth.

(*VB* 11)

Thus Bell's early instruction in painting was to subordinate technique to 'truth' however painterly the methods. 'Observation' was the by-word of this teaching.

By 1904, after their parents' death, Vanessa and her sister enjoyed a new freedom and independence. This is an important factor in her development as an artist, particularly because, as a woman artist in an art world dominated by men, she was usually made to feel irrelevant and inferior. 'All the members of [the New English Art Club]', she recalls, 'seemed somehow to have the secret of the art universe within their grasp, a secret one was not worthy to learn, especially if one was that terrible low creature, a female painter.'[27] The NEAC was an exhibiting society founded in 1886, which along with the Slade School of Fine Art encompassed the 'art universe' of the day. Bell had attended the Slade (under Henry Tonks) for a while but had found it not to her liking. In 1904, she visited Paris where she met Clive Bell who introduced her to various painters working there. Influenced by this, and having moved the family household from desirable Kensington to unfashionable Bloomsbury, she founded the Friday Club in 1905, a society where young and, at first, female, artists could meet, debate, and exhibit work. She married Clive Bell in 1907.

Vanessa Bell's *Iceland Poppies* (1908) was shown at the NEAC in 1909 and was much admired by Sickert. This painting, according to Watney, 'encapsulates her artistic education.' It owes much to Whistler's influence for its layering of paint, although Bell's paint is much thicker than his. She 'achieves a unity of tone more severe than any Whistler, since she does not sacrifice form, which is found in her subject matter itself, in the stark horizontals provided by the stems of the poppies, the edge of the table or shelf, and the design on the wall behind.'[28] Her sense of design and the bold handling of colour indicate the qualities Bell was to explore over the next ten or so years; but it is also worth noting that, except for rare cases, this is achieved by observations of nature. Complete flatness of design is avoided in *Iceland Poppies* mainly by the presence of shadows cast by the vase, bowl and bottle, but these shadows are so slight they seem to be included almost for decorative purpose rather than as suggestions of modelling in a traditional sense. The not 'undecorative' shadows are tending towards Sickert's 'prismatic chiaroscuro'.

In 1908 Bell records her conversations with the painter Henry Lamb (commissioned by Virginia to do a drawing of Vanessa): 'He is now painting without any medium (like us), and is using no black. His blacks he makes with blues, reds and greens – an expensive method.' (*VB* 75–76) But although Bell seems to admire this method, she goes on to describe the progress of her own portrait of Marjorie Strachey in which she talks of a more traditional handling of light and shadows (*VB* 77). The first Post-Impressionist show, as Bell testifies above, encouraged a new, colour-based approach, and she abandoned the old ways. Even so, one might expect Bell to emphasize the structural significance of the Picasso still-life she bought in 1911, but she writes to her sister: 'I wonder how you'll like it. It's "cubist" and very beautiful colour.' (*VB* 109)

Looking back on the impact of the second Post-Impressionist exhibition in 1922, Bell seems to suggest to Fry she took from the French influence an iconographic, rather than art-for-art's-sake, approach:

> the English seemed to be always thinking of the pictures they were producing and the French of . . . something they were trying to express by means of the pictures, which in themselves were unimportant to the painters. I thought then that it was very important to have the French attitude of mind. So it is odd that you should suggest now that that is more or less my attitude. Perhaps we all have it much more than we had, and it wouldn't now be the difference between French and English if one could see them together.
>
> (*VB* 268)

Bell's interest in the expressionistic suggests she saw herself as working away from a self-consciously aesthetic and formal approach to painting even when she was supposedly embracing it.

By the time of the second show she was increasingly introducing design-based geometric and architectonic elements into her paintings, often using heavy outlines around shapes and flat areas of colour, and rendering shadow with positive colours rather than dark tones. *Landscape with Haystack, Asheham* (the Woolfs' house), shown at the 1912 exhibition, is typical of this new freedom with colour and form. *Studland Beach* (Plate 7) (one of a series) of the same year is even more extreme in these respects. This is a flat representation of a shore-line which divides the picture plane diagonally, with two groups of figures situated on the opposite diagonal. A standing woman with children at her feet, is in the shelter of a tent at the shore-line (and therefore at the point of the intersection of the two diagonals). There is a 'compositional tension' between this and the other group in the diagonally opposite corner.[29] In Gauguin's *Vision After the Sermon* a similar diagonal – made by the trunk of a tree – divides one group of figures from another who seem to enact their inner spiritual experience (the Biblical story of Jacob wrestling with the angel). Caws invokes Gauguin's *Harvest at Le Pouldu* to comment on the 'disquieting mystery' and celebration of the 'uninterpretable' in Bell's painting.[30] Bell's 'whole scene is drastically pared down' for Watney, 'into two major areas of uncompromisingly flat colour, a "sea" of deep indigo painted over a red ground, and a "beach" of various cream and ochre tints'. These 'extremely simplified forms' surpass Matisse's work of the same period.[31] Bell's paintings 'from 1911/ 12 explore the possibilities of transforming a tradition of monochrome tonality into an art in which colour is built up from related tints. Having emptied her pictures of superfluous information, she was free to concentrate on the exciting potentialities of colour relationships explored for their own sake.'[32]

My comparison with Gauguin, however, lends weight to the argument that Bell, even when she reduces form to very simple geometric blocks of colour and abandons naturalistic effects such as shadow and modelling, does not subordinate 'content' to such formal aspects of her work. Like Sargent, in her own way, she seems to be somewhat against 'trying for an effect regardless of truth'. If anything, such abstractionism and reduction of form enhances the subject-matter of *Studland Beach*: 'This reduction of form to elemental shapes expresses a feeling which is often austere and remote, but is also . . . related to her maternal experience.'[33] This is not to suggest that this work is predominantly 'narrative' in content but that, however abstract, it is still figurative; and, however eternal the subject of motherhood, Bell portrays it in quite specific or personal terms.

In *Nursery Tea* (1912), for example, it has been argued that 'the human situation presented is totally subordinated to abstract considerations and conveys little of her affection for her children'.[34] Yet if one considers the rather hackneyed clichés which more conventional realist portraits of children could be, the attraction becomes obvious in portraying one's son as 'the one spot of satisfactory colour with his orange hair and bright pink dress.'[35] This 'rather comic' picture nevertheless represented to Bell an important phase in the development of her innovatory technique:

> I am trying to paint as if I were mosaicing – not painting in spots but by considering the picture as patches each of which has to be filled by the definite space of colours as one has to do with mosaic or woolwork, not allowing myself to brush patches into each other. It's amusing to make these experiments even if they don't succeed. I think this one *ought* to give one something of the life one seems to get with mosaic. I don't know if it will.
>
> (VB 119)

Bell's 'entirely new' mosaic technique is, in fact, one discussed, as we have seen, in both classic and romantic sources for Post-Impressionism: Denis and Meier-Graefe.

Bell, who worked closely with fellow-painter Duncan Grant for many years, was active in the Omega Workshops. It is likely that their involvement in design projects enabled Bell and Grant to arrive at a pure abstraction in their painting much earlier than many artists in Europe.[36] Her striking abstract work, entitled *Abstract* (Plate 8), comprises six rectangular patches of colour in a field of monochrome yellow. She also uses collage in other paintings of the time (1914/15) which may have been inspired by her use of *papier collé* in interior decoration (for example her nursery designs). Whatever the motivation, these works represent the brief moment in her career when Bell abandons all representational elements in her work, showing no differentiation between design and fine art. These works were the closest she came to a fulfilment of Fry's and her husband's theories: form and colour relationships are explored for their own sake and refer not to nature but only to themselves. They are self-reflexive and plastic just as Fry might have dictated; yet they seem to have been regarded by Bell herself as private experiments – something continued in her decorative design work but not in her painting. Her paintings do show an interest in formal design, but apart from the few purely abstract works, they are always rooted in representations of observed objects.[37]

As she moves on from this period of total abstraction, her painting reverts to more naturalistic imagery, but 'with hindsight her entire career bears down relentlessly on this point of technical and conceptual sophistication'.[38] Bell explains to Leonard Woolf why she could not ultimately abandon subject matter in favour of pure abstraction by citing her own experience of looking at a Picasso from whose 'forms and colours' she 'got quite a strong emotion':

> but it wasn't changed when weeks afterwards it was pointed out to me by chance that the blue was a lake. . . . The picture does convey the idea of form, of what you call secondary form I suppose, but not the idea of form associated with anything in life, but simply form, separated from life. As a matter of fact we do first feel the emotion and then look at the picture, that is to say, look at it from the point of view of seeing its tertiary form – at least I do. The reason I think that artists paint life and not patterns is that certain qualities of life, what I call movement, mass, weight have aesthetic value.
>
> (*VB* 133–34)

Bell does not regard form in painting as imitative – 'associated with anything in life' – but as something taken from nature or reality, and 'separated from life.' By this she acknowledges art is a fiction, but that it is constructed out of rhythms and movements the artist abstracts from life (material and historical). Bell regards 'flat patterns' as completely unconnected to such movements; they are separate, rather than separated, from life, therefore, they can only impose order upon it – not move with its pulse. Instead of insisting that form can be significant only at the expense of content/subject matter, as Fry and Clive Bell do, Vanessa Bell exploits the tension between the two, showing that form and content may cohere in a painting without making it imitative or 'descriptive': 'But where I quarrel with Clive . . . is when he says one gets the same emotion from flat patterns that one does from pictures. I say one doesn't because of the reason I have just given – that movement etc. give me important aesthetic emotions.'[39] Like Fry and Clive Bell, she does not regard art as a photographic resemblance of life, but, unlike them, she finds the sensual pleasures of artistic form and colour relations to be linked to forms and movements in life, and to have iconographic value. This is the irony of Fry's and Clive Bell's position: 'the one thing that the theory of Significant Form cannot cope with is the actual process of signification'.[40]

Whereas Fry proclaims subject matter is irrelevant to form and that, therefore, an image of a kitchen utensil is as significant as an image of Christ, Vanessa Bell's paintings often reveal a strong sense of subject, in spite of any declarations by her that her pictures are without meaning. Many of her paintings refer to women and children, and formal and colour relationships in her pictures often reflect upon the human. One such psychologically compelling piece is *The Tub* (1917) (Plate 9): a pensive, nude woman stands to the side of a round bath tub tilted towards the picture frame so that its rim forms an almost perfect circle. Behind is a vase with three flowers – one yellow, two red.

Spalding suggests a parallel with *Iceland Poppies* where, she claims, the motif of three flowers – one of which 'is separated by its colour from the rest'[41] – perhaps signifies Bell's jealousy of her sister's flirtation with her husband. *The Tub*, she says refers to a similar triangular relationship between Duncan Grant, David Garnett and Vanessa Bell (although the figure 'originally represented Mary Hutchinson, Clive's mistress'):[42] the woodcut of *The Tub*, executed some time later when Bell became pregnant by Grant, shows the nude overlapping the circle of the tub, and behind her two, not three, flowers. But this imagery may perhaps suggest the fulfilment of the woman's menstrual cycle, since the odd flower out in the painting may signify the unfertilized egg which is fulfilled in the woodcut. The shape formed by the stems and flower heads above the circle of the tub is reminiscent of that of a woman's ovaries and fallopian tubes above the womb. The closer position of the woman to the circle of the tub in the woodcut may be taken as an indication of pregnancy since her form breaks the circle just as the menstrual cycle is broken by pregnancy – she can be seen as part of the whole of the circle rather than isolated from it.[43]

Readings of these images may yield to the sensual pleasures of the medium, but technique may also be related to subject matter. Watney remarks on the 'numerous pentimenti in this large painting' which 'seem to reinforce the significance of the act of undressing before us, a curiously apt metaphor for this further paring down of her pictorial vocabulary, allowing her to pursue that distinctive dramatisation of the qualities of related brush-marks in the context of an extremely personal iconography which abstraction could never have allowed.'[44] Caws offers a sensitive analysis of *The Tub* as a meditation on subjectivity in which 'the tub has to be read at once in association with the bare female figure, gathered unto itself and yet not closed off from us, whom it faces, nor from the world of nature, manifest in the background in those flowers, nor from the world of intellect and art upon which – for all we know – it may be meditating.[45] The flowers, I suggest, are no mere emblems of nature.

Flowers are also of some importance in *A Conversation*, also known as *Three Women* (1913–16) (Plate 10). This schematized, but figurative picture, shows three women in conversation at a window in which is visible a cluster of brightly coloured flowers in a landscape comprising two bands of colour, one green, one orange. This is framed by two stylized white curtains which stand like columns at either side. In front are the figures of three women in rather sombre garb. There is no sense of depth in the painting, and the heads of the women lie flat against the window motif. Two of them listen while the other speaks. The two listening (one head overlaps the other) wear hats, one green and one orange like the background; the woman speaking is in profile against the flowers, whose brightness reflects her animation, which is also suggested by the stunning blue of her eye and the gesture of her hands.

The flowers, divided from the women by the plane of the window, seem to be 'the visual equivalent' of their chatter.[46] The women's heads may seem to overlap the flowers; but because of the flatness of the design – the lack of recession – the flowers may also seem to occupy the same picture plane as the women; so the less substantial reality of thought and conversation is given the same solidity and status as the more tangible mass of human form. The division suggested by the window is dissolved and what is seen on either side of it is not in opposition but united in the same pictorial surface.

This painting greatly impresses Woolf with its iconographic, not its formal, achievements:

> I am greatly tempted to write "Variations on a Picture by Vanessa
> Bell". . . . I should run the three women and the pot of flowers on a chair
> into one phantasmagoria. . . . I think you are a most remarkable painter.
> But I maintain you are into the bargain, a satirist, a conveyor of impressions
> about human life: a short story writer of great wit and able to bring off a
> situation in a way that rouses my envy. I wonder if I could write the Three
> Women in prose.
>
> (*L* III 498)

The essentially two-dimensional composition of Bell's painting, according to Gillespie, 'anticipates, in a general way, Woolf's use in *The Waves* of the circle as an image of human relationships. None of the women look out from Bell's painting; they look intently at each others' faces, which form a semicircle.'[47]

Woolf's story, 'A Society' (1921), 'and Vanessa Bell's woodcut illustration for it, are closely related to *The Conversation*. The sisters reproduce, each in her own medium, the intimacy of the women, their complete absorption in their discussion, their monumentality, and the unity of the design.'[48] Similarly, Dunn compares *A Conversation* with *A Room of One's Own*.[49] Woolf's response to Bell's pictures betrays a sense of common concern, not just with general human relations, then, but with women's space in particular.

In preparing for collaboration with Woolf on *Kew Gardens*, Bell writes:

> It's a relief to turn to your story, though some of the conversation – she says, I says, sugar – I know too well! But it's fascinating and a great success, I think. . . . I wonder if I could do a drawing for it. . . . It might not have much to do with the text, but that wouldn't matter. But I might feel inclined to do the two people holding the sugar conversation. Do you remember a picture I showed at the Omega of 3 women talking with a flower bed seen out of the window behind? It might almost but not quite do as an illustration.
>
> Now do send me your theories of aesthetics and feelings on looking at one of my works. I'm longing to hear them.
>
> (*VB* 214–15)

Bell sees parallels, then, between her sister's depiction of conversational exchange and her own. There are parallels also between Bell's painting and Woolf's *Walter Sickert. A Conversation*.[50] There is, not least, a common interest in expressing a sense of collective communication. Colours, moreover, are the common metaphor conveying this sense.

Woolf constantly draws parallels between writing and painting, and eagerly discusses both topics with writers, painters and theorists alike. She is inquisitive into the nature of painters' lives, as, for example, when she begs Bell to report from Paris: 'do describe a dinner at a cafe and how you artists talk.' (*L* II 472) She often uses vocabulary picked up from her painter friends to talk about her literary works: she says to Fry 'I'm not sure that a perverted plastic sense doesn't somehow work itself out in words for me'. (*L* II 285) Woolf's painterly analogies are strongest, however, in reference to Vanessa Bell, whom she readily acknowledges as an inspiration for her stories and characters. She makes frequent reference to 'writing Vanessa's life' (*L* II 325), most significantly in the guise of Katherine Hilbery, and Lily Briscoe. But Vanessa Bell is also an important source for Woolf's aesthetics: 'I'm going to write an account of my emotions towards one of your pictures, which gives me infinite pleasure, and has changed my view upon aesthetics.' (*L* II 257)

Bell, too, drew considerable inspiration from her sister; and both sisters recognized a common aim in their respective media. With regard to *The Waves*,

Bell writes to Woolf of 'an absurd great picture I've been painting off and on the last 2 years and if only I could do what I want to – but I can't – it seems to me it would have some sort of analogous meaning to what you've done.' Her explanation suggests she finds a common sense of intersubjectivity in their work:

> To me, painting a floor covered with toys and keeping them all in relation to each other and the figures and the space of the floor and the light on it means something of the same sort that you seem to me to mean. However, I know quite well that my painting will mean it to no one else. Only perhaps it helps me to understand what you're about.
>
> (*VB* 367–68)

Bell illustrated Woolf's stories and designed dust-jackets for most of her novels, but Woolf seems to have considered her sister's work at a deeper level than that of mere illustration. Not only is she concerned with the 'plasticity' of words, but Woolf is also 'always trying to get behind words' (*L* I 408), something she relates to colour: 'and then there's the whole question . . . of the things one doesn't say; what effect does that have? and how far do our feelings take their colour from the dive underground? I mean what is the reality of any feeling? – and all this is complicated by the form, which must sit tight.' (*L* II 320) Woolf shares her sister's aesthetic preoccupations: they both try to show non-physical experiences as formal realities, at the same time emphasizing and illuminating feminine experience. Both show communication between people as material events. Both relate this to colour.

Vanessa Bell's work has recently been recommended for fresh, feminist interpretation. The 'recurring, dissolving images of women in [her] work should be seen in the wider context of the much negotiated imagery of women in the suffrage campaigns of [the] period as well as in relation to the anomalous position of women in the Bloomsbury group,' according to Elliott and Wallace. 'From a feminist perspective', they suggest, 'there is more to Bell's choices than a purely formalist inclination.' Considering the challenge to traditional feminine roles by 'the suffrage campaigns and the political and industrial mobilization of women during the First World War', Bell, they say, 'may well have been drawn to such experimental modernist forms because they seemed especially appropriate for female subjects whom she found increasingly difficult to visualize in more concrete terms.'[51] Elliott and Wallace do not elaborate on this connection; and I would not like to follow them in attributing feminist intentionality or suffragist allusion to Vanessa Bell's work. But I do suggest that Woolf may well have looked at her sister's art with just this sort of contextually aware 'feminist perspective'.

12 'Her pictures stand for something': Woolf's forewords to Bell's paintings

Woolf's elegant, concise forewords to her sister's exhibition catalogues (1930; 1934), draw together observations on the status of women artists with explorations of literary analogies to the painterly. Reflecting on the sensual and iconographic power of Bell's colour, they also echo ideas and phrases from both *A Room of One's Own* and 'The Sun and the Fish'. These explorations of her sister's art, informed by (and informing) Woolf's literary engagement with gendered interpretations of light, dark and colour, expose the complexities and ambiguities of Woolf's position as a woman observing another woman's art in a man's world.

A woman artist in Bond Street

The 1930 'Foreword' opens with a humorous reminder of the new liberties enjoyed by women artists:

> That a woman should hold a show of pictures in Bond Street, I said, pausing upon the threshold of Messrs. Cooling's gallery, is not usual, nor, perhaps, altogether to be commended. For it implies, I fancy, some study of the nude, and while for many ages it has been admitted that women are naked and bring nakedness to birth, it was held, until sixty years ago that for a woman to look upon nakedness with the eye of an artist, and not simply with the eye of a mother, wife or mistress was corruptive of her innocency and destructive of her domesticity.
>
> (*F* 170)

Woolf dramatizes women's intervention in the traditionally masculine realm of art by positioning herself on the gallery's threshold. Poised between exclusion from, and possible submission to, this male bastion of the arts, she exploits the irony implicit in her sister's exhibiting there: woman as object of the artist's gaze has become its subject. Previously women have been permitted to look at nakedness only with the subordinate gaze of the mother, wife or mistress, and denied the look and subjective status implied by 'the eye of the artist'. The veiling of flesh from women's eyes was a moral imperative: 'Hence the extreme activity of women in philanthropy, society, religion and all pursuits requiring clothing.' (*F* 170) The possibility of a male nude as the object of a woman artist's gaze affirms a new sense of feminine subjectivity; and may also restore fleshly associations to the masculine (the male nude as object of the male gaze traditionally represents spiritual harmony and transcendence, rarely real flesh).

The woman artist comes to stand for the modern artist in pursuit of pure painting – art freed from morality, narrative or meaning; whereas Victorian attitudes to painting and to women artists in particular are represented by the skeleton in the cupboard of 'every Victorian family':

> an aunt who was driven to convert the native because her father would have died rather than let her look upon a naked man. And so she went to Church; and so she went to China; and so she died unwed; and so there drop out of the cupboard with her bones half a dozen flower pieces done under the shade of a white umbrella in a Surrey garden when Queen Victoria was on the throne.
>
> (*F* 170)

Queen Victoria and incongruous objects falling from a Victorian cupboard echo the 'amusing game'. Similarly, the observation, 'she died unwed', suggests that like the unwedded 'sights' of that game, the Victorian aunt is a figure of failed creativity. Yet her 'flower pieces' testify to women's artistic potential forced into the shade in the era of nineteenth-century imperialism. These introductory remarks set an oppositional and gendered model of light and dark (the woman artist works in 'the *shade* of a *white* umbrella') against which will emerge the figure of the modern woman artist: 'Mrs. Bell'.

Woolf shows a writerly trepidation at the door to this one woman show: 'These reflections are only worth recording because they indicate the vacillations and prevarications (if one is not a painter or a critic of painting) with which one catches at any straw that will put off the evil moment when one must go into the gallery and make up one's mind about the pictures.' (*F* 170) Hesitating over visits to exhibitions in general, Woolf also explores the particularly delicate status of the woman artist:

> But Mrs. Bell has a certain reputation it cannot be denied. She is a woman, it is said, yet she has looked on nakedness with a brush in her hand. She is reported (one has read it in the newspapers) to be "the most considerable painter of her own sex now alive". Berthe Morisot, Marie Laurencin, Vanessa Bell – such is the stereotyped phrase which comes to mind when her name is mentioned and makes one's predicament in front of her pictures all the more exacting. For what ever the phrase may mean, it must mean that her pictures stand for something, are something and will be something which we shall disregard at our peril. As soon not go to see them as shut the window when the nightingale is singing.
>
> (*F* 170)

This apparently evasive passage,[1] fraught with ambiguities, does suggest finally that Woolf finds Bell's pictures iconographic since they 'stand for something'. But Bell's talent may be overshadowed by her notoriety as a woman painter of nudes. As such she is considered a threat to male prowess (sexual and artistic): Woolf's depiction of her sister holding the 'phallic' brush contradicts the traditionally *macho* image of the artist encapsulated in the anecdote about Renoir;[2] Bell is a libidinous woman whose 'reputation' colours her work.

Yet 'brush' may also connote feminine sexuality: as 'the most considerable painter of her own sex', Bell is figured as a formidable woman artist capable of wielding a brush over a male object, possibly also suggesting here that she might sweep away (perhaps emasculate) what she sees. But she is simultaneously an artist whose subject matter *is* her own sex, and who inscribes her sexuality in art, the instrument no longer phallic but vaginal. Here the possibility of an autonomous feminine sexuality and art is intimated: woman as subject and object of the artistic gaze, is now able to 'illumine [her] own soul' (*AROO* 135). This liberating aspect is countered by the suggestion of Bell's possible confinement to the ranks of women artists stereotypically considered as secondary to the dominant male canon. Such contradictions throw the observer into an 'exacting' 'predicament' even before Bell's paintings have been glimpsed. Woolf's vacillations may also tempt deconstructive readings: endlessly transgressive, unable to settle on either side of the threshold, this playful text may undo art's fixed gendered oppositions. But Woolf's complex doorstep model is, I suggest, contextually sensitive and politically encoded.

The song of the nightingale

Woolf's predicament may be understood by careful consideration of her comparison of Bell's pictures to the song of the nightingale. To stay away from her sister's paintings is to ignore art, she implies. Birdsong is a fitting metaphor for art; but her choice of the nightingale's song, in particular, has special significance: the myth of Procne and Philomela, an appropriate allusion for Woolf's discussion of her sister's art, but not altogether a pleasant one.

> Tereus, pretending that [his wife] Procne was dead, asked that Philomela might be sent to him, and on her arrival raped or seduced her and then cut out her tongue to prevent her telling. She contrived to send her sister a piece of embroidery on which was woven her story. Procne found her and took revenge on Tereus by serving him at a meal with the flesh of his and her child Itys. Finding this out, he pursued the women, but the gods turned him into a hoopoe, Procne into a nightingale, and Philomela into a swallow (a later tradition, represented in Latin authors, reverses these last two).[3]

Philomela, the silent weaver of images, transformed into a nightingale, is an important figure in *The Waste Land* (which Woolf herself set in type for the Hogarth Press in 1923).

> Above the antique mantel was displayed
> As though a window gave upon a sylvan scene
> The change of Philomel, by the barbarous king
> So rudely forced; yet there the nightingale
> Filled all the desert with inviolable voice
> And still she cried, and still the world pursues,
> 'Jug Jug' to dirty ears.[4]

Woolf's reference to 'shutting the window when the nightingale is singing' may, then, suggest Eliot's window scene. But Philomela's 'Thracian web', woven according to Ovid, with 'purple signs on a white background'[5] and by which she 'tells the story of her wrongs', may also be taken as a model for feminist art.[6] Its origins lie in woman's suffering and anguished protest: 'in trouble cunning comes.'[7] Procne reads and acts upon her sister's message but 'says not a word'. Such art, then, speaks secretly to women in a public realm still dominated by men, and its decorative allure is deceptive for it becomes instrumental in the downfall of a tyrant.

The tapestry's purple and white colours provide retrospectively the accidental significance, almost, of a suffrage pennant; and we may even find a parallel in suffragette handkerchiefs embroidered by women on hunger strike in Holloway prison.[8] Anti-feminists also employed imagery which echoes (not necessarily consciously) that of the myth: for example, the postcard depicting the cutting out of a woman's tongue below the legend 'Beware of Suffragists'.[9] Philomela's tapestry, less seriously, may be suggested in Woolf's own hobby of embroidering tapestries from her sister's designs (*L* III 414–415). It may also prefigure her references to women's webs of fiction as 'the work of suffering human beings' (*AROO* 63). Yet Woolf also aspires to an art whose concerns go beyond such matters:

> It is fatal for a woman to lay the least stress on any grievance; to plead even with justice any cause; in any way to speak consciously as a woman. And fatal is no figure of speech; for anything written with that conscious bias is doomed to death. It ceases to be fertilised. Brilliant and effective, powerful and masterly, as it may appear for a day or two, it must wither at nightfall; it cannot grow in the minds of others.
>
> (*AROO* 157)

If a woman's art survives 'nightfall', we might gather, it is an art no longer articulated from the shade of oppression marked out for women by patriarchy.

Such an art may register its origins in oppression, but it does not plead or grieve, for it is an art transformed, articulating and claiming a new, and unshadowed, creative position for women. This new art, then, suggests not Philomela's tapestry, which in some versions of the story tells of its author's imprisonment among the slaves,[10] but the elegiac song of the nightingale, both art and artist having been transformed and freed. Yet this transformation may not be considered fully as liberation since, in order to survive, the woman artist relinquishes her own shape to find refuge in the shape of a bird. To compare her sister's pictures to the song of a nightingale may be for Woolf to recognize their painful triumph over the 'fatal' connotations of 'nightfall'.

In Keats's Ode, the nightingale is praised for transporting its audience back to the sunny, arcadian climes of 'the warm south' as it sings 'of summer' from its 'melodious plot/ Of beechen green, and shadows numberless'.[11] This suggests the shadows are too numerous to count but also subtly hints that, as the bird sings, they disappear (there are now none to count). The bird's song of summer contrasts with its dark surroundings, but at the same time dispels that darkness. We do not know whether this poem figured in Vanessa Bell's plan to illustrate some Keats for the Hogarth Press in 1921, for although Woolf thought her project 'a very brilliant one' (L II 491), it came to nothing.

Elsewhere,[12] Woolf considers the differences between Keats's nightingale and Eliot's to illustrate her point (as in her 'amusing game') that for modern tastes 'Beauty is part ugliness; amusement part disgust; pleasure part pain.' (E IV 433) Here she anticipates the liminal imagery of her foreword: 'Emotions which used to enter the mind whole are now broken up on the *threshold*' (my italics). In Keats's poem 'sorrow is the shadow which accompanies beauty. In the modern mind beauty is accompanied not by its shadow but by its opposite. The modern poet talks of the nightingale who sings "jug jug to dirty ears".' (E IV 433) This literary abandonment of shadow also fits with Post-Impressionism's colourist displacement of chiaroscuro.

Appropriately enough, after the nightingale allusion in her foreword, Woolf crosses the gallery's threshold to celebrate her sister's luminously colourful and shadowless art.

> But once inside and surrounded by canvases, this shillyshallying on the threshold seems superfluous. What is there here to intimidate or perplex? Are we not suffused, lit up, caught in a sunny glow? Does there not radiate from the walls a serene yet temperate warmth, comfortable in the extreme after the rigours of the streets? Are we not surrounded by vineyards and olive trees, by naked girls couched on crimson cushions, by naked boys ankle deep in the pale green sea?
>
> (F 170–71)

This savouring of colour, light and sensuousness delivers us from doorstep 'shillyshallying' over women's past subordination: the vision of the Victorian aunt's skeleton gives way to a vibrant celebration of flesh. The imagery of naked boys and girls may suggest the 'nuptials' Woolf describes in her vision of androgynous art (*AROO* 157). But Bell's art does more than merely counter Victorian prudery:

> Even the puritans of the nineteenth century might grant us a moment's liberty in this serene and ordered world. But it is not the puritans who move us on. It is Mrs. Bell. It is Mrs. Bell who is determined that we shall not loll about juggling with pretty words or dallying with delicious sensations.
>
> (*F* 171)

Bell's achievement is a directness of vision beyond the verbal: it is unmediated, and untroubled by 'the rigours of the streets' or, as in 'The Sun and the Fish', by 'the tumult of the world'. Left at the gallery door, tumult gives way to a 'serene and ordered world'. Bell's paintings seem to match the 'still rapture' of the lizard-tanks' classical 'squares of immortality'.

Woolf seems to find her advice to women writers to 'Think of things in themselves' awesomely enacted in paint by her sister.

> Ninety nine painters . . . would have caricatured and illustrated; would have drawn our attention to the antics of parrots, the pathos of old umbrellas, the archness of ankles, the eccentricities of noses. . . . But look round the room: the approach to these pictures is not made by that means. No stories are told; no insinuations are made. The hill side is bare; the group of women is silent; the little boy stands in the sea saying nothing.
>
> (*F* 171)

In contrast to declaring privately her sister 'a short story writer of great wit', as we saw earlier, Woolf explains publicly here Bell's 'uncompromising' (*F* 171) art as one free of literary associations, of narrative or of any meaning at all ('No stories are told'): these are stark classical images, now beyond the celebration of the flesh ('no insinuations are made'). Yet 'satire' is achieved – but by other means than narrative. Bell's apparent rejection of caricaturing nineteenth century 'umbrellas' and 'ankles' suggests her bold innovation as a modern painter, but also her dismissal of Victorian attitudes to women and their clothing: Woolf seems to be hinting at the satirical implications of her sister's direct, unshadowed, treatment of such subject matter. But if this sounds like a feminist interpretation creeping into her analysis, she closes the passage with a statement at odds with the idea of satire and more appropriate to the pages of Clive Bell's *Art*: 'If portraits there are, they are pictures of flesh which happens from its texture or its modelling to be aesthetically on an equality with the China pot or the chrysanthemum.' (*F* 171) This resembles Bell's account of the Post-Impressionist approach to a coal-scuttle as 'an end in itself, as a significant form related on terms of equality with other significant forms.'[13] Woolf, then, supplies the orthodox creed: subject matter is irrelevant; there is no meaning or narrative content; these are paintings about paintings. Yet, as her doorstep prevarications have intimated, how we read her observations becomes a matter of position: if we remain on the threshold between street and gallery, between Philomela and the nightingale, between the grief and protest of her tapestry and the purity and freedom of the birdsong, we cannot, since we have a foot in both camps, submit entirely to this declaration of significant form.

Woolf's initial caveat that her sister is exhibiting in male territory may suggest Bell as the nightingale singing of sunshine (a promise of feminine enlightenment) from the as yet unbanished shadows of patriarchy. Analysis of this is necessarily synæsthetic: it may appear to the male eye, in a realm dominated by men, that 'The hill side is bare' and 'the group of women is silent', but to a woman's eye such cold pastorals may speak volumes. There is then a double consciousness at work in Woolf's foreword; and this model of reading into Bell's paintings may also be profitably put to use in reading Woolf's words. Accordingly, we might reconsider Woolf's observations concerning the 'fatal' error of a woman who writes openly of 'any grievance'. Perhaps Woolf is recommending silence with the thought that Philomela's silent art and her sister's silent response are (not just enforced but) strategically necessary for survival and escape from tyranny. Woolf's foreword, too, is written from the contested space of Messrs. Cooling's gallery: the presence there of her sister's paintings suggests a challenge to the male orthodoxy but also imprisonment by it. The code between sisters may lie dormant or it may be activated, depending on the permutation of reading context and (gender) position.

Woolf's representation of Bell's art allows for it to be read according to the theory of significant form (the male domain), perhaps gently questioning whether this resembles the birdsong state (free of protest) into which women's art will transform itself. But she also discloses its iconographic (and feminist) potential. Rather than settling on either position exclusively, Woolf takes her doorstep vacillations into the gallery. No sooner has she invoked the terms of significant form than she declares it an interpretative dead end: 'Checked at that point in our approach (and the snub is none the less baffling for the beauty with which it is conveyed) one can perhaps draw close from another angle.' (*F* 171)

'Goddess and peasant'

Woolf next considers the paintings in relation to the artist's personality: 'Let us see if we can come at some idea of Mrs. Bell herself and by thus tresspassing, crack the kernel of her art.' This writerly approach, however, she finds 'rebuffed' by contradictions:

> One says, Anyhow Mrs. Bell is a woman; and then half way round the room one says, But she may be a man. One says, She is interested in children; one has to add, But she is equally interested in rocks. One asks, Does she show any previous knowledge of clothes? One replies, Stark nakedness seems to please her well. . . . Was she ever at a University? Does she prefer herrings or brussel sprouts? Is she – for our patience is becoming exhausted – not a woman at all, but a mixture of Goddess and peasant, treading the clouds with her feet and with her hands shelling peas? Any writer so ardently questioned would have yielded something to our curiosity.
>
> (*F* 171–172)

Woolf's humorous query on Bell's 'previous knowledge of clothes', suggests an awareness of women's historical struggle against oppression symbolized by the Victorian aunt forced into 'pursuits requiring clothing', a struggle we may read as a pre-eclipse phase of feminism. Bell also evokes the post-eclipse condition of 'stark nakedness', defying the history of oppression associated with clothing, celebrating a world of flesh uninhibited by patriarchy or puritanism. Yet Woolf communicates a sense of unease at total nakedness: it may not be desirable to discard the clothes of history altogether. As an artist Bell has apparently achieved a state of androgyny; her art reveals to Woolf that she has avoided the 'fatal' error of being a 'woman pure' for she seems to be a 'woman-manly' (*AROO* 157): she 'is a woman. . . . But she may be a man'. The questions about University attendance and food preferences echo Woolf's concerns in *A Room of One's Own* with the material conditions necessary for women's education and production of art. The figure of Bell as Goddess-cum-peasant, furthermore, resembles Woolf's portrait there of the 'very queer composite being', one we should pause to consider.

The male-dominated literary canon presents to Woolf an idealized order of femininity at odds with, but complicit in, the perpetuation of the historical realities of woman's suffering and oppression:

> She pervades poetry from cover to cover; she is all but absent from history. She dominates the lives of kings and conquerors in fiction; in fact she was the slave of any boy whose parents forced a ring upon her finger. Some of the most inspired words, some of the most profound thoughts in literature fall

from her lips; in real life she could hardly read, could scarcely spell, and was the property of her husband.

(AROO 66)

Woolf suggests how women writers might transform this hybrid monster bred of poetry and history, 'a worm winged like an eagle; the spirit of life and beauty in a kitchen chopping up suet', by 'keeping in touch with fact – that she is Mrs. Martin, aged thirty-six, dressed in blue, wearing a black hat and brown shoes; but not losing sight of fiction either – that she is a vessel in which all sorts of spirits and forces are coursing and flashing perpetually.' *(AROO 66– 67)* Recommending we think about women both 'poetically and prosaically', Woolf acknowledges the historical and material realities of Mrs. Martin's clothes, as well as the liberating potentialities of fiction. Similarly, in 'Poetry, Fiction and the Future', Woolf's poetic figure of 'the nightingale singing' is 'incongruously coupled' with the figure of an oppressed, vagrant, 'diseased old woman' whom she links to the 'dirty work' of prose *(E* iv 433–34). Just as Woolf's transformed composite being combines the figure of a historically determined, domestically imprisoned, clothed woman with that of a vessel brimming with contesting alternatives, so the figure of 'Mrs. Bell', emerging from the gallery wall, combines the peasant element of kitchen work with the Goddess element of liberated imagination. Just as 'Mrs. Bell' is a nightingale, so Woolf has given bird-like qualities to 'Mrs. Martin': not only does her name suggest the house martin, close relative of the swallow (and therefore subtly linked perhaps to the Procne and Philomela myth), but her clothes, too, suggest the blue-black plumage of these birds. Here we may see liberated imagination grounded in the material and historical: the woman artist is both woman and bird, Procne/Philomela and the nightingale/swallow; the origins of Mrs Bell's art, and the potential for women's escape and transformation, lie with the Victorian aunt.

The presence of Procne and Philomela may again be felt as Woolf expands upon the sense of impersonality communicated in her sister's work. Unlike a novelist,

> Mrs. Bell is as silent as the grave. Her pictures do not betray her. Their reticence is inviolable. That is why, if it be true that they yield their full meaning only to those who can tunnel their way behind the canvas into masses and passages and relations and values of which we know nothing – if it be true that she is a painter's painter – still her pictures claim us and make us stop. They give us an emotion. They offer a puzzle.

(F 172)

Woolf's tunnelling reference may be compared with Fry's favourite dictum from the painter Seurat: 'painting is "the art of hollowing out a canvas."' [14] Fur- thermore, and only if the myth of the two sisters remains dormant, we may also read this passage as a declaration of Bell's art as significant form, as art about art, abstract and remote. *The Times* reviewer makes use of Woolf's 'enchanting' foreword to confirm the view of Bell's art as a mixture of purist formal concerns and a mystical sense of common humanity, 'inviolable reticence' taking on the quality of holy innocence.[15] This is a less extreme version of the quasi-religious sentiments of significant form: art has nothing specific to say, but its very reticence allows us to contemplate our humanity in the terms of Clive Bell's 'aesthetic rapture'.

Whatever Woolf's sources for the term 'reticence' (Spalding suggests Fry's 1926 *Vogue* essay on Vanessa Bell),[16] Eliot's allusion to Philomela seems a likely precedent for her 'inviolable': here the nightingale is not credited with 'inviolable reticence', however, but with 'inviolable voice'. Such references suggest an alternative and contradictory set of allusions to the myth of Procne and Philomela is embedded in the foreword's paraphrased theories of significant form, so that both approaches may be simultaneously voiced and silenced. Woolf's teasing point that her sister's pictures might 'yield their full meaning only to those who can tunnel . . .' acknowledges Bell as a 'painter's painter', practising significant form, but also suggests her art conceals a hidden language akin to the secret communications between Philomela and Procne. I am not trying to suggest Vanessa and Virginia themselves communicated like this, or that Vanessa's paintings actually allude to the myth; but that Woolf seems to weave these references into her (writer's) interpretation of her sister's work.

Woolf's tunnelling reference also echoes her discussion of painting and writing in 'Pictures': the sensuous colour and light of Proust's imagery sets his reader 'tunnelling logically and intellectually into the obscurity of the young man's emotions' after 'a shred of meaning' with which to illuminate the darkness (*M* 141). This extenuated process of reading, I suggest, is one in which Woolf appears to be engaging as she considers her sister's pictures. Similarly, by 'tunnelling' (beyond the emotional) below the surface of her prose we have discovered 'shred[s] of meaning' in her mythical metaphors.

Woolf goes on, in her foreword, to emphasize that the strength of Bell's art lies in its signification beyond verbal language: 'their expressiveness has no truck with words'. The paintings 'offer a puzzle', which suggests both that they may embody a code to be deciphered and that, on the contrary, they may remain an enigma not reducible to any single solution or interpretation. 'Her vision excites a strong emotion and yet when we have dramatised it or poetised it or translated it into all the blues and greens, and fines and exquisites and subtles of our vocabulary, the picture itself escapes. It goes on saying something of its own.' (*F* 172) While declaring them beyond words, Woolf, nevertheless, finds in Bell's paintings a model for a new literary art surpassing that of Thackeray and Dickens (in her 'painting of the Foundling Hospital' (*F* 172)). We may interpret this as both a recognition of painting as beyond all literature and a suggestion that Bell's paintings challenge mainly the nineteenth-century literary and sentimental approach to art. Bell is also positioned as a woman innovator who breaks with a male-dominated past and language, and we may see her work as inspiration for a new women's literature. In suggesting Bell's picture itself escapes our vocabulary, Woolf may be alluding to a woman's art that escapes the male tyranny of the public realm, with 'our' ironically referring to the supposed universality of this realm. Likewise, if 'our emotion has been given the slip' (*F* 172), as she suggests, perhaps it may be the aesthetic emotion of the male-formulated significant form that this woman's art escapes in order to speak secretly to her sister. After the 'dust and ashes', after the destruction of the old world, 'Mrs. Bell' says 'Nothing' (*F* 172): again, this may mean that she says nothing to the universalizing male, but plenty to women.

Ostensibly Woolf finds Bell's awesome achievement of silence troubling, for it suggests a welcome freedom but also a fearful sterility. Bell's picture defies interpretation: 'It goes on saying something of its own', which has nothing to do with its author who has absented herself. Beyond even the urgent message hidden in Philomela's tapestry, we might gather, women's art perhaps continues more purely as art. This may be Woolf's aspiration for women's fiction. Even as she declares its permanence, Woolf hints that the calm enlightenment in Bell's 'serene and sunny, and very still' picture may be under threat: this depends on whether or not we read irony in her discerning 'no sense that this sunny day is perhaps the last' (*F* 172). Perhaps this woman's art banishes not merely shadows but nineteenth-century sunshine too.

Woolf closes her foreword with a consideration of Bell's art as simultaneously communicating emotion (perhaps associated with significant form) – 'And yet somehow our emotion has been returned to us. For emotion there is. The room is charged with it.' (*F* 172) – and remaining aloof. She writes as someone awed by, and somewhat alienated from, this painter's language ('it is always by her means, in her language, with her susceptibility, and not ours'); she becomes its interpreter to the uninitiated ('There is emotion in that white urn; in that little girl painting a picture . . .'); but her informed admiration also gives way to criticism.

> One feels that if a canvas of hers hung on the wall it would never lose its lustre. It would never mix itself up with the loquacities and trivialities of daily life. It would go on saying something of its own imperturbably. And perhaps by degrees – who knows? – one would become an inmate of this strange painters' world, in which mortality does not enter, and psychology is held at bay, and there are no words. But is morality to be found there? That was the very question I was asking myself as I came in.
>
> (*F* 172–173)

This complex response to Bell's art goes beyond the token genuflection to the doctrine of significant form David Dowling finds it.[17] Bell's artistic language is both a source of illumination to Woolf and something alienating and unknowable. She sees her sister imprisoned as an 'inmate of this strange painters' world': a sterile, permanently sunlit, and unchanging world. Woolf herself, on the other hand, enjoys the freedom to come and go, and to prevaricate at the gallery door. In contemplating her sister's pictures, she touches upon a dilemma in the avant-garde quest for a new transformational language: how far can it disconnect from the traditions it seeks to undermine before ceasing to communicate altogether? Woolf also shows that silence in one domain becomes eloquence in another; and the silence she attributes to her sister's art is one she invests, in her allusions to the myth of Procne and Philomela, with a feminist subtext. Her vacillations take us through positive and negative aspects to both conditions. They also leave us at the door with one resounding question: 'But is morality to be found there?'

The painter's art may be truly silent after all; and Woolf frequently calls painters 'inarticulate' (*L* I 60), 'as mute as mackerel' (*M* 143), and their art as 'tend[ing] to dumbness' (*L* II 382), even capable of depriving the observer 'of a tongue' (*E* III 163–64). These epithets echo Simonides' dictum that painting is mute poetry (and poetry a speaking picture);[18] and where tradition, following Plutarch, identifies an equal and common aim of imitation, Woolf often seems fondly to be advancing verbal over visual art. In likening visual artists to fish, inhabiting a 'sublime silent fish-world' (*L* IV 142), she recalls the limited and sterile world of the zoological aquarium. In 'Pictures', using a similarly 'piscine' vocabulary, she recognizes that to expect anything else of painters is to misunderstand their art:

> They must weave their spells like mackerel behind the glass at the aquarium, mutely, mysteriously. Once let them raise the glass and begin to speak, and the spell is broken. A story-telling picture is as pathetic and ludicrous as a trick played by a dog, and we applaud it only because we know that it is as hard for a painter to tell a story with his brush as it is for a sheep-dog to balance a biscuit on its nose. Dr. Johnson at the Mitre is much better told by Boswell; in paint, Keats's nightingale is dumb; with half a sheet of notepaper we can tell all the stories of all the pictures in the world.
>
> (*M* 142)

Woolf's assertion of the writer's superiority over the painter may also betray a feminist undercurrent: the reference to Dr. Johnson in close proximity to dog tricks is a reminder of his notorious remarks on women preachers, cited by Woolf to show that 'even in the nineteenth century a woman was not encouraged to be an artist' (*AROO* 82–83). In 'Pictures', then, Woolf playfully positions painters in the place traditionally marked out by patriarchy for women. Her remark that 'in paint, Keats's nightingale is dumb' is one she goes on to contradict when introducing her sister's paintings. In comparing her pictures to that birdsong, Woolf may imply that Bell has for the first time in paint made the nightingale sing. On the other hand, Woolf may be suggesting herself as the songster, lyrically – *verbally* – transporting us from the silent subaquatic world of her sister's art. Perhaps Woolf, adapting as a feminist vehicle Eliot's modernist nightingale, inscribes a morality where she finds none.

It may take Procne to read Philomela's art as iconographic rather than as significant form. In the light of Woolf's vacillations, the answer to her final question depends on who is looking, and from where. Gillespie finds Woolf articulating 'the layperson's uncertainties' in posing this question, but these may also be the professional concerns of the (feminist) writer. Gillespie also rightly notes that the painter's 'reticence both intrigues and repels Woolf',[19] and we can now begin to see in more detail how these effects operate in Woolf's writing, not least from a feminist perspective: for as the mythical subtext to her foreword reveals, Woolf is capable of finding a specifically feminist eloquence at work beneath the public silence of her sister's painting. Her 'layperson's uncertainties' may also be regarded as sophisticated prevarications upon the strategies available to women artists exhibiting (and women writers reviewing) in a man's gallery. This context informs Woolf's question about morality and in posing it, she both voices the doubts of the uninitiated about significant form, and puts forward a specifically feminist question, one that keeps in play both the silent protest of Philomela's tapestry and the inviolable song of the nightingale.

'Character is colour'

Woolf's 1934 'Foreword' demonstrates her understanding of Bell's iconographic colourism. She begins by pleading ignorance, while roundly, but also knowledgeably, dismissing the approach to Bell's art she expects from the critics:

> As Keats wrote to Haydon, "I have never been too sensible of the labyrinthian path to eminence in Art . . . to think I understand the emphasis of painting." Let us leave it to the critics to pursue the exciting adventure which awaits them in these rooms; to trace the progress of the artist's brush beginning, shall we say, with the chocolate-faced nursemaid and the monolithic figures of 1920; to note the birth of other sensibilities; how blues and oranges trembled into life; how this mass mated itself with that; how the lines grew taut or slack; how with an infinitude of varied touches the finished picture came into being.

(*F2* 1)

Woolf's invocation of Keats gives her a writer's alibi to depart from a painter's or art critic's approach;[20] but she, nevertheless, shows off, in her familiar sexually explicit argot ('mated'), a fair understanding of the integral relations of colour and mass. She now turns to her own response, in which she includes the reader too. Here she again remarks on the silence of her sister's paintings; but while she makes it clear that they are quiet verbally, she shows that nevertheless their colour makes them visually loquacious.

> For us the experience has its excitement too. A meaning is given to familiar things that makes them strange. Not a word sounds yet the room is full of conversations. What are the people saying who are not sitting on that sofa? What tune is the child playing on her silent violin? Nobody moves and yet the room is full of infinite relationships. People's minds have split out of their bodies and become part of their surroundings. Where does the man end and Buddha begin? Character is colour, and colour is china, and china is music. Greens, blues, reds and purples are here seen making love and war and joining in unexpected combinations of exquisite married bliss. A plant bends its leaves in the jar and we feel that we too have visited the depths of the sea.
>
> Cornfields bask in the sun of man's first summer; the haymakers are primeval men. Everywhere life has been rid of its accidents, shown in its essence. The weight of custom has been lifted from the earth. Hampstead is virginal; Ken Wood ecstatic. The onions and the eggs perform together a solemn music. Flowers toss their heads like proud horses in an Eastern festival. In short, precipitated by the swift strokes of the painter's brush, we have been blown over the boundary to the world where words talk such nonsense that it is best to silence them. And yet it is a world of glowing serenity and sober truth. Compare it, for example, with Picadilly Circus or St. James's Square.
>
> (*F2* 1)

Woolf communicates great pleasure in the overflowing of her sister's colours and forms out of art and into life and then into music, and so on. This sense of overflowing is heightened by the ambiguity of her references to 'conversations', which the art both participates in, and depicts. (She is, furthermore, actually portrayed by her sister in conversation.)[21] *The Times* review again makes use of Woolf's foreword and, picking up on her conversational analogies, emphasizes that 'though [Bell] can make a picture, anyhow, she is most happy when she makes it out of colour. . . . In the more recent paintings the colours, while preserving their decorative individuality, have entered into general conversation – a matter of allusions, responses, protests, and exclamations rather than reportable language.'[22] But if Woolf finds the language of Bell's pictures unreportable, she does not suggest it has nothing to say. She identifies in Bell's art, the language of colour, and attempts a verbal account of its messages, coming very close, in the process, to her own model of verbal language: the 'amusing game'. Just as there, 'sights marry, incongruously, morganatically,' and just as in 'Craftsmanship' the English language goes 'a-roving'; so here, colours ('greens, blues, reds and purples') are 'seen making love and war and joining in unexpected combinations of exquisite married bliss'. Just as words express character, so too 'character is colour'. Yet words remain alien to paint: they do not belong to this world of pure, direct sun, untouched by 'custom' (and presumably history).

Woolf, no longer 'shillyshallying' (as in the earlier foreword) at the gallery's threshold, makes strong connections between verbal language and the language of colour, the latter sometimes articulating what the former cannot. Her comparison of Bell's art with the metropolitan world outside suggests that she considers her sister's paintings, no longer remote, to challenge (not merely escape) the values of urban commerce. Colour seems to be the means of this challenge, one that in Woolf's realm at least may become feminist. Her sister's world is for her a composite one of 'glowing serenity and sober truth'; and in this Woolf has apparently moved on from her previously prevaricating view of Bell's 'serene and sunny, and very still' art: now she seems to find not only serenity and light but, in the endless movement of colour in conversation, a suggestion of the 'morality' she was earlier seeking.

13 *To the Lighthouse*: purple triangle and green shawl

Colour, silence and 'flying phrases'

'All your pictures are built up of flying phrases', Woolf writes to her sister 'mistress of the phrase', in 1927. Bell's colour she singles out for special praise: 'your colour intrigues me, seduces, and satisfies me exquisitely. I should like you to paint a large, large picture; where everything would be brought perfectly firmly together, yet all half flying off the canvas in rapture.' (*L* III 340–41) Woolf celebrates Bell's pictures here in terms that recall the woman artist's technique in her latest novel: 'Beautiful and bright it should be on the surface, feathery and evanescent, one colour melting into another like the colours on a butter-fly's wing; but beneath the fabric must be clamped together with bolts of iron.' (*TL* 264) Colour is luminous and structural: both solid and fragile like post-eclipse colours. Woolf envisages an art that is both self-contained and over-flowing, reflecting the 'tumult' and 'still rapture' of 'The Sun and the Fish', as well as the silence of the imprisoned Philomela's art and her flight into the nightingale's song. Woolf encapsulates this dual condition when she praises Bell's paintings for being as 'firm as marble and ravishing as a rainbow' (*L* V 236), just as she suggests writing should be 'granite and rainbow' (*E* IV 478). Bell, however, is less certain of such inter-artistic analogies: for her, writing is 'all to do with life',

> "whereas in painting one seems to get into another world altogether, separate from the ordinary human emotions and ideas. Perhaps that's only an illusion, however. But it may be an illusion that helps. It seems such a relief to have this other world to plunge into."
>
> (*VB* 392)

Bell's view of the visual arts as a retreat from life may support readings of Woolf's *künstlerroman* as 'escaping' the real world (or 'futile and anarchic history'), plunging the reader deep into aesthetics.[1] The politically explosive era of modernism attracted some to the new religion of art as a respite from conflict; but as the initial reception of Post-Impressionism illustrates, avant-garde art might also be understood as politically engaging and disruptive. If Bell's paintings constitute for her aesthetic escape from life, then, they become for Woolf, I suggest, an inspiration for writerly intervention.

I have been suggesting that when Woolf likens her painter sister to a dumb fish, and admires her sunlit pictures, there is at play both a surface meaning (painterly silence) and a feminist subtext (sisterly code). I will be reading *To the Lighthouse* and *The Waves* with Woolf's feminist articulation of the painter's silence in mind. The allegedly 'silent' significant form some critics[2] find in Woolf may, I suggest, conceal its own feminist interruptions; silence enigmatically 'illuminates women's presence' for one critic,[3] but it may yield a more specific, contextually sensitive, materialist feminism. As Woolf's foreword has shown, context and position as well as structure may help determine our interpretations. My feminist reading itself, of course, can only be partial.

Woolf herself seems to support an orthodox silent reading of her novel, however, when she writes to Fry in terms suggestive of significant form:

> I meant *nothing* by The Lighthouse. One has to have a central line down the middle of the book to hold the design together. I saw that all sorts of feelings would accrue to this, but I refused to think them out, and trusted that people would make it the deposit for their own emotions – which they have done, one thinking it means one thing another another. I can't manage Symbolism except in this vague, generalised way. Whether its right or wrong I don't know, but directly I'm told what a thing means, it becomes hateful to me.
>
> (*L* III 385)

Although appealing to Fry's aesthetics, Woolf does not dismiss altogether the possibility of meaning; it may have been important for her in the process of writing not to 'think out' its emotional significance, but it is something she expects her readers to engage in; and she herself seems unhappy with only restricted meaning. Her reticence, however, is at odds with her private statements on her intentions to write an elegy, and her decision to put her father's character at its centre (*D* III 18–19). Woolf later worries, in a letter to a woman friend, that she has been 'critical' and 'irreverent' (*L* III 374) about him, suggesting the accrual to her novel's 'central line' of some specific and personal meanings.

Woolf, then, broadening out from the closely biographical, seems to have understood this work as challenging a remembered sense of patriarchy, and as celebrating the survival and flourishing of its author's feminist creativity: her father's life, she decides, 'would have entirely ended mine. What would have happened? No writing, no books; – inconceivable.' (*D* III 208) This is helpful in the critic's task of 'think[ing] out' meanings in connection to Woolf's central design. In telling Fry she 'meant *nothing* by The Lighthouse', Woolf may present to him a silence that in other contexts and from other perspectives may speak volumes. Mrs Ramsay, for example, serves up at her pre-war nuptial banquet 'Boeuf en Daube' (*TL* 152–63), one of Roger Fry's culinary specialities,[4] a dish the Post-Impressionist painter Lily Briscoe, nevertheless, as we may gather from her opposition to her hostess's promotion of marriage, finds difficult to swallow. Its dominant brown tones seem opposed by her more prismatic palette. Eliza Haywood's advice to women in a man's world seems applicable to the novel's ambiguities: 'whenever we would truly conquer, we must seem to yield.'[5] If *To the Lighthouse* yields to readings of significant form, then, it may yet simultaneously disclose a conquering feminism. There may be more to Woolf's painterly analogies than the purely 'aesthetic emotions' she voices to Fry.

Engaging photological and prismatic tropes in *To the Lighthouse*, Woolf draws on the English Post-Impressionism of her sister, Vanessa; but perhaps also on the politically pyrotechnical aesthetics of her sisters in the suffrage movement. She brings together in her elegy the new language of Post-Impressionist colour with a new feminist language of colour. *To the Lighthouse* may undermine notions of significant form (an emotional understanding of form for form's sake), then, with a materialist feminist exploration of colour.[6] There are allegoric aspects to Woolf's 'poetical attitude',[7] I suggest, as well as emotional ones. Woolf herself notes that when she reads poetry 'the Colour Sense is first touched: roused' (*RN* 13), just as, perhaps, Mrs Ramsay reads poetry: 'words, like little shaded lights, one red, one blue, one yellow, lit up the dark of her mind.' (*TL* 183) Her novel, whatever Woolf's protestations to Fry, may be invested with a poetry of colour, one more appropriately understood in relation to the novel's elegiac discourse. I will trace its related manipulation of patriarchal chiaroscuro and feminist colour tropes. My reading takes seriously Woolf's estimate that *To the Lighthouse* is an elegy.

'But what? Elegy?'

(But while I try to write, I am making up "To the Lighthouse" – the sea is to be heard all through it. I have an idea that I will invent a new name for my books to supplant "novel". A new — by Virginia Woolf. But what? Elegy?)

(*D* III 34)

I have argued elsewhere that *To the Lighthouse* follows some conventions of pastoral elegy,[8] which here I will relate to the novel's engagement with tropes of colour, light and shade. The movement of an eclipse, as we have seen, suggests that of elegy in its transition from light to darkness to light again; and the three parts of *To the Lighthouse* echo this 'triadic'[9] movement: 'The Window', suggesting a means of natural illumination and its reception, gives an account of one day and a candle-lit and moon-lit evening in the period before the Great War; 'Time Passes' is characterized mainly by darkness; 'The Lighthouse', again suggestive of illumination, this time artificially generated rather than passively received, describes one (post-war) day leading to vision and enlightenment. As in Woolf's eclipse story, then, the source of illumination seems to undergo a transformation: from window to lighthouse, in broad terms. The 'down-pouring of immense darkness' (*TL* 195) in the middle part is a kind of eclipse since it marks the occlusion of one way of life, or one sense of subjectivity, and leads to the emergence of another. This elegiac movement may be considered in terms of gendered and contested subjectivity. If the first part presents a study of old order, pre-war, values (the promotion of marriage and children as the social norm, careers and intellectual pursuits as the public domain of men, and domestic duties as the private realm of women), then the final part shows their considerable erosion: Lily Briscoe the artist (along with others) dissents from the pre-war, marital prospectus pushed by Mrs Ramsay, the housewife, whose death in the intervening years comes to stand for the passing of those values.

That Woolf admits to having exorcised the ghosts of her parents (*D* III 208; *MB* 90) and that, somewhat conversely, her sister thanks her for having resurrected them, by writing *To the Lighthouse* (*VB* 317), has encouraged critical assessments of the novel as 'frankly biographical'[10] and a tendency to regard it only in vague terms as an elegy.[11] Because Woolf also expresses interest in formal questions about combining prose and poetry ('But can prose . . . chant elegy?'(*E* IV 436)), critics have acknowledged her references to elegy in generalized discussions about the self-reflexively lyric nature of her narrative, without attending to more specific issues of the genre (such as meaning). Peter Knox-Shaw is almost unique in providing 'an exposition of the novel's elegiac structure'[12] but he does not relate his ideas to feminism and understands the novel's sense of consolation to arise from reinstatement rather than transformation of the past.[13] This implies that the old order values of Mrs Ramsay are preserved rather than challenged by Lily Briscoe's art in the post-war part of the novel, a view I dispute.

In *To the Lighthouse* Woolf breaks new ground not only in putting a woman artist at the centre of a modernist *künstlerroman*, but also in positioning her in a, previously male-dominated, elegiac tradition.[14] In Lily's painting, and Woolf's novel, both the subject and object of the artist's gaze is feminine. This displacement raises the important factor of the 'pathetic fallacy': if nature is personified as feminine and other in this tradition,[15] how can a woman elegist's lyric celebration of self function without reinscribing her as part of the object-world? The allegoric structure is thrown into collapse, for allegory depends on the otherness of its vehicle; the vehicle cannot also be the tenor ('the thing in itself').[16] The role of photological tropes in elegy, as we have seen, also presents problems relating to gender: if the loss of solar light communicates the loss of the (always and already) masculine subject, it cannot function in the same way for the feminine (traditionally associated with darkness). But as we have seen, the photological or solar trope of elegy may be refigured for feminism. Lily Briscoe's colourist painting is to be understood as prismatic feminist elegiacs.

'The Window': 'She would move the tree'

The elegiac emblem of a storm-struck tree is circuitously achieved by Lily's elimination in her second picture of the tree at the centre of her first composition. In pastoral poetry the tree is the symbol of patronage – political and literary – and under its shade ('umbra'), pastoral figures have languished from Theocritus to the present. Pastoral tradition signifies the turn from idyll to elegy[17] (the main movement of *To the Lighthouse*) with a storm-struck tree[18] and the loss of its 'umbra':[19] the descent of darkness in 'Time Passes' echoes this motif.

But at first Lily decides to 'put the tree further in the middle' (*TL* 132): the thought returns at dinner as she is haunted by Charles Tansley's refrain 'Women can't write, women can't paint.' (*TL* 134–135) Lily's aesthetic contemplation is informed by the context of her (social and political) struggle with Tansley's chauvinism: to see this contemplation as purely an issue of significant form is to ignore this context. Under unspoken pressure from the socially ameliorative Mrs Ramsay to 'say something nice to that young man there', Lily takes refuge from these dominant gender codes in her deliberations about painting (*TL* 144, 159). Inspired by and transforming the domestic accoutrements of feminine servility (embroidered tablecloth and salt cellar), Lily mentally manipulates the figures of her painting in terms that suggest their compositional significance and their constructedness.

Yet, if Lily finds refuge from Mrs Ramsay's marital schemes in making the tree more central in her composition, the paradox of this artistic gesture is revealed when, after dinner, Mrs Ramsay herself identifies *her* ambition with the sight of a tree, leading her to conclude that 'Paul and Minta would carry it on when she was dead.' (*TL* 176) She identifies with the tree as a natural, unifying sign of an old-order status quo. She is complicit with this status quo, but her subordination to it is signalled by her association with shadow imagery. Her 'crepuscular' (*TL* 189) position is in the 'umbra' of patriarchal patronage, conceptually cast by the light of Mr Ramsay's solar intellect and power:[20] 'she could feel his mind like a raised hand shadowing her mind; and he was beginning now that her thoughts took a turn he disliked – towards this "pessimism" as he called it – to fidget.' (*TL* 189)

Ramsay's luminous mind betrays a physically violent aspect not normally associated with his cerebral reputation. This 'splendid' enlightenment mind is part of a larger canon of enlightened masculine subjectivity: 'His own little light would shine, not very brightly, for a year or two, and would then be merged in some bigger light, and that in a bigger still. (He looked into the darkness, into the intricacy of the twigs.)' (*TL* 59) Conceptually his wife is (in) his shadow: she is 'a wedge-shaped core of darkness, something invisible to others' (*TL* 99), which may be taken as the pastoral umbra as well as the umbra of a solar eclipse. The novel, then, charts the eclipse of Mr Ramsay's solar position, and the emergence of a new constellation of subjects, symbolically glimpsed by Mrs Ramsay at the close of the first part, when she sees 'the stars . . . trying to flash out from behind the edges of the leaves' (*TL* 175). Significantly, a tree blocks her view. Lily's final mark on the canvas at the novel's close is not recounted as a tree, but as 'a line there, in the centre' (*TL* 320); the tree has vanished.[21] This possible sense of a lost umbra may be interpreted in relation to the dispersal of the Ramsays' chiaroscuro by the intervening progress of Lily's Post-Impressionist colourism.

Bright violet and staring white

Lily's transformative vision is already evident in her first painting where she depicts Mrs Ramsay and son as a 'triangular purple shape'. Here, the 'wedge-shaped core of darkness' turns purple under Lily's gaze. Compare the novel's opening description of mother and son: a vignette of family values, implicitly connected (in the image of the Army and Navy catalogue and in Mrs Ramsay's ambitions for her son) with imperialism and colonialism (*TL* 11). James seems already inducted into this masculine realm, which separates him from his mother by a 'private code'; and he might almost be considered to be practising the art of pastoral in his development of a private internal language fixed on the natural and object world outside. This 'secret language' (*TL* 12) suggests a self-consciousness in the narrative: perhaps it, too, is encoded, allegorical. In this scene's deployment of colour, for example, we may discern the red, white, and blue of a Union Jack, an apt reflection of the imperialist subtext: James's eyes are 'fierce blue' and 'impeccably candid' (which may signal white), and his mother imagines 'him all red and ermine on the Bench or directing a stern and momentous enterprise in some crisis of public affairs.' (*TL* 12)

Lily erects her easel in a space vulnerable to intrusion: she dreads the overbearing presence of Mr Ramsay who 'almost knocked her easel over, coming down upon her with his hands waving.' (*TL* 32) Attempting to produce her art in a space defined and contested by male presence and opinion, Lily finds

William Bankes's presence more tolerable, however, in spite of Mrs Ramsay's matchmaking designs. But nevertheless he does force her to take 'her eyes off her picture'.

> The jacmanna was bright violet; the wall was staring white. She would not have considered it honest to tamper with the bright violet and staring white, since she saw them like that, fashionable though it was, since Mr Paunceforte's visit, to see everything pale, elegant, semi-transparent. Then beneath the colour there was the shape. She could see it all so clearly, so commandingly, when she looked: it was when she took her brush in her hand that the whole thing changed. It was in that moment's flight between the picture and her canvas that the demons set on her who often brought her to the edge of tears and made this passage from conception to work as dreadful as any down a dark passage for a child. Such she often felt herself – struggling against terrific odds to maintain her courage; to say: "But this is what I see; this is what I see", and so to clasp some miserable remnant of her vision to her breast, which a thousand forces did their best to pluck from her.
>
> (*TL* 34)

Lily's vision arises from a process of artistic tension, echoing that of childbirth (suggested by 'conception' and the reference to the child's dark passage; there is also the sense of suckling in Lily's vision being clasped to the breast); and this figures as a move from women's traditional function of creativity (childbearing) to the new possibility (some might argue, substitute) of her artistic creativity. Lily's desire to remain 'honest', furthermore, may suggest something other than a desire for naturalism.

Her struggle for self-expression in male dominated environs coincides with her vision of 'bright violet' and 'staring white'. These colours seem to defy the masculine presences overshadowing her work, and may even offer a glimpse of suffrage colours. The moment might be taken, then, as a metaphor for the woman artist's politically contested position. Lily's prismatics stand as an alternative to the patriarchal chiaroscuro threatening to engulf her: caught in the conflict of emotional and social subordination and self-doubt (*TL* 35), she puts down her brushes to go with Bankes. As she does so the colours seem to recede:

> "It suddenly gets cold. The sun seems to give less heat," she said, looking about her, for it was bright enough, the grass still a soft deep green, the house starred in its greenery with purple passion flowers, and rooks dropping cool cries from the high blue. But something moved, flashed, turned a silver wing in the air. It was September after all . . . and past six in the evening.
>
> (*TL* 35)

The range of colours here suggest a Post-Impressionist mosaic of oppositional planes; yet at the same time we may chart in them a movement away from the flickering glimpse of green and purple to the dark omen of the rooks. The unnamed bird, apparently on the wing in September, may be a house martin or swallow, its silver glint almost supplying the white of the suffrage tricolour to go with the purple and green. With or without a feminist subtext, however, this passage brings a sense of cooling off, auguring the onset of the evening, of the winter, and of the war and devastation to come. The colours may thus also be interpreted as part of the novel's elegiac vocabulary.

Compare Tansley's earlier view of Mrs Ramsay 'against a picture of Queen Victoria wearing the blue ribbon of the Garter'; she has 'stars in her eyes and veils in her hair, with cyclamen and wild violets'. (*TL* 27) Lily offers a transfiguration of this patriarchal image. She departs from the Victorian Pre-Raphaelite version of ethereal femininity that Mrs Ramsay seems to present to Tansley.

Green shawl and purple shadow

We find another cluster of prismatic (and potentially feminist) colours when Mrs Ramsay notes Lily's 'white puckered . . . face' (*TL* 45); next she flings a 'green Cashmere shawl over the edge of a picture frame' as she measures up her knitting against James's leg (its colour not stated here) (*TL* 47); then purple appears: 'as, after a flight through sunshine the wings of a bird fold themselves quietly and the blue of its plumage changes from bright steel to soft purple. [Mrs Ramsay] had stood there silent for there was nothing to be said. He had cancer of the throat.' (*TL* 48) The man's cancer seems to stop her voice, as if she normally spoke with his (a mouthpiece for patriarchy). Yet into this verbal silence Woolf introduces a visual message in the language of oppositional colour, which both registers a change to the darker in emotional tone, but which may also signal a reference to feminist colours: from 'sunshine' to 'soft purple' may both chart a movement from light to dark, and from masculine 'solar' light to feminist colour. Again this double signification suggests both Mrs Ramsay's complicity with patriarchy and her potential to overthrow it.

Out of this contradictory state, a resolution may arise, perhaps glimpsed at the section's closing vignette. In this classical mother-and-son composition, sanctioned by the presence of an 'authenticated master-piece by Michael Angelo', Mrs Ramsay, 'knitting her reddish-brown hairy stocking' (*TL* 51),[22] is occupied in an act of Victorian 'philanthropy . . . requiring clothing'. But the presence of 'the green shawl which she had tossed over the edge of the frame' (*TL* 51), breaking its gilt line, seems silently to hint at alternative possibilities somewhere between art and life. The liberational potential, however, is far from realized by Mrs Ramsay herself, who later takes the 'green shawl off the picture frame' to go to her husband ('for he wished, she knew, to protect her') and she wears it while smoothing over a difference with him (*TL* 104). Lily notices her wearing the shawl when she catches sight of the Ramsays 'in the dusk standing, looking, the symbols of marriage, husband and wife.' (*TL* 115)

Mrs Ramsay again makes use of the shawl as a means of familial amelioration when she wraps it around the skull in her children's bedroom: 'She could see the horns, Cam said, all over the room. It was true. Wherever they put the light (and James could not sleep without a light) there was always a shadow somewhere.' (*TL* 176–177) Mrs Ramsay's daughter cannot sleep with the skull in the room, casting shadows; her son wants the light on and the skull where it is. Mrs Ramsay's solution bears the seeds of social and artistic progressiveness. Her green shawl imposes a Post-Impressionist colourist solution to the play of light and dark of skeletal structure. This may also be a proto-feminist act: the chiaroscuro which keeps women in the shadow of masculine light has perhaps been obliterated by a green cover potentially suggestive of a suffrage banner. Significantly the shawl remains there (albeit somewhat tattered) during the dark interlude of 'Time Passes'.

Mrs Ramsay emerges from these contradictory moments both as a shadow to the light of patriarchy, and as a potential source of counter-illumination. On the one hand, as 'a wedge of darkness' (*TL* 100) she finds her thoughts photologically shaped by the Lighthouse beam (*TL* 101); but on the other, she, herself, is a 'column of spray . . . burning and illuminating'. (*TL* 62) Lily, furthermore, finds, in Mrs Ramsay, a secret message, accessible in close bodily proximity (*TL* 82). It is 'nothing that could be written in any language known to men'. (*TL* 83)

This meditation on a secret unifying language between women comes just before Lily's discussion of her picture with Bankes, who asks: 'What did she wish to indicate by the triangular purple shape just there?' In replying Lily explains nothing about her secret woman's language, but, instead, resorts to compositional terms; nor does she offer a colourist explanation. Instead she refers to the need for a sort of chiaroscuro:

> It was Mrs Ramsay reading to James, she said. She knew his objection –
> that no one could tell it for a human shape. But she had made no attempt at
> likeness, she said. For what reason had she introduced them then? he asked.
> Why indeed? – except that if there, in that corner, it was bright, here, in
> this, she felt the need of darkness. Simple, obvious, commonplace, as it
> was, Mr Bankes was interested. Mother and child then – objects of universal
> veneration, and in this case the mother was famous for her beauty – might
> be reduced, he pondered, to a purple shadow without irreverence.
>
> (*TL* 84–85)

The suggestion of balancing brightness and darkness encourages Lily to call the purple triangle a purple shadow;[23] and in her further elaboration to Bankes it becomes a colourless shadow: 'A light here required a shadow there.' (*TL* 85) Lily's respect for the logical representation of light and shade in accordance with nature, is in keeping with Impressionist plein-air techniques; but her departure from the concept of direct depiction of her subject matter suggests the Post-Impressionist abstractive technique of dreaming before nature (the purple triangle). Yet, in talking to a *man* about this, Lily seems to move from a colourist explanation towards one based on chiaroscuro. The colour purple retreats further into shadow, the longer the discussion continues; and Lily, furthermore, rather as Woolf herself writes to Fry, explains to her male audience the 'question' of 'relations of masses, of lights and shadows' in terms of significant form, 'subduing' in the process, 'all her impressions *as a woman* to something much more general.' (*TL* 86; my italics) Lily, avoiding the authorial error of thinking of her sex, hides her considerations of intimacy with Mrs Ramsay (and all it implies for a feminist aesthetics), then, in a discussion which draws on both significant form and a sense of androgyny.

Ironically the section closes with Lily's gratitude to the Ramsays for a small social miracle: 'This *man* had shared with her something profoundly intimate.' (*TL* 86; my italics) Here she seems to come close to succumbing to Mrs Ramsay's match-making, but it is the exchange about art she has enjoyed; and her response masks a desire for a rather different intimacy. This man also appears to have stopped Lily painting, for she abandons her work and shuts her paint-box (*TL* 87). Lily is not actually seen to paint again until the novel's final part. But colour is important in the story that Mrs Ramsay earlier in the day reads to her son.

'A shadow was on the page'

Mrs Ramsay reads 'The Fisherman and His Wife' from *Grimm's Household Tales*[24] (Andrew Lang's introduction to which includes criticism of Max Müller's 'Solar method' of interpretation).[25] This 'parable of egotism'[26] charts the increasing opacity of the sea, as the fisherman repeatedly returns to ask an enchanted flounder to grant the wishes of his insatiably acquisitive wife. Significantly, Mrs Ramsay, dutifully feeling herself inferior to her husband ('she did not like, even for a second, to feel finer than her husband' (*TL* 65)), and aware of Augustus Carmichael, himself a victim of uxorial excess (*TL* 66–67), notices his 'shadow was on the page' (*TL* 66).

At first the fisherman finds the sea 'all green and yellow, and no longer so smooth';[27] but it turns dark grey when his wife decides if he 'won't be King, I will' (*TL* 90). After Emperor and Pope, the wife finally wants to be God, the ultimate sovereign. The woman's desire for the highest subjectivity results in both man and wife being rudely returned to their humble origins where, as Mrs Ramsay tells James, 'they are living still at this very time.' (*TL* 98) The raging 'pitch black' sea of the story (*TL* 97) prefigures the dark storm at the centre of *To the Lighthouse*, and echoes the movement of elegiac eclipse. In the story, however, the rise of woman's subjectivity, associated with augmenting colour and then blackness, causes the eclipse of her own sovereignty, and a patriarchal status quo seems to be restored at its end (although both husband and wife suffer penury). It serves as a warning against uxorial ambition, and implicitly recommends the containment of feminine desire. This is not the outcome of *To the Lighthouse* but Woolf's novel does seem to rework the story for feminism; its colour deployment feeds into Woolf's gendered allegoric vocabulary. The story's function as part of patriarchal enlightenment seems confirmed by 'the light of the Lighthouse' appearing in James's eyes as 'the interest of the story died away in them' (*TL* 98); but its colours continue to resonate with feminist potential.

'The Window' closes with the chiaroscuro vision of the Ramsays, the wife in the shadow of her husband, triumphantly submitting to his will, murmuring an appropriate line from a Shakespearean sonnet: 'As with your shadow I with these did play.' (*TL* 187)[28] If Mrs Ramsay's shadowy image in this first part may be seen as a quiescent pastoral 'umbra' – a shaded space of patriarchal patronage under which she languishes and around which Lily, less happily, hovers – then the 'downpouring of immense darkness' of the middle part may be seen as the augmenting of this subdued shadow into the more devastating umbra of an eclipse. As we have noted, it is possible to see the storm/eclipse as a means of reaffirming and reinvigorating the status quo, in which case we might read the third part of *To the Lighthouse* as a reinstatement of the values of the first.[29] But as the transformational movement of elegy allows, and Woolf's feminist refiguration of the eclipse has shown, the passage from darkness into new light may mark a transition to new values.

'Time Passes': 'So with the lamps all put out'

In 'Time Passes', a gender-based transition is effected in a figure of enlightenment (or photological trope): it begins with the extinguishing of lights in the pre-war house,[30] the last light belonging to the poet Mr Carmichael 'who liked to lie awake a little reading Virgil, [and who] kept his candle burning rather longer than the rest' (*TL* 195); and it ends with Lily's waking in a new dawn light. Enlightenment has transferred from masculine experience to feminine.

For this to occur, as in 'The Sun and the Fish', the relationship and gendering of traditional subject-object oppositions undergo considerable change ('Not only was furniture confounded; there was scarcely anything left of body or mind by which one could say "This is he" or "This is she." ' (*TL* 196)). The turning point in this process comes, I suggest, at the end of section six where we learn that 'the mirror was broken' and, in parenthesis, that Mr Carmichael 'brought out a volume of poems in the spring'. (*TL* 208) This marks a moment of rupture and recovery after which appears, in tandem with the restorative work of Mrs McNab and fellow workers, a difference in gender relations discernible in Woolf's tropes of light, shade and colour:

> With the sunset sharpness was lost . . . loosely the world shook itself down to sleep, darkly here without a light to it, save what came green suffused through leaves, or pale on the white flowers by the window.
> [Lily Briscoe had her bag carried up to the house late one evening in September. Mr Carmichael came by the same train.]
>
> (*TL* 219)

The colours of green and white illuminate the darkness heralding Lily's arrival: they communicate the pastoral message of renewal as well as flash two suffrage colours. Purple, the remaining suffrage colour, shines in the next and final section of 'Time Passes':

> Through the open window the voice of the beauty of the world came murmuring . . . entreating the sleepers . . . if they would not actually come down to the beach itself at least to lift the blind and look out. They would see then night flowing down in purple; his head crowned; his sceptre jewelled; and how in his eyes a child might look.
>
> (*TL* 219–220)

Instead of the individual seeking reflection in the natural world, as before (and 'Time Passes' has shown the disintegration of that relationship) (*TL* 199), the world itself now seems to beckon people; instead of 'the mystic, the visionary' looking to beach and ocean as mirror (*TL* 203–204), they are to look to the night sky. Darkness, unlike earlier manifestations, is now masculine, majestic and benign. The gender of subjectivity seems to have become unfixed in this image: not only has darkness become masculine, but its purple dress is both a sign of old-order male sovereignty (part of a king's regalia) as well as of new feminist subjectivity. This may mark, not the endless deferral of the signification of subjectivity, but a point of transition from a model of exclusively masculine subjectivity to a collective one inclusive of the feminine. The darkness does not engulf or obliterate differences and individuals as in the much cited opening passages of 'Time Passes' (*TL* 196), so much as tenderly embrace them;

but there is a sinister aspect to the 'curtains of dark wrapp[ing] themselves over the house', suggesting that to 'acquiesce and resign' would be to give up the struggle too early, and it is against its comforting 'folds' that the sun (whose gender is thrown into question by the night's apparent masculinity) rouses Lily from the precipice of sleep: 'the sun lifted the curtains, broke the veil on their eyes, and Lily Briscoe stirring in her sleep clutched at her blankets as a faller clutches at the turf on the edge of a cliff. Her eyes opened wide. Here she was again, she thought, sitting bolt upright in bed. Awake.' (*TL* 220–21) 'Time Passes' ends with the rousing to consciousness of a woman artist in an object world that has been refigured and regendered. It has moved from the chiaroscuro of Mr and Mrs Ramsay to the collectively informed prismatics of Lily Briscoe, explored in the final part of the novel.

'The Lighthouse': silent resistance

'The Lighthouse' examines the novel's central masculine subject now deprived of his feminine foil: Ramsay's enlightenment mind has lost its uxorial shadow, and it becomes a collective effort on the part of his children and guests to resist his demands for sympathy (and a replacement). By the close, he himself has become part of a new configuration of plural subjectivity: Mrs Ramsay's shadow is overcome by Lily's Post-Impressionist colours; his notion of the ever-expanding solar ball of masculine enlightenment (*TL* 59) is challenged by her less apocalyptic understanding of enlightenment as interstellar: 'little daily miracles, illuminations, matches struck unexpectedly in the dark.' (*TL* 249)

The arrival at the Lighthouse of Mr Ramsay, Cam, James, and the Macalisters, coincides with Lily's completion (in Carmichael's presence) of her painting recording the loss of Mrs Ramsay and the assertion of her own artistic subjectivity. Cam's presence on this voyage is significant. Feminine participation was barred from the earlier expedition; in this sense, at least, the voyage is not the exact fulfilment of the aspirations in the first part. Similarly, although in some ways a completion of the one she started in the first part of the novel (*TL* 228), Lily's painting is a new one (*TL* 231, 243–44). As in the first case, however, she constructs her art in a position threatened by male presence; and in seeing her canvas as a means 'to ward off Mr Ramsay' (*TL* 231), Lily may be again practising a feminist aesthetics: 'A woman, she had provoked this horror; a woman, she should have known how to deal with it. It was immensely to her discredit, sexually, to stand there dumb. . . . In complete silence she stood there, grasping her paint brush.' (*TL* 236) The contrast between Lily's silent resistance to Mr Ramsay's implicit demands for sympathy and the compliant response she imagines would be made by Mrs Beckwith, 'that kind old lady who sketched' (*TL* 236), suggests Woolf's distinction between the submissive art of the Victorian aunt and the defiantly silent art of 'Mrs Bell'. Indeed the feminist import of the woman artist's verbal silence is underlined by Lily's refusal to console Mr Ramsay – and perhaps also her refusal of sexual advances implicit in the analogy of 'draw[ing] her skirts a little closer round her ankles' (*TL* 236) – while she clutches her brush, the instrument that renders her articulate in the realm of paint. (Cam and James also use silence against Mr Ramsay's 'tyranny' (*TL* 252).) Yet, as a 'skimpy old maid, holding a paintbrush on the lawn' (*TL* 278) she may appear a transitional and composite figure made out of Victorian aunt and defiant feminist.

Lily appears to reject Ramsay in order to focus, as she paints, on the memory of his wife, especially her silent moment of intimacy: 'The moment at least seemed extraordinarily fertile. She rammed a little hole in the sand and covered it up, by way of burying in it the perfection of the moment. It was like a drop of silver in which one dipped and illumined the darkness of the past.' (*TL* 265) The hole suggests both feminine sexuality ('intimacy' and 'fertile' contributing to this) and vocality – a mouth to be silently enjoyed and silenced. Mrs Ramsay points to a physical realm beyond the verbal where intimate communication is possible.

'Green paint on her brush'

But Lily also entertains blasphemous sentiments about Mrs Ramsay. 'Squeezing her tube of green paint' (*TL* 266), she imagines the triumphant pleasure in informing Mrs Ramsay of the Rayleys' failed marriage. The green paint has become invested with the fantasy of overcoming Mrs Ramsay.[31] Its possible suffrage significance makes the colour green appropriate as a mark of defiance against this arch propagandist for marriage, although as a sign also of fertility it remains ambiguously linked with Mrs Ramsay's shawl. This ambiguity is reflected in the fact that the feminist Lily 'had only escaped by the skin of her teeth' (*TL* 271) Mrs Ramsay's 'mania . . . for marriage' (*TL* 270).[32] But Lily, brandishing her green paint, celebrates the passing of Mrs Ramsay: 'We can over-ride her wishes, improve away her limited, old-fashioned ideas.' (*TL* 269) Suggesting a political consequence to her aesthetic practice,[33] Lily recalls her earlier exultant resolution to 'move the tree to the middle, and need never marry anybody': 'She had felt, now she could stand up to Mrs Ramsay – a tribute to the astonishing power that Mrs Ramsay had over one. Do this, she said, and one did it. Even her shadow at the window with James was full of authority.' (*TL* 271) Here Lily realizes in artistic terms that Mrs Ramsay, oppressed and overshadowed by patriarchy, nevertheless, perpetuates its values: her 'Do this' is a repetition of her husband's 'Do this' recalled by Cam; and Lily seems to paint to defy this (*TL* 262). Her pre-war tactic to centre the tree seems impossible now, for she discovers 'the whole wave and whisper of the garden became like curves and arabesques flourishing round a centre of complete emptiness.' (*TL* 275) The compositional gap left by the departed Mrs Ramsay – 'the empty drawing-room steps' (*TL* 275) – suggests the loss of a pastoral umbra: 'Was there no safety? . . . No guide, no shelter, but all was miracle, and leaping from the pinnacle of a tower into the air?' (*TL* 277). The overwhelming desire to fill the space forces Lily to break her turbulent silence with a tearful invocation of Mrs Ramsay (*TL* 277–278) – a gesture at odds with her desire to overcome the woman.

The parenthetical account of the mutilation of fish, interrupting her cry (yet possibly simultaneous with it), is a complex reflection on Lily's artistic dilemma: '[Macalister's boy took one of the fish and cut a square out of its side to bait his hook with. The mutilated body (it was still alive) was thrown back into the sea.]' (*TL* 277–78) The boy's cutting of the fish may represent the artist's act of creation: cutting out a square of nature and framing it – the square brackets themselves acting as frame. Suggestive of a literalist 'slice-of-life' naturalism, however, it does not fit with Lily's 'tunnelling' method. Perhaps this mutilated fish constitutes a grotesque reworking of the 'flounder' in the story Mrs Ramsay earlier read to her son. But Mrs Ramsay may be a fish that Lily herself also wants, partially, to retrieve and (less brutally) transform.

Lily's recurrent memory of Mrs Ramsay 'raising to her forehead a wreath of white flowers' and 'stepping . . . across fields among whose folds, purplish and soft, among whose flowers, hyacinths or lilies, she vanished' (*TL* 278, 279), links her with purple and white flowers suggestive of elegy[34] and of suffrage; but she also recalls her as 'going unquestioningly with her companion, a shadow, across the fields.' (*TL* 279) Mrs Ramsay is no longer seen a shadow but obliviously accompanies one: as if a colourist version of the woman is haunted by a shadow version, the former positive, the latter negative. These are the two versions of Mrs Ramsay we earlier saw disappearing and emerging in the discussion between Lily and Bankes, where she is first referred to as a 'triangular purple shape' and, eventually, reduced to merely 'a shadow' (*TL* 84–85).

Green light and purple foot

The narrative focus switches to Cam's 'green thought in a green shade':[35] 'her mind made the green swirls' and 'wandered in imagination in that underworld of waters where the pearls stuck in clusters to white sprays, where in the green light a change came over one's entire mind and one's body shone half transparent enveloped in a green cloak.' (*TL* 281) Linked with Lily's paint, the green light and green cloak also connect Cam's thoughts to her mother's green shawl over the skull, and suggest a bodily, material source of colour.

James, meanwhile, imagines his father as a wheel running over a 'foot, purple, crushed' (*TL* 284), and its colour corresponds with Mrs Ramsay's purple shadow (and Mr Tansley's 'purple book' (*TL* 247)); but James only obliquely refers to his mother as the victim, and his father now rides 'over his foot, over Cam's foot, over anybody's foot. One sat and watched it.' (*TL* 285) James is here both victim of 'paternal tyranny'[36] and a bystander, identifying the oppressed in the patriarchal quest for enlightenment (Mr Ramsay's mission to the Lighthouse) as both male and female: purple becomes associated with both sexes. James is aligned with his mother in being shadowed by Ramsay: 'Something, he remembered, stayed and darkened over him.' (*TL* 285) He remembers his father's words falling 'like a blade, a scimitar, smiting through the leaves and flowers even of the happy world and making them shrivel and fall.' This suggests an elegiac moment: it recalls Ramsay's earlier verbal 'pelt of jagged hail' (*TL* 54) and the 'drench of hail' sent in 'Time Passes' (*TL* 199), as a deliberate act of divine spite.[37]

That enlightenment is a masculine province is suggested by James's memory of the Lighthouse as 'a silvery, misty-looking tower with a yellow eye that opened suddenly and softly in the evening' (*TL* 286): its yellow eye, like the dominant yellow veiling James's thoughts of the past (*TL* 285), may be taken as a sign of masculine subjectivity.[38] But now he has a new perspective: 'He could see the white-washed rocks; the tower, stark and straight; he could see it was barred with black and white' (*TL* 286). James's discovery that 'nothing was simply one thing' (*TL* 286), then, shows two versions of this figure of enlightenment: one yellow-eyed, suggesting his father's oppression of his mother (later, Mr Ramsay reads a book of 'yellowish pages' (*TL* 292)); the other black and white, perhaps indicative of James's countering of paternal tyranny, a challenge, which, if successful, might merely replicate it.

Sinking ship and wave of white

Lily's parenthetical observation on 'the sea without a stain on it' (*TL* 289), suggests a return to clear waters, as in the Grimms story. The sea seems to have 'swallowed up' the father-and-son struggle going on in the boat (*TL* 289). As if picking up on this, Cam tells herself 'a story of adventure about escaping from a sinking ship.' (*TL* 289) Her pleasure in this change is characterized in terms of chiaroscuro: 'And the drops falling from this sudden and unthinking fountain of joy fell here and there on the dark, the slumbrous shapes in her mind; shapes of a world not realised but turning in their darkness, catching here and there, a spark of light; Greece, Rome, Constantinople.' (*TL* 290) Cam's understanding of the dormant dark shapes in her mind, linked in the novel's lexis to Mrs Ramsay, seems to come both from the fountain and from the spark of light; 'turning in their darkness' suggests their transformation, as if they will slip the bonds of darkness. But the passage also implies that the darkness itself results from, as well as is illuminated by, the light of successive (patriarchal) empires. This poignant moment of a woman's self-realization rests on the paradox of her 'little island' of enlightenment emanating from the very system that also oppresses the feminine as darkness – 'it had, she supposed, a place in the universe.' (*TL* 290) This is confirmed by Cam's thoughts on her father in his study (*TL* 290), for her a haven of learning; and she comes to see him as 'most wise; he was not vain nor a tyrant'. (*TL* 291) Cam is not necessarily yielding to her father's tyranny but assessing his enlightenment tradition for her own ends and position. Her admiration for this tradition is mixed with indications of its decline. As she goes on 'telling herself about escaping from a sinking ship' (*TL* 293), we might recall the capsizing light of the eclipse, and the potential for feminist emergence from this dying patriarchy.

If the sea 'swallow[s] up' something of the patriarchy from the land, then the shore seems to have a gift from the sea in the shape of Mr Carmichael who is 'puffing and blowing like some sea monster'. (*TL* 294) He presides over Lily's meditations as she feels herself 'standing up to the lips' in 'unfathomably deep' waters into which (like the 'amusing game') 'had spilled so many lives. The Ramsays'; the children's; and all sorts of waifs and strays of things besides. A washerwoman with her basket; a rook; a red-hot poker; the purples and grey-greens of flowers: some common feeling held the whole together.' (*TL* 295) Lily's aquatic sense of commonality (intersubjectivity, perhaps) brings a prismatic alternative to Cam's earlier thoughts in chiaroscuro. But this new formation is reflected in the now 'unsatisfactory' positions of the boats in the bay: 'The disproportion there seemed to upset some harmony in her own mind . . . she could not achieve that razor edge of balance between two opposite forces; Mr Ramsay and the picture; which was necessary.' (*TL* 296)

Lily is no longer painting in the same social and political space, a space contested by Ramsay's patriarchy. In this new configuration, Mr Carmichael, poet and sea-monster, seems a transformed Pythian creature. He does not threaten, but seems, muse-like, to assist Lily's progress: her picture must come, not from opposition to Ramsay, but from her new sense of collectivity. She must also reconsider the object of her gaze: 'something . . . evaded her when she thought of Mrs Ramsay. . . . But what she wished to get hold of was that very jar on the nerves, the thing itself before it has been made anything.' (*TL* 297) To get back in touch with her object, Lily begins to reflect on Carmichael's dislike of

Mrs Ramsay (*TL* 299). Significantly, she defines her special silent affinity with him as 'the slopes of a hill running purple down into the distant heather. She knew him in that way.' (*TL* 299) Purple is now linked to Carmichael as well as Mrs Ramsay. Interestingly, Lily, possibly introducing the figure of Procne, characterizes Mrs Ramsay's philanthropy (despised by Carmichael (*TL* 300)) as solar: 'like the swallows for the south, the artichokes for the sun' (*TL* 301).

In painting, she also overcomes Tansley's negative influence: 'There he was, lean and red and raucous, preaching love from a platform (there were ants crawling about among the plantains which she disturbed with her brush – red, energetic ants, rather like Charles Tansley).' (*TL* 302) Lily's intrusion of her brush is not an act of destruction but of disruption – she seeks to transform with the feminine Tansley's political world, force it to address what has been excluded. And it is a social, multi-subjective view of Mrs Ramsay that she comes to desire: 'Fifty pairs of eyes were not enough to get round that one woman with.' (*TL* 303)

Recalling Mrs Ramsay 'knitting, talking, sitting silent in the window alone' (*TL* 303), actions which suggest a silent, artistic code, she focuses on the passionate conflict of the marriage which 'tired' and 'cowed' Mrs Ramsay (*TL* 306), but brings out the sinister irony of Mrs Ramsay's preparing her daughter, Prue, for 'that same happiness' (*TL* 308). Prue's sacrifice to such ambitions, is recalled in the imagery of 'valleys, white, flower-strewn' (*TL* 309), and, when Lily suddenly finds Mrs Ramsay restored to her, white dominates the palette: somebody causes the window to whiten and throw 'an odd-shaped triangular shadow over the step' which 'altered the composition of the picture a little'. (*TL* 309) And with a 'wave of white' returns 'the old horror' of desire for Mrs Ramsay: 'Mrs Ramsay . . . knitted her reddish-brown stocking, cast her shadow on the step. There she sat.' (*TL* 310)

This imagery may be read in terms both of significant form and of feminist iconographic colourism. On the one hand, Lily's emotional response to Mrs Ramsay is translated into the formal democracy of 'ordinary experience . . . on a level with the chair, with the table' (*TL* 310); and the white and shadow, bereft of social significance, are co-opted to compositional demands to create significant form. On the other hand, Mrs Ramsay *as Mrs Ramsay* is the central focus of Lily's picture, the feminine object of a feminine gaze. Even her shadow has a political, as much as formal, significance, as we have seen, and here it may be read as a sign of her oppression. But 'cast' may suggest both the forming and the discarding of this shadow; and the fact that Mrs Ramsay is described as actively casting her own shadow, points both to her complicity in patriarchy and to her possible rejection of it. The simultaneous presence and absence of shadow, then, marks a point between chiaroscuro and colourism, the threshold of public and private feminist aesthetics. The image changes with context.

Tantalizingly, we are not told whether Lily actually paints in a purple triangle: is it implicitly there, or no longer necessary? The predominant white, now associated with Mrs Ramsay, unites in its wave a past, tragic image of feminine creativity (the daughter lost in childbirth) and a new more hopeful one (the woman artist about to find a new social sense of self).

Sun and shipwreck: green and blues

Lily, having reached this new compositional threshold, now wants to include Mr Ramsay, 'as if she had something she must share', rather than resist him (*TL* 310). Similarly, the 'glaring white and black' of the male province of the Lighthouse includes, in the next section, a sign of feminine/feminist presence: 'a dab of white' on one of the windows 'and a little tuft of green on the rock' (*TL* 311). This green tuft may correspond to Cam's (green-linked) presence on the journey to the Lighthouse: unlike the mistaken 'old ladies . . . at home' scoffed at by James, she is there to see the Lighthouse, close up (*TL* 312).

Significantly, it is Mr Ramsay, saying ' "Come now" ' and 'shutting his book', who rouses Cam to the possibilities of 'fresh woods, and pastures new':[39] 'Come where? To what extraordinary adventure? She woke with a start.' (*TL* 313) Echoing the sun's role in awakening Lily, his rousing of Cam may suggest the contribution of (previously masculine) enlightenment traditions to the process of women's emancipation. Observing that 'it seemed as if they were doing two things at once', Cam indicates the transformative powers of this solar influence as well as its very transformation: 'they were eating their lunch here in the sun and they were also making for safety in a great storm after a shipwreck'. (*TL* 314) The mundane and the imagined co-exist in the same moment: Cam experiences the patriarchal sunshine at the same time as she is caught up in the aftermath of its demise.

Looking at her father, while the water 'became greener', Cam sees the island as a 'dwindled leaf-like' and 'frail blue shape' (*TL* 317), and this sense of delicate fragility of colour anticipates the moment revealing non-transcendence in 'The Sun and the Fish'. Just as, there, the refiguring of masculine solar subjectivity opens up a space into which a plural and prismatic subjectivity intrudes, so, here, Mr Ramsay's last recorded moment in this solar journey opens the way for a new subjectivity: 'He rose . . . for all the world, James thought, as if he were saying, "There is no God," and Cam thought, as if he were leaping into space, and they both rose to follow him as he sprang, lightly like a young man, holding his parcel, on to the rock.' (*TL* 318) At the Lighthouse, the idea of a transcendent, masculine, solar subject (God) is put in question, and the space filled by contesting and interconnecting subjects, masculine and feminine. Mr

Ramsay seems to show the way towards a materialist understanding of this moment of enlightenment by his grip on the parcel containing supplies for the Lighthouse men ('grossly material things', perhaps (*AROO* 63)) and his connection with the solid rock.

The final switch back to Lily and Carmichael shows the emergence of colour-based enlightenment rather than chiaroscuro. In a moment of elegiac consolation, Lily imagines Carmichael, in the guise of an old pagan god, 'crowned the occasion': 'when his hand slowly fell, as if she had seen him let fall from his great height a wreath of violets and asphodels which, fluttering slowly, lay at length upon the earth.' (*TL* 319) The falling hand echoes Mr Ramsay's in the boat – 'He only raised his right hand mysteriously high in the air, and let it fall upon his knee again as if he were conducting some secret symphony' (*TL* 288) – and marks a moment of relinquishment: a man's hand, previously seen to cast a shadow on the mind of Mrs Ramsay, now gives way to the earth's taking on colour.

At the centre of Lily's picture is recounted no tree, nor purple shadow, but instead, 'all its green and blues, its lines running up and across, its attempt at something.' We are not told the colour into which she has dipped her brush when, 'with a sudden intensity, as if she saw it clear for a second, she drew a line there, in the centre. It was done; it was finished. Yes, she thought, laying down her brush in extreme fatigue, I have had my vision.' (*TL* 319–320) The line suggests the feminist reclamation of the first person.[40] Lily's first person is a colourist illumination of the feminine umbra behind the masculine solar subject. As such it contests and transforms this understanding of subjectivity with a feminist and collective model. Just as the momentary intrusion of suffrage colours at the eclipse of masculine solar subjectivity, heralds the return of a wider spectrum of colour, so, too, we have seen in *To the Lighthouse* a feminist intervention in a narrative of subjectivity which moves from the chiaroscuro of the Ramsays to the feminist prismatics of Lily Briscoe.

14 *The Waves*: purple buttons and white foam

Whereas *To the Lighthouse* closes in a burst of triumphant feminist prismatics, *The Waves*, which Woolf first issued in purple boards beneath a Vanessa Bell dust-wrapper, may be understood more sombrely as an elegy on their demise.[1] In this solar elegy, feminist colours may console, but they do not conquer. The 1930s saw a period of feminist reflection on women's gains in political and civil rights, poignantly registered in a context of economic decline.[2] 'For English women, [this period] provided no great political opportunity. . . . Feminists were unable to participate in a drive for fresh legislation that would benefit their sex. Campaigns still continued and feminist associations survived, but politicians beset by domestic and foreign challenges did not hesitate to downgrade women's issues.'[3] Woolf, too, was taking stock of her own past involvement in 'the cause'. My reading partly draws on an essay, imbued in feminist prismatics, written during the composition of *The Waves* (D III 304, 307): 'Memories of a Working Women's Guild'.[4]

Following feminist views of *The Waves*, I will focus on Rhoda as a counterpoint to Bernard whose final, dominant expression is considered to suppress hers. Whereas all three male speakers develop openly literary ambitions, taking themselves seriously as writers, authors in the world (*W* 89, 102), the women function at a different level of self-knowledge and social expectation, perhaps experiencing 'more fundamentally threatening' crises.[5] Susan and Jinny are rural and urban versions of women subordinated to the male order. Rhoda does not fit, yet, nor does she fight for her place. Rhoda is not an active or perhaps even conscious feminist: she does not successfully intervene in the material world but more and more retreats from its indifference. Her visions, informed by feminist prismatics, are spaces from which a feminism may arise but they become increasingly remote, abstract and enclosed.

To talk of 'separate people' in *The Waves* is perhaps to miss the point: 'The six characters were supposed to be one. I'm getting old myself . . . and I come to feel more and more how difficult it is to collect oneself into one Virginia.' (*L* IV 397) Woolf puts forward a sense of contested subjectivity, suggesting perhaps the Absolute Subject ('one Virginia') may never fully interpellate the self, which appears a site rather of perpetually conflicting interpellation. This is relevant to understanding the novel's alternation between soliloquies and interludes. For some critics, Bernard is author of the interludes,[6] for others, each character echoes phrases from them;[7] but although Bernard does come to dominate, he does not, nor does any other individual speaker, recount every-thing that occurs in these 'prose poems'.[8] The interludes are not 'objective' phenomenological accounts of the natural world, but pastorals over whose interpretation the various voices vie (including the reader's).[9] They tell many stories, identifiable both with individual soliloquies and beyond; they do not merely confirm the bleak vision of Bernard's final dominion. The reader, then, engages in a process of interpreting the interludes, both separately, and in rela-tion to the soliloquies. I do not propose one set way of reading, accounting for every element, but after discussing the solar and colour tropes in the broad shape of the interludes and Bernard's final eclipse imagery, I will explore the novel by following one strand: Rhoda's visions. My reading traces close tex-tual connections with classical mythology, Romantic poetry as well as Woolf's Women's Guild essay. But first, let us consider the novel's feminist allegoric potential.

'Some semi mystic very profound life of a woman'

> Yet I am now & then haunted by some semi mystic very profound life
> of a woman, which shall be told on one occasion; & time shall be utterly
> obliterated; future shall somehow blossom out of the past. One incident
> – say the fall of a flower – might contain it.
>
> (*D* III 118)

Woolf's early glimpse of *The Waves* is intriguing, for it seems to bear little resemblance to the novel published five years later. If this work originates in a vision of a woman's life (*D* III 114, 128) encapsulated in a momentary incident somehow outside history, by 1931 it almost ends in historical specificity, as an elegiac tribute to Woolf's brother, Thoby. Resisting this temptation, Woolf focuses on symbolic technique and 'the freedom & boldness with which my imagination picked up used & tossed aside all the images & symbols' which she used 'not in set pieces . . . but simply as images; never making them work out; only suggest. Thus I hope to have kept the sound of the sea & the birds, dawn, & garden subconsciously present, doing their work under ground' (*D* IV 10–11). Rather than think of Woolf's initial idea to chart 'some semi mystic . . . life of a woman' as having 'gradually evaporated'[10] by the time of the novel's completion, perhaps we might find it still present, suggested at this 'under ground' level of imagery. 'Mystic', as well as referring to sacred, obscure reli-gious feelings, may also suggest (see Chambers Twentieth Century Dictionary) 'a secret meaning hidden from the eyes of the ordinary person, only revealed to a spiritually enlightened mind: allegorical'. My reading of photological and colour tropes draws on both senses: Woolf's 'semi mystic' text is explored for references to a quasi-sacred mythology, and as partly allegorical. Woolf's qualification is significant: the woman's life is to be *'semi* mystic'. A later projection suggests the novel to be about her *struggle* to 'come to terms with these mystical feelings' (*D* III 203). Woolf also expresses ambitions for a less abstract project: 'I want to write a history, say of Newnham or the womans movement in the same vein. The vein is deep in me – at least sparkling, urgent.' (*D* III 203) These feminist aspirations, although addressed in *A Room of One's Own*, may extend to the similarly multivocal text, *The Waves*.

If ultimately 'no two people think alike about it' (*L* v 144), many agree that *The Waves* is a high modernist text, the culmination of (or inevitable dead-end to)[11] Woolf's experimentation in lyric prose,[12] and a virtuoso performance 'devoted to abstraction'.[13] For the same qualities, Woolf gleefully reports, *The Waves* was less politely considered by Vita Sackville-West, 'so bad that only a small dog that had been fed on gin could have written it'. (*L* IV 401) But Vanessa Bell's response has come to dominate (after being 'completely submerged in The Waves', she finds herself 'gasping, out of breath, choking, half-drowned . . . so overcome by the beauty' (*VB* 361)); so have observations on the novel's eloquent silence,[14] 'symbolic universality',[15] and sense of 'cosmic unity'.[16] But beyond aesthetic emotion *The Waves* may yet say more. Emotional, mystical readings tend to emphasize Bernard as spokesman for Woolf's own artistic vision,[17] and to find harmony between characters.[18] But I want to suggest the characters as contesting, and Bernard's role as ambivalent.[19] In exploring the novel's feminist subtext,[20] I will suggest Woolf's writerly engagement with colour may encourage iconographic readings of those elements previously understood to comply with orthodox tenets of significant form. The orthodox view of the novel's alternation between objective, impersonal interludes and subjective soliloquies, as a study in phenomenology and existentialism,[21] has influenced readings of colour in predominantly psychological terms.[22] McLaurin's model of colour locks into his informative analysis of the novel's repetitional aesthetics,[23] but his argument does not allow for the possibility of an iconographic or allegoric (not to mention feminist) deployment of colour.

Marcus, dropping her earlier mystical reading, sees *The Waves* as a 'marxist novel that is not realist' and its characters as imperialist ideologues, and understands its deployment of colour in relation to imperialism. 'Woolf exposes', she rightly observes 'the way that white women are implicated in . . . [the] imperialist project'. Countering feminist arguments 'that Bernard's fluency depends upon the suppression of Rhoda, that her silence is necessary for his speech', she emphasizes that 'in their roles as victims, silenced subjects, the women still participate in imperialist practice'.[24] But Rhoda's suicide, I suggest, although hardly a tempting, political solution, may mark unhappy, powerless dissent, and unwillingness to continue in complicity. Her silence, likewise, may be read as evidence of both complicity and resistance. Rhoda's vision of a 'white arm', Marcus interprets as that of 'a Britannia in endless surveillance of conquerable lands. . . . The mighty white arm of empire and civilization.' I will interpret Rhoda's visions, conversely, as possible sites of dissent. Marcus' emphasis on Britannia's origins as a sign of imperial subjugation,[25] may be undermined by the fact that the figure was part of suffrage iconography too.[26] But in *The Waves'* field of contested iconography and contested subjectivity, I suggest, such emergent feminist elements remain subordinate, their promise unfulfilled.

The interludes

As the relationship of sun, shade and colours develops in the interludes, we may discern the sense of an old order chiaroscuro containing, contesting, and defining itself against, an oppositional play of colour. The first interlude, often compared with Genesis, describes dawn bringing division into a world previously without light: '*The sun had not yet risen. The sea was indistinguishable from the sky.*' The '*woman couched beneath the horizon . . . rais[ing] a lamp*' (*W* 5) suggests both woman as enslaved functionary of the patriarchal order, and woman as appropriating the icon of masculine subjectivity (the sun). This imagery fits with suffrage iconography: for example, the white, green and yellow blades of the sun may perhaps recall the white, green and gold of the Women's Freedom League.[27] 'Woolf's sun is no Apollonian figure but a woman', it has been suggested, 'no father but a girl';[28] and the interludes have been identified as a 'woman-centred cosmogony' presided over by a goddess,[29] but I would propose that, although the sun's gender is contested in *The Waves* (as the possible allusions to suffrage iconography allow), the sun remains predominantly patriarchal.

The colours' subordination to light is perhaps impressionistic, whereas the use of colour to express shadow suggests a Post-Impressionistic abandonment of chiaroscuro: yet the sense of chiaroscuro *is* retained along with the colour, as in, for example, '*a blue finger-print of shadow*' (*W* 6). The use of simile and metaphor suggests going beyond impressionism to the visionary and allegoric. '*The birds sang their blank melody outside*' (*W* 6), may indicate an existential meaninglessness and absurdity, but, on the other hand, may provoke the reader to find (or supply) a hidden message. In the interludes, then, colours are contained by an '*uncompromising, undeniable*' sun, which also gives '*to everything its exact measure of colour . . .'* (*W* 160). This imperial solar realm of colour is not without shadow: '*Behind their conglomeration hung a zone of shadow in which might be a further shape to be disencumbered of shadow or still denser depths of darkness.'* (*W* 162) There is a cyclical movement of chiaroscuro in the interludes where light '*driving darkness before it*' (*W* 180), eventually yields to an all-covering darkness (*W* 258–59), only to return us to the beginning of the cycle. Colour, bright as a Fauve painting[30] at the sun's height, remains subordinate, its feminist potential perhaps signalled but not fulfilled.

Subjectivity, elegy and eclipse

If not, after all, a 'shrine to Thoby's memory',[31] *The Waves* is an elegy marking the death of Percival, 'heroic man of Empire',[32] solar hero (or Absolute Subject).[33] Like 'The Sun and the Fish' and *To the Lighthouse*, it charts the decline of masculine subjectivity using photological tropes: the death of Percival, 'himself a sun',[34] is reported after the sun has reached its zenith in the (almost Müllerian) solar narrative of the interludes. Bernard, in his summing up (following sunset in the interludes), likens his sense of self-loss to a solar eclipse. Percival's 'mantle passes to Bernard':[35] if the preceding interlude ends in darkness, Bernard is in the last instance aware of 'something rising beneath me like a proud horse', perhaps echoing Milton's 'day-star' which 'yet anon repairs his drooping head . . .'.[36] Less assuredly, Bernard reports the possible return of the sun: 'There is a sense of the break of day. I will not call it dawn.' (*W* 324) Although tentative, this suggests the resurrection of a masculine solar subject ('it is Percival's horse Bernard rides')[37] rather than his transformation under the influences of feminism. This view seems augured in imagery suggestive of the traditional, mythic victory over the python: Louis's belt is fastened by a petrified 'brass snake' (*W* 10); birds spike '*the soft, monstrous body of the defenceless worm*' and '*the sticky mixture*' of slugs (*W* 79–80); the '*gusts of dead smells*' (*W* 80) may even suggest 'the rotting of the serpent's corpse' at Pythian Delphi.[38]

Bernard's description of the sun going out on a solitary, masculine self, suggests that in losing himself, he also seems to lose the world: 'The scene beneath me withered. It was like the eclipse when the sun went out and left the earth, flourishing in full summer foliage, withered, brittle, false. . . . The woods had vanished; the earth was a waste of shadow. . . . A man without a self, I said. A heavy body leaning on a gate. A dead man.' (*W* 311, 312) This expression of individual, masculine, subjective loss, differs from the communal sense of loss and the triumphant overcoming of masculine subjectivity in 'The Sun and the Fish'. Colours (associated with the non-verbal), furthermore, seem to inhibit the radiance of Bernard's self: 'But how describe the world seen without a self? There are no words. Blue, red – even they distract, even they hide with thickness instead of letting the light through.' (*W* 314) Yet their feminist potential is subsumed. The masculine solar subject, whatever the 'ambivalence' of Bernard's gender[39] ('Nor do I always know if I am man or woman' (*W* 123)), seems to survive. The novel, nevertheless, to some extent, dissents from Bernard's imperialist attempts to 'sum up' (*W* 260) all identities.

The return of the self seems to accompany that of the light. Perhaps more emphatically than Woolf's eclipse essay, Bernard dwells on a sense of fragility; and the palpableness of light and colour is developed from the fruit simile to the more animate image of a sponge:

> Miraculously. Frailly. In thin stripes. It hangs like a glass cage. It is a hoop to be fractured by a tiny jar. There is a spark there. Next moment a flush of dun. Then a vapour as if the earth were breathing in and out, once, twice, for the first time. Then under the dullness someone walks with a green light. Then off twists a white wraith. The woods throb blue and green, and gradually the fields drink in red, gold, brown. Suddenly a river snatches a blue light. The earth absorbs colour like a sponge slowly drinking water. It puts on weight; rounds itself; hangs pendent; settles and swings beneath our feet.
>
> (*W* 313)

The colours, rather than lyrically orchestrating the 'epiphenomena of self',[40] are pitted against a reviled, transcendent, masculine 'self' now contemplated as absent. Unlike the colours in the essay's corresponding passage, which may be read as a positive, materialist, feminist, alternative to the masculine self, these colours do not transform the self, but, instead, remain in obeisance to it: 'So the landscape returned to me; so I saw fields rolling in waves of colour beneath me.' (*W* 313) Bernard apparently contains and orders the colour as he dominates the land. The solar eclipse here reverts to its traditional significance as a ritual testing and reaffirmation of masculine sovereignty. Masculine, solar subjectivity, then, returns to dominate at the close of *The Waves*, just as Terence remains dominant, surviving the death of his fiancée, at the close of *The Voyage Out*. But inside the elegy on Percival, I suggest, we may find one on Rhoda, whose suicide Bernard reports (*W* 307) just prior to the eclipse passage.[41]

White ships and purple buttons

The six characters begin imaginatively to explore their world in pastoral terms. Louis, for example, 'left standing by the wall among the flowers' makes them vehicles of his imagination (*W* 10); Bernard and Susan frighten themselves with sinister figures (the 'lady writing' and 'the gardeners sweeping') in their imaginary 'Elvedon' (*W* 15–16). Rhoda emerges as highly creative in this respect, developing inside an imaginary world of her own ('a short space of freedom'), unable to concentrate and integrate as well as the others. 'All my ships are white,' she declares as she creates a pastoral world in which she manipulates carefully selected objects, inventing a story about a shipwrecked sailor – a piscatory elegy perhaps (*W* 17).[42]

The novel describes the common and then segregated education of the two sexes. But the women present in the characters' early lives may elliptically gesture towards feminism. The recurrent image of 'the lady writing', for example, has been interpreted as Woolf's model of a feminist writer, the implicit counter-type to Bernard, and the true author of *The Waves*.[43] Given that Bernard's imaginary 'Elvedon' may be based on the schoolroom, this 'lady writing' may be the teacher, Miss Hudson. We might also infer from the 'purple buttons on her bodice' (*W* 19), which are in keeping with suffragist dress codes, that Miss Hudson is in sympathy with the cause.[44] The connection seems plausible: the period may be dated by the mention of Queen Alexandra's portrait (*W* 22, 34) as some time in the first decade of the century, the period of high suffrage agitation. Miss Hudson's purple buttons may be referred to Woolf's essay, 'Memories of a Working Women's Guild', the composition of which coincided with that of *The Waves*. In this careful exploration of her contradictory feelings in relation to class and the feminist movement, Woolf, introducing the Guildswomen's letters, seems to make specific reference to the pictorial language of suffrage colours.

The Guild was a powerful force for working-class women (from 1916 Woolf ran the Richmond Branch (*D* 1 76)); it enjoyed strong links with the suffrage movement, displaying a Rainbow Flag on marches.[45] The essay reflects on a 1913 conference in Newcastle where Woolf heard working-class women speakers demand 'divorce, education, the vote – all good things . . . higher wages and shorter hours' in 'a public hall hung with banners and loud voices' (*LAW* xviii, xxiii). Woolf seems, playfully, to refer to suffrage colours in her description of the typist, Miss Kidd, who 'was dressed in a peculiar shade of deep purple. . . The colour seemed somehow symbolical.' (*LAW* xxiv)

In 1913, as we have seen, the colour purple was indeed 'symbolical', and Woolf's account seems playful acknowledgement of this. She continues in the same vein when she describes Lilian Harris, whose 'dress . . . was coffee coloured', and directly addresses Margaret Llewelyn Davies:[46] 'you now emerged from an inner room, and if Miss Kidd was in purple and Miss Harris was coffee coloured, you, speaking pictorially (and I dare not speak more explicitly) were kingfisher blue and as arrowy and decisive as that quick bird' (*LAW* xxiv, xxv). Woolf's attention to the colour of the women's clothes and her cryptic aside, humorously recalling perhaps the *frisson* of intrigue and danger associated with the early suffrage years, suggest she may be referring playfully to different shades of feminist colours; and in 'speaking pictorially', as well as echoing Simonides, she points to an awareness of this visual feminist language. The allusion to arrows may, perhaps, refer to the arrow motif on suffrage banners and handkerchiefs denoting imprisonment.[47] Kingfisher blue may suggest Davies's (Girton) collegiate allegiance: it is the predominant colour of the Cambridge Alumnae suffrage banner.[48]

Woolf closes her exploration of the Guildswomen's letters with the example of Miss Kidd's 'fragment of a letter', reminding us once more of her symbolical 'sombre purple' attire:

> "When I was a girl of seventeen . . . my then employer . . . sent me to his home one night . . . and before he would allow me to leave he forced me to yield to him. At eighteen I was a mother." Whether that is literature or not literature I do not presume to say, but that it explains much and reveals much is certain. Such then was the burden that rested on that sombre figure as she sat typing your letters . . .
>
> (*LAW* xxxviii–xxxix)

Woolf quotes Kidd's letter as a means of explaining, even decoding, her 'sombre purple figure' (*LAW* xxxviii), behind which, echoing the myth of Procne and Philomela, is revealed a secret history of oppression and rape. Miss Kidd's own words break the silence and, with reference to them, Woolf translates verbally the pictorial message of this woman writing in purple attire. Compare Woolf's fictional description of the Suffrage society worker, Mrs Seal, 'dressed in plum-coloured velveteen' (*N&D* 78).

To speak 'pictorially' suggests we may talk silently using pictures, but also that we may voice in words what we see in the silent pictorial realm. In this preface which may be even more 'crafted and crafty' than one reader suspects,[49] Woolf seems to engage in both practices. In the context of a feminist project for working-class women, we have seen Woolf engage in the 'symbolical' language of colour as a means of (silently) voicing women's past experience and past suffering. Woolf's 'kindness' (*D* iii 307) in contributing to *Life As We Have Known It*, although in some ways a tiresome interruption ('With great plodding I have managed to write about the Women's Guild' (*D* iii 304)) to her rather more advanced literary project of *The Waves*, may, then, provide a key to feminist readings of the novel. In the sophisticated pictorial language of *The Waves*, I suggest, a similar feminist subtext may lie in the deployment of colour. Like Miss Kidd's purple attire, then, Miss Hudson's purple buttons may also be read symbolically. Perhaps this is the source of the 'unhappy, purple waves' earlier sensed by Bernard (*W* 15).

This imagery continues in the description of the girls' new teachers. The structuring of the soliloquies invites comparison between male and female experience at school: if Bernard, Louis and Neville turn to the solar figure of Percival, perhaps Rhoda's vision of Miss Lambert may be considered as an alternative to this masculine vision of subjectivity. She notes 'the purple light . . . in Miss Lambert's ring' which passingly illuminates 'the black stain on the white page of the Prayer Book' with a 'vinous' and 'amorous' light that seems to counter the implicitly dichotomizing patriarchal inscriptions of this religious text (*W* 34–35). It is not the ring that alienates Rhoda but the sitting 'under maps of the entire world', the writing 'exercises in ink', and the enforced anonymity of 'brown serge' (*W* 35): images suggestive of education as submissive inscription into empire. The ink and map are linked to the black and white of the prayer book. Against this shines the purple ring. Women are seen here, then, as complicit with imperialist ideology; but there is also an indication of opposition and resistance in the symbolism of the ring.

Rhoda's desire to escape these confines is manifest in her search for a kind of Absolute Subject ('a composed, a monumental face') capable of restoring her lost identity; and she locates this in her vision of 'a dingle in a wood' (*W* 35), the development of which is central to our understanding of Woolf's feminist subtext. Here, 'all is solemn, all is pale where she stands, like a statue in a grove. She lets her tasselled silken cloak slip down, and only her purple ring still glows, her vinous, her amethystine ring.' (*W* 48) Miss Lambert possesses transformative powers: 'things are changed under her eyes' (*W* 47), and she becomes incorporated into the grove vision. The ambiguous syntax makes it unclear where her purple ring glows – in the imaginary grove or in the 'private garden', to which Rhoda sees Miss Lambert admit a clergyman (*W* 47) – and it becomes a way from one world into another. Rhoda may be positioning Miss Lambert as her role model or Absolute Subject; but the idea of somehow replacing a patriarchal supreme subject with a female version is challenged by Miss Lambert herself.

Rhoda imagines becoming the ultimate female imperial subject, a counterpart to Percival (a position perhaps later occupied by the more earthy feminine figure of the '*magna mater*' Susan):[50]

> I will let the Russian Empress's veil flow about my shoulders. The diamonds of the Imperial crown blaze on my forehead. I hear the roar of the hostile mob as I step out on to the balcony. . . . I am waving my fist at an infuriated mob. "I am your Empress, people." My attitude is one of defiance. I am fearless. I conquer.
>
> (*W* 59–60)

In this fantasy, suggestive of Empress Alexandra at the storming of the Winter Palace, Rhoda's classroom sense of alienation is reversed: she assumes a guise of absolute sovereignty and designates the crowd or mob as faceless. That this is an unsatisfactory solution to Rhoda's lack of self assurance, becomes clear with the intervention of Miss Lambert: 'But this is a thin dream. This is a papery tree. Miss Lambert blows it down.' (*W* 60) Rhoda's rejection of the 'Empress dream' seems to contradict Marcus' understanding of her grove vision as consistently imperialist. Miss Lambert and her purple ring are at the heart of Rhoda's grove at this point, and Rhoda's vision of an alternative identity evolves around images of Miss Lambert's opposition to imperialist subjectivity.

The Waves does not, then, naively reinscribe imperial tropes, as Marcus suggests, but rather appropriates and adapts them for feminism. Suffragist art, again, provides a precedent in the Women's Coronation Procession of 1911, a colourful 'counter-hegemonic' pageantry in opposition to official celebrations of renewed male sovereignty. The suffragists' 'Pageant of Empire' (which included Indian suffragettes)[51] was a central element: 'The whole tableau was intended to symbolise the unity of the British Empire, a reinhabiting by women of the allegorical female figures by which such sentiments were conventionally expressed (as in the Victoria Memorial, unveiled the same year . . .).' Although effective, this allegorical tactic was unsettling in its contradictory positioning of women in opposition to, yet struggling for better representation within, Empire.[52] Rhoda's (and indeed the novel's) flirtation with imperial insignia reflects this historical dilemma for feminism.

'Nymph of the fountain'

After rejecting the Empress dream, Rhoda turns to Shelley, and her speech begins to echo his poem, 'The Question' (*W* 60),[53] whose gift of moonlight flowers of 'mingled' and 'opposed' hues, may be taken in contrast to the solar imagery associated with Percival, emblem of masculine subjectivity. If Shelley's speaker is unsure as to whom the flowers are to be given, Rhoda says she will 'lay them on the desk's shiny surface', perhaps intending them for her teacher Miss Lambert. Rhoda does not specify Shelley's 'flag-flowers, purple pranked with white' and 'reeds of such deep green',[54] but their coincidental suffrage significance may fit with the idea of a hidden, feminist potential in colours associated with Miss Lambert. Perhaps the elusiveness of such connections reflects Woolf's own sense of the 'under ground' workings of her imagery.

Other poems by Shelley come to mind as Rhoda continues. 'I faint, I fail' (*W* 61) echoes a line from 'The Indian Serenade' ('I die! I faint! I fail!'); but

Rhoda's references to the flowing and flooding stream that 'pours in a deep tide' (*W* 61) echoes the imagery of 'Arethusa'.[55] Arethusa was an attendant nymph to Artemis/Diana who, to rescue her from the amorous river-god Alpheus, transformed Arethusa into a fountain that eventually emerged (after going underground to the sea) at Ortygia.[56] Alpheus, as Shelley's poem recounts,[57] in pursuing Arethusa through the ocean, tries to mingle his waters with hers.[58]

Woolf's allusions to this myth feed into the elegiac aspects of *The Waves* since both Arethusa and Alpheus are invoked in *Lycidas*.[59] For Bernard, Rhoda is 'the nymph of the fountain' (*W* 126, 283), but Rhoda herself frequently signals identification with Arethusa. Her closing words to the first soliloquies seem to fit with Arethusa's oceanic experiences: 'Let me pull myself out of these waters. But they heap themselves on me; they sweep me between their great shoulders; I am turned; I am tumbled; I am stretched, among these long lights, these long waves, these endless paths, with people pursuing, pursuing.' (*W* 28) Rhoda's sense of alienation from social convention does not diminish with the passing of childhood: Susan, in contemplating for herself a future of rural motherhood, notes 'Rhoda's strange communications when she looks past, over our shoulders' (*W* 106). Resistant and evasive, Rhoda looks beyond Susan's conventional understanding of herself as part of a natural cycle, and Jinny's urban version of feminine subordination to a male hegemony (yet Jinny is also linked to Philomela (*W* 192)), and finds respite in visiting 'furtively the treasures I have laid apart'. These are 'marble columns and pools on the other side of the world where the swallow dips her wings.' (*W* 113) Again the swallow suggests Procne and Philomela: Rhoda's grove is now a haven from the sexual advances – and 'scorn' – of men. The moon, sign of Artemis/Diana, along with Arethusa's connections with this virgin goddess, suggest Rhoda's grove approximates to Diana's sacred grove. Only in imagining such a place, does Rhoda feel stable and unified: outside in the social world she feels a failure.

Unlike the successfully interpellated, socialized Susan and Jinny, Rhoda finds herself 'broken into separate pieces' by their world (*W* 115), the world of men. Rhoda's sense of unity, available through havens of artistic invention – 'Alone, I rock my basins' (*W* 115) – seems connected to a sense of remaining inviolate. Her closing vision, before the fourth interlude, appropriately, then, comes by the 'sudden effulgence of moon':

> I also see the railings of the square, and two people without faces, leaning like statues against the sky. There is, then, a world immune from change. When I have passed through this drawing-room flickering with tongues that cut me like knives, making me stammer, making me lie, I find faces rid of features, robed in beauty. The lovers crouch under the plane tree. The policeman

stands sentinel at the corner. A man passes. There is, then, a world immune from change.

(W 115)

Rhoda's vision may suggest a cold pastoral, an unchanging, and timeless, classical world, beyond the world of people and language, and, perhaps, stands for the realm of art, cordoned off from life, as well as for virginity. But as a place 'where I can display my assortment of curious treasures', it seems to change every time Rhoda recalls it: this world immune from outside change, is one she may yet manipulate. In this particular vision, the lovers' sexuality is not specified, and the policeman's role is also ambiguous: is he guarding the lovers, or are they hiding from him and the passing man? Perhaps, then, this world without faces may be free of conventional gender codes. It is the place from which Rhoda may draw (and reject) a sense of self, as we have seen, yet, so far, she has not found one to sustain her in the social, and verbal, world:

> But I am not composed enough. . . . I am to be broken. I am to be derided
> all my life. I am to be cast up and down among these men and women, with
> their twitching faces, with their lying tongues, like a cork on a rough sea. Like
> a ribbon of weed I am flung far every time the door opens. I am the foam
> that sweeps and fills the uttermost rims of the rocks with whiteness; I am
> also a girl, here in this room.

(W 115–16)

Rhoda figures her sense of violation and dispersal as flotsam and jetsam in the social tide, and ultimately as white foam; imagery appropriate to her identification with Arethusa.

Her connection to whiteness in this context, furthermore, supplies an interesting interpretation of her vision of facelessness: Alpheus, it transpires, pursued not only Arethusa but Diana herself who, on reaching Ortygia, avoided capture by daubing her face and the faces of her nymphs with white mud, so that Alpheus could not pick her out from the group.[60] In connection with this myth, 'Artemis's most famous statue at Athens was called "White-browed" ',[61] an epithet we might also apply to Rhoda. Rhoda's imaginary attempt to escape the world to which Susan and Jinny have readily submitted, then, is informed by these myths, suggesting a desire to avoid the sexual advances of men, and to find refuge in the anonymous companionship of women. Again, this fits with feminist iconography, since the suffragist dress code for demonstrations required women to wear predominantly 'white frocks'. They also paraded in pageants dressed as famous heroines and goddesses from history and mythology.[62]

Rhoda's concluding sentence shows she is thinking 'poetically and prosaically' at the same time: as well as not losing sight of fiction – 'I am the foam . . .' – she keeps in touch with historical fact – 'I am also a girl, here in this room.' The white foam, then, reminds us of Woolf's vision of woman as 'a vessel in which all sorts of spirits and forces are coursing and flashing perpetually' (*AROO* 66–67), of Arethusa's fountain-waters mingling with the ocean, of Diana's refuge among her nymphs, and of a predominant suffragist colour.[63] As well as signalling oppression, these images may also be taken as sources of creative strength and resistance.

White arm and purple flame

At the dinner party in honour of Percival, Rhoda's alternative vision of anonymous, communal subjectivity is countered by the central, solar hero, but she endures her friends' cruelty because 'there is always some name, some face, which sheds a radiance, which lights her pavements and makes it possible for her to replenish her dreams'. (*W* 130) Rhoda's visions are socially generated not produced in a vacuum. She refers to an image of feminine retreat from voraciousness: 'the tiger leapt, and the swallow dipped her wings in dark pools on the other side of the world' (*W* 137); and this may be the social mechanism by which she replenishes her dreams. The tiger may not be tied to one specific interpretation, but it seems to stand for Rhoda's perpetual sense of social panic and oppression: 'if I fall under the shock of the leap of the moment you will be on me, tearing me to pieces'. (*W* 141) The leap of the tiger in one world forces the appearance of a swallow in another.

Rhoda's imagery suggests the Dionysian myths of Actaeon and Orpheus, and she positions herself as a hero torn to pieces by hounds or bacchantes, but then seems to shift between the former and the latter:

> But there is no single scent, no single body for me to follow. And I have no face. I am like the foam that races over the beach or the moonlight that falls arrowlike here on a tin can, here on a spike of the mailed sea holly, or a bone or a half-eaten boat. I am whirled down caverns, and flap like paper against endless corridors, and must press my hand against the wall to draw myself back.
>
> (*W* 143)

The arrow-like moonlight (suggestive of Diana's hunting skills, as well as the suffrage arrow motif), the declared facelessness, and the dispersing foam, again, point to Rhoda's identification with Artemisian cults. This vision does not focus on an individual, solar hero but on the tactical dispersal of identity. Rhoda admits to needing her friends' company to stay this process of dispersal, but also to give her a sense of anonymous communality. The solar hero is not a direct source of illumination to Rhoda, but she is warmed by the incidental 'general blaze' (*W* 142) from those who gather round him. At its height, she sees this in terms of 'queer ambiguous tints', which are not vibrant but on the point of decadence; the beautiful fruit of light has a bloom of decay about it. Jinny too describes musty 'Membranes, webs of nerves that lay white and limp,' veiling the dinner-table discourse from the material world beyond. Louis notes 'The roar of London . . . is round us' (*W* 146), and Neville that: 'lit up' and 'many coloured', 'we are walled in here. But India lies outside.' The diners, then, inhabit a luminous, yet slightly dingy, imperialist halo, outside which lies the subject nation, India, for which their solar hero is destined. From this dank cocoon Bernard projects his vision of Percival as imperial overlord 'applying the standards of the West' (*W* 147).

In Rhoda's parodic counter to Bernard's eulogy, Percival appears an ominous figure: she describes him first as 'a stone', then as a source of light, creating dominion over a dark world, and finally, Woolf's slippery syntax allows, as a vulture 'that feeds on some bloated carcass' resembling the 'shrivelled' world that 'rounds itself' into view (*W* 148). This world, as Percival's (and, vicariously, his friends') carrion filling out below him (and them), darkly anticipates Bernard's famous eclipse simile.

Rhoda offers an alternative vision to this, when Neville, seeing her look 'far over our heads, beyond India', asks her to speak.

> There . . . I see a shape, white, but not of stone, moving, perhaps alive. But it is not you; not Percival, Susan, Jinny, Neville or Louis. When the white arm rests upon the knee it is a triangle; now it is upright – a column; now a fountain, falling. It makes no sign, it does not beckon, it does not see us. Behind it roars the sea. It is beyond our reach. Yet there I venture. . . .
>
> (*W* 150–151)

Rhoda's grove, no longer graced with a purple glow, but dominated by an anonymous and fluctuating white figure, may still resemble the Ortygian grove of Artemis/Diana. Rhoda's insistence that she sees the grove always beyond the figures of her friends ('between your shoulders, over your heads'), suggests they somehow cause it, but we may wonder whether she ventures there to confirm, or escape, their patriarchal values: 'these pilgrimages, these moments of departure, start always in your presence, from this table, these lights, from Percival and Susan, here and now. Always I see the grove over your heads.' (*W* 151) Perhaps this is a space of both resistance and refuge, itself marked out by the patriarchy photologically identified with Percival and Susan.

Artemisian connections and Dionysian imagery, again, appear in the parenthetical conspiracy between Rhoda and Louis 'forebod[ing] decay'. The 'dance of savages', 'stags blar[ing] in the thicket', and the 'bleeding limbs . . . torn from the living body' (*W* 152), seem to augur the death of the solar hero (as the sun's zenith is reached in the interludes); and we might see Rhoda's oppositional grove vision (Actaeon's offence was against Diana, we recall) as part of the cycle by which the solar subject will eventually be renewed. Yet Rhoda and Louis, in predicting his death, almost seem to plot it: 'The shadow slants. We who are conspirators, withdrawn together to lean over some cold urn, note how the purple flame flows downwards.' (*W* 152) The Roman flavour to this suggests the purple flame as a classical symbol of imperial power, and its downward slant, an ill omen for the ruler; but it may also connect with the purple glow Miss Lambert brings to Rhoda's grove.

Violets, squares and oblongs

When Percival dies, Rhoda's grove appears to have changed too: 'Now the shadow has fallen and the purple light slants downwards. The figure that was robed in beauty is now clothed in ruin. . . . as I told them when they said they loved his voice on the stair, and his old shoes and moments of being together.' (*W* 172) This is a puzzling passage. Rhoda has previously asserted that the white figure is not Percival (or anyone else), but are we now to see it as him? 'His voice' refers to Percival but does it refer to the figure? Do the fallen shadow and purple light symbolically reflect or somehow cause the figure's ruin? According to the text, Rhoda has told only Louis about the shadow and purple light, but now she talks as if her statement were more public. Yet we might detect antipathy in her admonitory tone, for she does not align herself with those who 'loved his voice'.

Percival represents the material basis of Rhoda's visionary existence, and her response to his death seems painful acknowledgement of a material world now bereft of his presence. Her shopping trip reveals the class divisions of the world left by Percival and reminds us of the material wealth underpinning Rhoda's position: her 'intellectual freedom depends upon material things'. (*AROO* 162–163) She buys luxuries from shopgirls she seems to despise and expresses a loathing for the urban masses. Yet Rhoda's purchases connect her to the very people she calls 'coarse, greedy, casual' and whose 'dirty fingers' make 'our love impure' (*W* 173). Rhoda's attitude to the material world she sees as Percival's legacy seems ambivalent: 'Percival, by his death, has made me this present, has revealed this terror, has left me to undergo this humiliation.' (*W* 173) Is the world reduced to 'grossly material things' because it is bereft of Percival's powers of transcendence, or without him is Rhoda seeing for the first time, less glamorously, the capitalist economy he actually helped to construct? This ambiguity is also felt in Rhoda's bitter retort: 'This is my tribute to Percival; withered violets, blackened violets.' (*W* 174)

Rhoda's visit to a concert supplies a moment of (literally lyric) consolation when a 'sea-green woman comes to our rescue' with 'the note, "Ah!"' (*W* 176) This is a possible moment of feminist consolation and transformation. But the imagery of containment and over-ripeness echoes that of the preceding interlude where the sun strikes and seems to melt and marshal colour: just as the '*plums swelled out their leaves*' (*W* 162), so the woman is 'swollen but contained in slippery satin' (*W* 176). These colours remain part of the solar cycle; they do not overcome or transform it.

Yet Rhoda's grove-vision, now more abstract, seems to lose its purple glow and white figure to an apparently consoling vision of oblongs and squares (*W* 177), an acknowledgement, perhaps, of significant form. It becomes for Rhoda her 'end'; and, in setting out on her pilgrimage, 'lurch[ing] down Regent Street' to Greenwich she no longer exudes misanthropy. The acceptance of life as it is, 'mean streets' and all, as a universal 'dwelling-place' (*W* 177), is seen alongside a more historically specific description of the economy in Regent Street. Rhoda seems to yield to Percival's world, where previously she has sought escape; and perhaps this is a yielding to the religion of significant form. But James Naremore detects 'an extremely bitter irony' and 'almost a sneer'[64] in Rhoda's acknowledgement of the dwelling-place of squares and oblongs, a reading confirmed by her 'withered violets'. In her moment of apparent consolation and reconciliation to such an order, however, emerges another potentially feminist sense of release, as she watches a ship on the river:

> A woman walks on deck, with a dog barking round her. Her skirts are blown; her hair is blown; they are going out to sea. . . . Now I will relinquish; now I will let loose. . . . We will gallop together over desert hills where the swallow dips her wings in dark pools and the pillars stand entire. Into the wave that dashes upon the shore, into the wave that flings its white foam to the uttermost corners of the earth, I throw my violets to Percival.
>
> (*W* 178)

The woman seems connected to Rhoda's sense of release. We might wonder where the ship is going – perhaps India, perhaps not – and whether Rhoda refers to the woman or to Percival when she says 'we will gallop together'. Although, in an earlier draft, Rhoda refers to 'when I am thundering with Percival on the edge of the world,'[65] the final version does not specify such a union, but maintains a sense of ambiguity and, as we have seen, tends to dramatize Rhoda's otherworldly visions as generated in opposition to what Percival seems to represent for her peers.

We might see two journeys imagined here: one to India, and one to 'where the swallow dips her wings'. When Rhoda throws the violets to Percival she throws them into the white foam we have come to identify with her Arethusa persona; but the wave itself seems to suggest the far-reaching bounds of the empire, the sea through which Arethusa is pursued by the river-god (the Thames may suggest Alpheus' presence). This conjunction of elements may offer a model of Rhoda's position within the imperial economy: just as the white foam is its product and is pushed around by its tides, so Rhoda is bound up in a system which, although she may despise it, controls and disperses her. Rhoda's throwing of violets into the white foam seems a poignant moment of capitulation, and, like a bruise rising, we may see the momentary coincidence of potentially feminist colours; but as Rhoda's subsequent life and suicide suggest, she seems to abandon the emblem to the overwhelming wave.

White spaces, cliffs and green light

Certainly when next we encounter Rhoda she speaks in defeat and contempt: 'Oh, life, how I have dreaded you . . . oh, human beings, how I have hated you!' (*W* 222) Her contempt for the masses seems to return her to the Empress dream; and she conflates the mob with her peer group in recounting the tide of conformism overpowering her: 'How you chained me to the spot. . . . How you snatched from me the white spaces that lie between hour and hour and rolled them into dirty pellets and tossed them into the waste-paper basket with your greasy paws. Yet those were my life.' (*W* 221–22) Noting the absence of 'even a blue feather pinned to a hat' (incidentally a favourite accessory of Margaret Llewelyn Davies), Rhoda accuses the world of a drabness – perhaps, then, a political colourlessness – ('All were dressed in indeterminate shades of grey and brown'), which defiles her visionary 'white spaces'. But, she also acknowledges her own complicity:

> But I yielded. Sneers and yawns were covered with my hand. I did not go out into the street and break a bottle in the gutter as a sign of rage. Trembling with ardour, I pretended that I was not surprised. What you did, I did. If Susan and Jinny pulled up their stockings like that, I pulled mine up like that also.
>
> (*W* 222)

In the context of conforming to the whims of Susan's and Jinny's dress code, and hiding behind 'shade after shade' (*W* 222), Rhoda's failure to participate in violent acts of dissent may be understood, more specifically, as a failure to join women in political action against their traditional lot. 'I yielded' also suggests giving in to sexual advances, and when Rhoda mentions 'I left Louis; I feared embraces', we may again be reminded of Arethusa's flight from Alpheus.[66] Rhoda then makes more explicit her acceptance of the status quo and her air of capitulation at Greenwich: 'Then in some Hall I parted the boughs of music and saw the house we have made; the square stood upon the oblong. "The house which contains all."' (*W* 223) But in opposition to this, Rhoda's journey up the hill (on a mule-back she imagines as her bed) to 'see Africa' seems her final pilgrimage, one steeped in a possibly feminist mythology:

> The good woman with a face like a white horse at the end of the bed makes a valedictory movement and turns to go. Who then comes with me? Flowers only, the cowbind and the moonlight-coloured May. Gathering them loosely in a sheaf I made of them a garland and gave them – Oh, to whom? We launch out now over the precipice. . . . The cliffs vanish. Rippling small, rippling grey, innumerable waves spread beneath us. I touch nothing. I see nothing. We may sink and settle on the waves. The sea will drum in my ears. The white petals will be darkened with sea water. . . . Rolling me over the waves will shoulder me under. Everything falls in a tremendous shower, dissolving me.
>
> (*W* 225)

The 'woman with a face like a white horse' may be an Artemis figure; but since she seems to leave Rhoda she may not be included in the 'we' who 'launch out now over the precipice'. This action suggests the myth of Arethusa – particularly Rhoda's description of finding herself dissolving into water[67] – but it may also suggest Sappho's legendary 'Leucadian Leap' or 'lovers' leap' (from a white rock).[68]

Rhoda's imaginary leap, then, suggests both flight from unwanted advances in its links with Arethusa, and a suicidal jump due to unrequited love, if connected to Sappho. Rhoda's binding of violets may also connect her to Sappho whose epithet was 'violet-weaving';[69] likewise Neville's description of Rhoda as 'fl[ying] with her neck outstretched and blind fanatic eyes, past us' (*W* 215) may suggest Sappho's legendary mid-air transformation into a swan;[70] and Rhoda's white spaces and fragmentary visions may suggest the famous lacunæ and fragmentary nature of Sappho's surviving œuvre. Perhaps Rhoda, Sappho-like, represents a half-lost, woman's poetics, even a 'semi mystic life of a woman'.[71] Woolf's allusions in the drafts to Arethusa, Artemis and Sapphic sexuality, it has been suggested, may also reveal a more 'overtly lesbian' aspect to Rhoda's visions than survives into the published version of *The Waves*.[72]

But whatever the nature of Rhoda's imaginary flight, it is juxtaposed with her recognition of the material world she simultaneously inhabits: 'Putting my foot to the ground I step gingerly and press my hand against the hard door of a Spanish inn.' (*W* 225) Rhoda finds herself on a threshold where intervention seems to meet with resistance; we are not sure whether she is to be accepted, excluded or contained by the hard door.

At Hampton Court, steeped in the symbolism of male sovereignty,[73] as well as of its demise,[74] Rhoda seems to have learnt a more direct, less fearful, approach to her peers (*W* 243). But she also recognizes her continuing exclusion from their values: 'you . . . are committed, have an attitude, with children, authority, fame, love, society; where I have nothing. I have no face.' Rhoda's facelessness seems connected to her refusal 'to accept the shadow of the trees and the pillar-boxes' (*W* 243), suggesting her defiance of the place allocated to her gender by traditional values of chiaroscuro. Yet, she still extracts her alternative vision from the material presence of her friends: 'Behind you is a white crescent of foam.' Rhoda's simultaneously poetic and prosaic thoughts show an imperial centre of sovereign subjectivity in relation to classical, pastoral motifs. She juxtaposes imagery of distant 'Parrots shrieking' in 'the intense stillness of the jungle' with that of industrial progress – '(Here the trams start.)'; and conversation in one realm – '(Here we talk.)' – with a silent mythical imagery of oppression in another: 'The swallow dips her wings in midnight pools.' (*W* 243–44)

But in her torment Rhoda again has compensatory glimpses of a different model:

> Yet there are moments when the walls of the mind grow thin; when nothing
> is unabsorbed, and I could fancy that we might blow so vast a bubble that the
> sun might set and rise in it and we might take the blue of midday and the
> black of midnight and be cast off and escape from here and now.
>
> (*W* 244–45)

As an alternative to hierarchized relations between self and peers, Rhoda sees a potentially non-solar model of subjectivity in her vision of an alternate temporality. This bubble, decentring the solar round, echoes the post-eclipse world in 'The Sun and the Fish', and may be seen as an alternative to the world returning to Bernard's solar subjectivity at the close of *The Waves*. That Rhoda's vision yields to his, is confirmed not only by his reporting of her suicide, but by her own poignant last words:

> "Now," said Rhoda, "as they pass that tree, they regain their natural
> size. They are only men, only women. . . . Pity returns, as they emerge into
> moonlight, like relics of an army, our representatives, going out every night
> (here or in Greece) to battle, and coming back every night with their wounds,
> their ravaged faces. Now light falls on them again. They have faces. They
> become Susan and Bernard, Jinny and Neville, people we know. Now
> what a shrinkage takes place!. . . . Yet they have only to speak, and their first
> words, with the remembered tone and the perpetual deviation from what one

expects, and their hands moving and making a thousand past days rise again in the darkness, shake my purpose."

(*W* 254–55)

This recalls Woolf's description of her companions' return to size from the statuesque after the eclipse (*D* III 144). McLaurin finds Rhoda 'uncompromising in her love of the geometrical, abstract, and dehumanised'; but we have seen how this may read ironically; how it differs from her potentially feminist visions of purple and white. Rhoda's visions, furthermore, are not static (the square and oblong, like the purple glow, are not constant), nor does she always seek stasis:[75] she also looks for change. We might wonder also whether she 'hates individuality'[76] *per se* or whether her more distant, abstract view of her friends allows Rhoda to see their collective potential, one which might produce less disappointing, perhaps less cruel, individuals than the 'people we know'.

What does seem to unify Rhoda's visions, is a sense of negativity or dissent: they are generated by an anguished dissatisfaction with the status quo. Her unhappiness with her peers seems to lie with their 'perpetual deviation' from her vision. She depicts them in a sinister chiaroscuro: as 'our representatives', they form part of a wave of militaristic enlightenment from classical times on, battling against darkness. Bitter irony seems to inform these observations, for Rhoda's experiences show she is not represented by these people, and their illumination brings darkness too. Everything they do is at odds with her vision: their actions make 'a thousand past days rise again in the darkness' and shake her purpose.

In recognizing in Rhoda a limited sense of subversiveness ('she subverts through her silences'), critics have suggested her inevitable tacit complicity in an order which destroys her; and her whiteness, in its apparent 'affinity with feelings of isolation, loneliness, desolation, and silence',[77] is seen as a mark of this self-destructiveness. But such arguments, ignoring Rhoda's other colours and offering a limited understanding of her whiteness, draw on a deterministic, psychoanalytical model of language as functioning by the suppression of the feminine.[78] They disallow the possible connection of whiteness with a materialist feminism, along with the mythic and political allusions to colour we have explored: 'Sensing only intermittancy and rupture, Rhoda leaves the novel in one of those white spaces so terribly familiar to her, an unspecified gap in the text that is only retroactively filled in by Bernard's mournful respect.'[79] Rhoda's suicidal depression may come from the knowledge of a lost potential for material change, I suggest, not merely from a sense that, in tandem with the (always and already) suppressed feminine of language, the status quo remains immutable. In *The Waves*, then, we glimpse one woman's possibly feminist 'new colours' as, Arethusa-like, they appear – only to 'run underground' again (*GR* 82).

An image from one of Woolf's earliest projections about the work that was to become *The Waves* seems appropriate here:

> Then the day fell into the sea: the sun went down.
> & those who watched it saw no green light.[80]

At one point Rhoda does glimpse, in the gold spot of the sun fading between trees at Hampton Court, 'a slice of green . . . elongated like the blade of a knife seen in dreams, or some tapering island on which nobody sets foot.' (*W* 235) But, like her other 'green oases' (*W* 20), this potentially feminist colour[81] is lost, perhaps not permanently, to the dominant solar cycle of *The Waves*.

15 Conclusion

In exploring Woolf's tropes of light and colour in relation to iconographic colourist and suffragist traditions and contexts, I have sought to revise the critical emphasis on aesthetic emotion, psychological volume, and significant form, as characteristic of her Post-Impressionism; and to identify in that dominant discourse, a green oasis, perhaps. A prismatic, materialist, feminism may be at work in Woolf's Post-Impressionism. Exploiting both the 'interaction and [the] inevitable tension between the spheres of "feminism" and "aesthetics"',[1] Woolf's feminist aesthetics utilise the politics of the visual by engaging with art both on gallery walls and on the street.

It is the interrelation between these two spheres of colourism I have tried to exploit in my readings. If the 'red flowers . . . with the thin green leaves' Rachel Vinrace picks in the shade of a tree (*VO* 205) suggest a prismatic feminist intervention in pastoral-elegiac discourse, the discovery that these flowers, in an earlier draft of *The Voyage Out*, are 'purple and white' (tenderly arranged by Rachel 'white next to purple'),[2] may indicate a suffragist colourism underpinning the text's published prismatics. I have preferred, however, in reading her later work, to focus on the range of colourism (encompassing both spheres) Woolf does put into print (a process of uncovering, nevertheless). The oppressive moment of traditional patriarchal chiaroscuro in 'The Moment: Summer's Night', which initiated my investigation, is succinctly countered by feminist prismatics in another luminous moment, from the story 'Moments of Being: "Slater's Pins Have no Points"', with which it seems appropriate to close since it was constructed by Woolf as she was finishing *To the Lighthouse* and ruminating on that 'semi mystic very profound life of a woman' to be contained in 'one incident – say the fall of a flower', which was to become *The Waves*:

> Fanny had surprised her in a moment of ecstacy. She sat there, half turned away from the piano, with her hands clasped in her lap holding the carnation upright, while behind her was the sharp square of the window, uncurtained, purple in the evening, intensely purple after the brilliant electric lights which burnt unshaded in the bare music room. . . . All seemed transparent for a moment to the gaze of Fanny Wilmot, as if looking through Miss Craye, she saw the very fountain of her being spurt up in pure, silver drops. She saw back and back into the past behind her. She saw the green Roman vases stood in their case. . . . She saw Julia open her arms; saw her blaze; saw her kindle.

> Out of the night she burnt like a dead white star. Julia kissed her. Julia
> possessed her.

> (*CSF* 220)[3]

This intimate 'Sapphist' (*L* III 431) moment of prismatic enlightenment, set in the private aesthetic sphere of the music room, is shot through with the feminist colours that simultaneously position it in the public sphere of politics.

Positing an avant-garde, feminist colourism in her revision of photological tropes, I have explored how this new language opens up a spectrum of possible interpretations from the narrow, political significance of specific colours to a broader sense of feminist prismatics. If the appearance of suffrage colours in Woolf's writing suggests historical, materialist and transformative aspects to her feminist aesthetics, we have also seen how Post-Impressionist colourism, itself, may be understood in these feminist terms. Woolf's wider range of prismatics, then, may be linked to an historical, feminist politics of the visual. But it may also offer, simultaneously, a provisional, and potent, language by which we might imagine a future liberated from all such historical and political concerns. However we seek to understand their imaginative possibilities, Woolf's colour tropes should be read in relation to the aesthetic and political contexts they emerge from as well as contest.

Notes

1 Introduction: interrupted moments

1 Woolf, 'Moments of Vision' (1918), *E*, II, pp. 250–51.
2 Alex Zwerdling, *Virginia Woolf and the Real World* (Berkeley, Los Angeles and London, 1986).
3 Woolf, 'The Moment: Summer's Night', *M*, p. 9.
4 Hermione Lee, 'A Burning Glass: Reflection in Virginia Woolf', *Virginia Woolf: A Centenary Perspective*, ed. Eric Warner (London and Basingstoke, 1984), p. 16.
5 Lee, 'A Burning Glass', p. 25.
6 Harvena Richter, *Virginia Woolf: The Inward Voyage* (Princeton, 1970), p. 27.
7 Shiv K. Kumar, *Bergson and the Stream of Consciousness Novel* (London and Glasgow, 1962), p. 69. See Josalba Ramalho Vieira, 'Henri Bergson's Idea of Duration and Virginia Woolf's Novels', *Ilha do Desterro: A Journal of Language and Literature*, 24 no.2 (1990), 9–20.
8 Henri Bergson, *Time and Free Will: An Essay on the Immediate Data of Consciousness* (1889), trans. F.L. Pogson (London, 1971), pp. 108, 116, 231–232.
9 See Randall Stevenson, *Modernist Fiction: An Introduction* (Hemel Hempstead, 1992), pp. 104–5.
10 Kumar, *Bergson*, p. 101.
11 James Hafley, *The Glass Roof: Virginia Woolf as Novelist* (Berkeley and Los Angeles, 1954), pp. 166, 43–44.
12 Tony Inglis, 'Virginia Woolf and English Culture', first published in French in *Virginia Woolf et le groupe de Bloomsbury*, ed. Jean Guiguet (Paris, 1977); first English version in *Virginia Woolf*, ed. Rachel Bowlby (London and New York, 1992), p. 48.
13 Thomas Hann, 'The Bergsonian Heritage', *The Bergsonian Heritage*, ed. Thomas Hann (New York and London, 1962), p. 6.
14 Wyndham Lewis, *The Art of Being Ruled* (London, 1926), p. 391.
15 See, Alice Van Buren Kelley, *The Novels of Virginia Woolf: Fact and Vision* (Chicago, 1973); Nancy Topping Bazin, *Virginia Woolf and the Androgynous Vision* (New Brunswick, 1973); Carolyn Heilbrun, *Towards Androgyny* (London, 1973).
16 Walter Benjamin, *Charles Baudelaire: A Lyric Poet in the Era of High Capitalism*, trans. Harry Zohn (London and New York, 1983), pp. 144–45.
17 Karl Kraus (1912); Thomas Szasz, *Karl Kraus and the Soul-Doctors* (London, 1977), p. 159.
18 Lucio P. Ruotolo, *The Interrupted Moment: A View of Virginia Woolf's Novels* (Stanford, Calif., 1986), pp. 2–3.

19 Jean Guiguet, 'A Novelist's Essay: "The Moment: Summer's Night" by Virginia Woolf', *Der Englische Essay: Analysen*, ed. Horst Weber (Darmstadt, Germany, 1975), p. 301.

20 Madeline Moore, 'Nature and Community: A Study of Cyclical Reality in *The Waves*', *Virginia Woolf: Revaluation and Continuity*, ed. Ralph Freedman (Berkeley, 1980), p. 226.

21 Benjamin, 'Theses on the Philosophy of History', *Illuminations*, ed. Hannah Arendt, trans. Harry Zohn (New York, 1969), p. 255.

22 See Patricia Maika, *Virginia Woolf's 'Between the Acts' and Jane Harrison's Conspiracy* (Ann Arbor, 1987), pp. 7–8.

23 Jane Ellen Harrison, *Themis: A Study of the Social Origins of Greek Religion* (Cambridge, 1912), pp. viii, 534–35. She cites Bergson's *L'Évolution Créatrice* (1907) and *La Perception du Changement*, Conférences faites à l' Université d'Oxford (1911), p. 18.

24 M.C. Bradbrook, 'Notes on the Style of Mrs Woolf' (1932), *Virginia Woolf: The Critical Heritage* (London, 1975), ed. Robin Majumdar and Allen McLaurin, pp. 310–11.

25 Bradbrook, 'Notes,' p. 309.

26 Michael Hollington, 'Svevo, Joyce and Modernist Time', *Modernism*, ed. Malcolm Bradbury and James McFarlane (Harmondsworth, 1985), p. 43.

27 Bradbury and McFarlane, 'The Name and Nature of Modernism', *Modernism*, p. 25.

28 Ibid., p. 26.

29 Allen McLaurin, *Virginia Woolf: The Echoes Enslaved* (Cambridge, 1973), pp. 110–121.

30 Karin Stephen, *The Misuse of the Mind: a Study of Bergson's Attack on Intellectualism* (London, 1922).

31 McLaurin, *Virginia Woolf*, pp. 70–84.

32 Astradur Eysteinsson, *The Concept of Modernism* (Ithaca and London, 1990), p. 240.

33 Peggy Kamuf, 'Penelope at Work: Interruptions in *A Room of One's Own*', *Novel* 16 (1982), p. 17.

2 Virginia Woolf: heliotropics, subjectivity and feminism

1 Woolf, 'The Sun and the Fish', *Time and Tide*, 9, 5 (3 February 1928) 99–100; reprinted *New Republic*, New York, 8 February 1928, pp. 321–23; *CDB*, pp. 193–99.

2 Susan Dick, *CSF*, p. 299.

3 Jacques Derrida, *Writing and Difference* (London, 1978), p. 27.

4 Derrida, *Margins of Philosophy*, trans. Alan Bass (Hemel Hempstead, 1982), p. 271.

5 Gillian Beer, 'The Victorians in Virginia Woolf: 1832–1941', *Arguing with the Past: Essays in Narrative from Woolf to Sidney* (London and New York, 1989), pp. 151, 153–54, notes that Woolf's 'favourite reading as a girl' included John Tyndall's *On Radiation* (London, 1865) and *Six Lectures on Light* (London, 1873).

6 Shakespeare, *Cymbeline*, IV.ii.258.

7 For example: David Daiches, *Virginia Woolf* (London, 1945), pp. 55–92; Jean O. Love, *Worlds in Consciousness. Mythopoetic Thought in the Novels of Virginia Woolf* (Berkeley, Los Angeles and London, 1970), pp. 180–94; Perry Meisel, *The Absent Father: Virginia Woolf and Walter Pater* (New Haven and London, 1980), chapters 2 and 3.

8 Toril Moi, *Sexual/Textual Politics* (London, 1985), p. 13.

9 Genesis 1.i-iv, *The Holy Bible*, Authorized Version (Oxford, 1908).

10 Julia Kristeva, 'About Chinese Women', *The Kristeva Reader*, ed. Toril Moi (Oxford, 1986), pp. 139–40.

11 Hélène Cixous, 'Sorties', *New French Feminisms*, ed. Elaine Marks and Isabelle de Courtivron (Brighton, 1981), p. 90.

12 Sigmund Freud, 'Notes on a Case of Paranoia', *The Pelican Freud Library* (Harmondsworth, 1979), vol. 9, pp. 190 and 222. The sun is also addressed as female in Leadbelly's (chain gang) blues number, 'Go Down, Old Hannah'.

13 Cixous, 'Sorties', p. 90.

14 Genevieve Lloyd, *The Man of Reason: 'Male' and 'Female' in Western Philosophy* (London, 1984), p. 2.

15 Moi, *Sexual/Textual Politics*, pp. 105–06, p. 13.

16 Makiko Minow-Pinkney, *Virginia Woolf and the Problem of the Subject* (Brighton, 1987), pp. 92, 8–9.

17 Louis Althusser, 'Ideology and Ideological State Apparatuses (Notes towards an Investigation)', *Lenin and Philosophy and Other Essays*, trans. Ben Brewster (London, 1971), p. 168.

18 Luce Irigaray, 'Any Theory of the "Subject" Has Always Been Appropriated by the "Masculine"', *Speculum of the Other Woman*, trans. Gillian C. Gill (New York, 1985), pp. 133–34.

19 Minow-Pinkney, *Virginia Woolf*, p. 92.

20 J. Hillis Miller, 'Mr. Carmichael and Lily Briscoe: The Rhythm of Creativity in *To the Lighthouse*', *Modernism Reconsidered*, ed. Robert Kiely and John Hildebidle (Cambridge, 1983), p. 187.

21 Irigaray, *Speculum*, p. 136.

22 Judith Butler, *Gender Trouble: Feminism and the Subversion of Identity* (London, 1990), pp. 2–3, 148.

23 Christine Di Stefano, 'Dilemmas of Difference: Feminism, Modernity, and Postmodernism', *Feminism/Postmodernism*, ed. Linda J. Nicholson (London, 1990), p. 76.

24 Lloyd, *The Man of Reason*, pp. 104, 105.

25 Jürgen Habermas, 'Modernity – An Incomplete Project', *Postmodern Culture*, ed. Hal Foster (London and Sydney, 1985), p. 5.

26 Pauline Johnson, 'From Virginia Woolf to the Post-Moderns: Developments in a Feminist Aesthetic', *Socialism, Feminism and Philosophy. A Radical Philosophy Reader*, ed. Sean Sayers and Peter Osborne (London and New York, 1990), p. 104.

27 Ibid., pp. 119, 120.

28 Habermas, *The Philosophical Discourse of Modernity*, trans. Frederick Lawrence (Cambridge, 1987), pp. 302–03, pp. 338, 296.

29 Ibid., p. 297.

30 See Allison Weir, 'Toward a Model of Self-Identity: Habermas and Kristeva', *Feminists Read Habermas: Gendering the Subject of Discourse*, ed. Johanna Meehan (New York and London, 1995), pp. 263–282.

31 For discussion of the Scottish ballad, 'Mary Hamilton', see Jane Marcus, 'Sapphistry: Narration as Lesbian Seduction in *A Room of One's Own*', *Virginia Woolf and the Languages of Patriarchy* (Bloomington, Ind., 1987).

32 William Blake, 'The Marriage of Heaven and Hell', Plate 3, *Complete Writings*, ed. Geoffrey Keynes (Oxford, 1966), p. 149. Blake's considerable influence on Woolf is discussed by Diane Filby Gillespie, *The Sisters' Arts. The Writing and Painting of Virginia Woolf and Vanessa Bell* (Syracuse, NY, 1988).

33 Blake, *Milton*, 2, Plate 40, ll.32–36, p. 533.

34 Jane Marcus, *Virginia Woolf: A Feminist Slant* (Lincoln, Nebr. and London, 1983), p. 7.

35 Caroline Emilia Stephen, *The Light Arising: Thoughts on the Central Radiance* (Cambridge, 1908), and *The Vision of Faith* (Cambridge, 1911).

36 Marcus, *Virginia Woolf*, pp. 23, 28, 26.

37 Ibid., p. 27.

38 Ibid.. See Catherine Smith, 'Jane Lead: Mysticism and the Woman Cloathed with the Sun', in *Shakespeare's Sisters: Feminist Essays on Women Poets* (Bloomington, Ind., 1979).

39 Madeline Moore, *The Short Season Between Two Silences. The Mystical and the Political in the Novels of Virginia Woolf* (Boston, 1984), p. 27.

40 Ibid., pp. 27, 35: The main source is Lead's *A Fountain of Gardens Watered by the River of Divine Pleasure and Springing Up in all Variety of Spiritual Plants . . .* (London, 1697–1701), I, p. 27.

41 Ibid., p. 27.

42 Marcus, *A Feminist Slant*, p. 28.

43 For example, Jack F. Stewart, 'Light in *To the Lighthouse*', *Twentieth Century Literature*, p. 377.

44 Moi, *Sexual/Textual Politics*, p. 16 (Moi's italics).

3 The astonishing moment

1 *The Times*, Monday 27 June 1927, p. 14.

2 Ibid., pp. 14, 21.

3 Ibid., p. 14.

4 *The Times*, Tuesday 28 June 1927, p. 17.

5 *The Times*, Friday 7 November 1919, p. 12.

6 Ibid.

7 Alfred North Whitehead, *Science and the Modern World* (Cambridge, 1926; 1956), p. 13; Jeremy Bernstein, *Einstein* (Glasgow, 1973), p. 119.

8 *The Times*, Tuesday 28 June 1927, p. 17.

9 *The Times*, Thursday 30 June 1927, p. 18.

10 W.H. Auden, 'Musée des Beaux Arts', line 12, *Collected Poems*, ed. Edward Mendelson (London, 1976), p. 147.

11 Blake, *Jerusalem*, Plate 70 (c.1820), *The Illuminated Blake*, ed. David V. Erdman (London, 1975), p. 349.

12 Benjamin, *The Origin of German Tragic Drama*, trans. John Osborne (London, 1977), p. 178.

13 *The Times*, 30 June 1927, p. 17.

14 Ibid.

15 William Wordsworth, *The Prelude, or, Growth of a Poet's Mind*, (1850); *The Prelude, 1799, 1805, 1850. Authorative Texts, Context, and Reception, Recent Critical Essays*, ed. Jonathan Wordsworth, M.H. Abrams, and Stephen Gill (New York and London, 1979), p. 85.

16 Wordsworth, *The Prelude*, II, lines 357–58, 362–67.

17 Ibid., lines 178–82.

18 *The Times*, 30 June 1927, p. 18.

19 Ibid., p. 17.

20 Joseph Conrad, 'Author's Note', *The Shadow Line* (London, 1920).

4 The amusing game

1 A point noted by one of the few critics to analyse 'The Sun and the Fish', Sharon Louise Wood Proudfit, 'The Fact and the Vision: Virginia Woolf and Roger Fry's Post-Impressionist Aesthetic', The University of Michigan, PhD. (1967), p. 194.

2 Margaret Haig Thomas (1883–1958).

3 Johanna Alberti, *Beyond Suffrage. Feminists in War and Peace, 1914–28* (Basingstoke, 1989), p. 138.

4 Ibid.; Alberti quotes Octavia Wilberforce's autobiography, pp. 253–54, and *Time & Tide*, 14 May 1920.

5 Ibid., p. 137; Alberti quotes Rhondda, *This Was My World* (London, 1933), p. 294.

6 Rhondda, *This Was My World*, p. 304.

7 Zwerdling, *Virginia Woolf and the Real World*, p. 212.

8 Compare Woolf's fictional treatment of the suffrage movement in *N&D*, p. 76ff. Mary Datchet who at first works for a suffrage society later moves to one dedicated to a more general socialist agenda.

9 *Time and Tide*, 10, 4 (22 November 1929) 1403–04; 10, 5 (29 November 1929) 1434–36.

10 For example, Woolf published under Strachey's editorship, 'The Plumage Bill', *Woman's Leader*, 23 July 1920, pp. 559–60; Appendix II, *D*, II, pp. 337–38; see also *Our Freedom and Its Results, by Five Women*, ed. Ray Strachey (London, 1936).

11 See Malachi 4.ii: 'The Sun of Righteousness'.

12 Cixous, 'Sorties', p. 287.

13 'Human Beings – and Females', *Time and Tide*, 9, 5 (3 February 1928) 97.

14 See M.H. Abrams, *The Mirror and the Lamp: Romantic Theory and the Critical Tradition* (New York, 1953), p. 235ff.

15 Weir, 'Toward a Model of Self-Identity: Habermas and Kristeva', p. 264.

16 Paul Cézanne, Letter to Emile Bernard, 15 April 1904, *Paul Cézanne: Letters*, trans. Marguerite Kay, ed. John Rewald (London, 1941), p. 234.

17 V.N. Voloshinov [M.M. Bakhtin], 'Discourse in Life and Discourse in Poetry', trans. John Richmond, *Bakhtin School Papers*, ed. Ann Shukman (Oxford, 1983), p. 17.

5 The gathering crowd

1 See Gaston Bachelard, *The Poetics of Space*, trans. Maria Jolas (New York, 1964); Derrida, 'White Mythology', *Margins of Philosophy*.

2 Revelation 5.xii.

6 The chasing of the sun and the victory of the colours

1 Andrew Marvell, 'To His Coy Mistress', lines 45–46, *Complete Poems*, ed. George deF. Lord (London, 1984), p. 25.

2 James George Frazer, *The Golden Bough*: Part Three: *The Dying God*, vol. 4 (London, 1911), pp. 212–213.

3 Robert Graves, *The Greek Myths* (Harmondsworth, 1962), vol. 1, sec. 22.1, p. 85; sec. 28.2, p. 114.

4 Ovid, *Metamorphoses*, III.247–252, trans. Frank Justus Miller, Loeb Classical Library (London, 1926), vol. 1, pp. 141, 143.

5 Ibid., XI.20–26, 37–43, vol. 2, pp. 121, 123.

6 Lloyd, *The Man of Reason*, p. 106.

7 Woolf, 'Professions for Women', *DM*, p. 151.

8 Ruth Padel, 'Women: Model for Possession by Greek Daemons', *Images of Women in Antiquity*, ed. Averil Cameron and Amelie Kuhrt (London and Sydney, 1983), pp. 5–6.

9 Frazer, *The Golden Bough*: Part Seven: *Balder the Beautiful*, vol. 10 (London, 1913), p. 162.

10 Ibid., p. 70.

11 Padel, 'Women', p. 7.

12 See, Arthur S. Way, *Euripides* (London, 1919), vol. 3, p. 3.

13 R.Y. Tyrrell (ed.), *Bacchae* (London, 1892), pp. xxiii–xxiv.

14 Ibid., pp. xxiv–xxv.

15 Plato, Symposium 211b, *The Dialogues of Plato*, trans. Benjamin Jowett, vol. 2 (Great Britain, 1970), p. 225.

16 Plato, Philebus 55b, *The Dialogues of Plato*, trans. Benjamin Jowett, vol. 3, p. 102.

17 Lloyd, *The Man of Reason*, pp. 22, 37.

18 Tyrrell, *Bacchae*, pp. xxv–xxvi.

19 Ibid., pp. xxviii–xxx.

20 Frazer, vol. 1, p. 311; vol. 10, pp. 70, 162; vol. 4, p. 73.

21 Lisa Tickner, *The Spectacle of Women: Imagery of the Suffrage Campaign 1907–1914* (London, 1987), p. 265. Tickner quotes from Emmeline Pethick-Lawrence, 'The Purple, White and Green', *Programme*, Prince's Skating Rink Exhibition (London, 1909).

22 Tickner, *The Spectacle of Women*, p. 93.

23 Mary Lowndes, 'On Banners and Banner-Making', *The Englishwoman*, 7, 20 (1910), pp. 172, 173.

24 Tickner, *The Spectacle of Women*, p. 94; Emmeline Pethick-Lawrence, 'The Purple, White and Green', *Programme*, Prince's Skating Rink Exhibition (London, 1909).

25 Pethick-Lawrence, editorial, *Votes For Women*, 1908; quoted by Diane Atkinson, *Suffragettes in the Purple, White and Green, London 1906–14*, Museum of London (London, 1992), p. 15.

26 Tickner, *The Spectacle of Women*, p. 294.

27 Museum of London, *Suffragettes in the Purple, White and Green, London 1906–14* (September 1992–June 1993).

28 Atkinson, *Suffragettes in the Purple, White and Green*.

29 In Chapter 14, I discuss Woolf's possible references to the pictorial symbolism of suffrage colours in her 1931 essay, 'Memories of a Working Women's Guild'.

30 Tickner, *The Spectacle of Women*, p. 57.

31 Rhondda, *Leisured Women*, pp. 56–57.

32 Thorstein Veblen, *The Theory of the Leisure Class* (New York, 1899, 1912; 1963), p. 69.

33 Ray Strachey, *'The Cause': A Short History of the Women's Movement in Great Britain* (London, 1928), p. 313.

34 Tickner, *The Spectacle of Women*, p. 74.

35 Strachey, *Women's Suffrage and Women's Service: The History of the London and National Society for Women's Service* (London, 1927), p. 21.

36 Gillespie, *The Sisters' Arts*, p. 17; quoting 'Our Vortex', *Blast* 1–2 (1914–15), pp. 151–52.

37 Tickner, *The Spectacle of Women*, p. 74 (my italics).

38 *The Common Cause*, 25 November 1909, p. 433, quoted by Tickner, *The Spectacle of Women*, p. 265.

39 Tickner, *The Spectacle of Women*, p. 265.

40 The Suffrage Atelier Broadsheet (1913), Museum of London; Tickner, *The Spectacle of Women*, p. 22.

7 Elegiacs: capsizing light and returning colour

1 Claire M. Tylee, *The Great War and Women's Consciousness* (London, 1990), p. 14.

2 D.H. Lawrence, *Lady Chatterley's Lover* (1928) (New York, 1957), p. 237.

3 Kate Millett, *Sexual Politics* (London, 1972), p. 238.

4 D.H. Lawrence, *Study of Thomas Hardy and Other Essays*, ed. Bruce Steel (Cambridge, 1983), pp. 82, 70, 71.

5 *Votes For Women*, 18 February 1909, p. 365; Tickner, *The Spectacle of Women*, p. 16.

6 Tickner, *The Spectacle of Women*, p. 18.

7 Ibid.

8 Guillaume Apollinaire, 'Les Fenêtres' (1912), *Calligrammes, Poèmes de la paix et de la guerre (1913–1916)* (Gallimard, 1925), p. 26.

9 Mark Hussey, *The Singing of the Real World. The Philosophy of Virginia Woolf's Fiction* (Columbus, 1986), p. 166.

10 Andrew Rosen, *Rise Up, Women! The Militant Campaign of the Women's Social and Political Union 1903–1914* (London and Boston, 1974), pp. 138–139. pp. 152–156.

11 H.N. Brailsford and Dr J. Murray, *The Treatment of the Women's Deputations by the Metropolitan Police, A Copy of Evidence Collected by Dr Jessie Murray and Mr H.N. Brailsford, and forwarded to the Home Office by the Conciliation Committee for Woman Suffrage, in support of its Demand for a Public Inquiry* (London, 1911), pp. 9, 8–9.

12 Antonia Raeburn, *The Militant Suffragettes* (London, 1973), pp. 154, 155.

13 M.H. Abrams, *A Glossary of Literary Terms*, Third Edition (New York, 1971), p. 46.

14 John Milton, *Lycidas*, lines 165–85, *The Poems of John Milton*, ed. John Carey and Alastair Fowler (London and New York, 1978), pp. 252–53.

15 See Dorothy Brewster, *Virginia Woolf* (New York, 1962), p. 97.

16 Woolf, 'A Dialogue upon Mount Pentelicus', *CSF*, p. 66.

17 Milton, *Lycidas*, lines 186–93.

18 Abrams, *A Glossary of Literary Terms*, p. 45.

19 Eric Smith, *By Mourning Tongues. Studies in English Elegy* (Suffolk, 1977), p. 110.

20 Ibid., p. 111.

21 Milton, *Lycidas*, lines 100–02.

22 Virgil, *Georgics* 1.464–68; Shakespeare, *Lear* 1.ii.112–13, *Hamlet*, 1.i.118–20, *Othello* v.ii.99–101; Milton, *The Works of John Milton*, vol. 10: *History of Britain*, ed. G.P. Krapp (New York, 1932) p. 169; see A.S.P. Woodhouse and D. Bush, editors, *A Variorum Commentary on the Poems of John Milton*, vol. 2, *The Minor English Poems* Part Two (London, 1972), pp. 669–70.

23 See Woodhouse and Bush, *Variorum*, p. 670: One theory, G.G.L., 'Milton: "Built in the eclipse"', *Notes and Queries*, 179 (1940), p. 9, is that '*eclipse* must mean the eight days of the moon's waning or the *interlunium* . . . as no ship could be built in the short time of an eclipse'; another, T.O. Mabbott, 'Milton: "Built in the eclipse"', *Notes and Queries*, 179 (1940), pp. 141–142, is that 'the allusion is purely astrological: some part of the work was done in an eclipse and brought ill luck to the vessel'.

24 M. Mack, *Milton* (New York, 1950); Woodhouse and Bush, *Variorum*, p. 670.

25 Michael Lloyd, 'The Fatal Bark', *Modern Language Notes* 75, (1960) pp. 103–08; Woodhouse and Bush, *Variorum*.

26 Petronius, *Satyricon*, quoted in original Latin by T.S. Eliot, *The Waste Land* (1922), *The Complete Poems and Plays of T.S. Eliot* (London, 1969), p. 59.

8 The death of the sun and the return of the fish

1 Max Nordau, *Degeneration* (London, 1895), pp. vii–viii. Nordau, incidentally, is author of a novel about the marriage between a German royal and an American businessman, entitled *Morganatic*, trans. Elizabeth Lee (London, 1904).

2 Nordau, *On Art and Artists*, trans. W.F. Harvey (London, 1907).

3 Oswald Spengler, *The Decline of the West*, Volume ii, *Perspectives of World-History* (originally published in German 1922), trans. Charles Francis Atkinson (London, 1928), p. 105.

4 Ibid.

5 Ibid., pp. 327–28.

6 Gillian Beer, '"The Death of the Sun": Victorian Solar Physics and Solar Myth', *The Sun is God. Painting, Literature and Mythology in the Nineteenth Century*, ed. J.B. Bullen (Oxford, 1989), p. 159.

7 See, for example, William Thomson, 'On a Universal Tendency in Nature to the Dissipation of Mechanical Energy', *Philosophical Magazine*, 4 (1852), p. 306: 'most probably the sun was sensibly hotter a million years ago than he is now'. See also, Richard A. Proctor, 'Suns in Flames', *Myths and Marvels of Astronomy*, new edition (London, 1876), p. 190: arguing the other way, he assures that 'the sun will continue steadily to discharge his duties as fire, light, and life of the solar system'. (Beer, *The Sun is God*, pp. 162, 163).

8 Max Müller, *Lectures on the Origin and Growth of Religion* (London, 1878), p. 278; Beer, *The Sun is God*, p. 164.

9 Müller, *Lectures on the Science of Language*, Second Series (London, 1864), p. 516.

10 Ibid., pp. 518–19, 520.

11 Ibid., pp. 523, 524.

12 Beer, *The Sun is God*, p. 164.

13 Frances Power Cobbe, *Darwinism in Morals and Other Essays* (London, 1872), p. 343; Beer, *The Sun is God*, p. 165.

14 Beer, *The Sun is God*, pp. 175, 180.

15 Charles Darwin, *The Formation of Vegetable Mould, Through the Action of Worms, with Observations on their Habits* (London, 1881), pp. 305, 313, 155.

16 Leslie Stephen, *Swift*, English Men of Letters Series (London, 1882), p. 200; Beer, *The Sun is God*, p. 178; Woolf's research for her essay 'Swift's Journal to Stella' (1925), began with this book by her father: see *RN*, p. 50.

17 Beer, *The Sun is God*, p. 178. She cites Andrew Lang, *Custom and Myth* (London, 1985), p. 103.

18 Beer, *The Sun is God*, p. 179. She cites Darwin, *Earthworm*, p. 312.

19 Joseph Fontenrose, *Python: A Study of Delphic Myth and its Origins* (Berkeley and Los Angeles, 1959), p. 1, 515ff., 13–14.

20 Ibid., p. 14.

21 Ibid., pp. 14, 15.

22 Harrison, *Themis*, pp. 429, 437.

23 A.W. Verrall, *The 'Choephori' of Aeschylus*, trans. A.W.Verrall (London, 1893), note

to line 32, p. 5. Woolf summarizes Verrall's note on [Phoebus], line 32: *BERG* 6, M 19.

24 Beer, *The Sun is God*, p. 179: 'in 1850, turning away from the dragon or serpent, Landor had written an "Ode to the Worm".'

25 Fontenrose, *Python*, p. 231; see pp. 117, 142f., 282f.

26 Blake, 'Marriage of Heaven and Hell', Plate 8, *Complete Writings*, p. 151.

27 Proudfit, 'The Fact and the Vision', p. 201.

28 Eliot, *The Complete Poems and Plays*, p. 15.

9 Post-Impressionism: the explosion of colour

1 Julius Meier-Graefe, *Vincent Van Gogh. A Biographical Study*, Volume Two, trans. John Holroyd Reece (London, 1922), pp. 106–107.

2 'Manet and the Post-Impressionists', Grafton Gallery, London, 8 November 1910–14 January 1911.

3 Woolf, unsigned review of *The Tragic Life of Vincent Van Gogh* by Louis Piérard, trans. Herbert Garland (London, 1925), *E*, IV, p. 249.

4 Woolf, 'Character in Fiction' ['Mr Bennett and Mrs Brown'] (1924), *E*, III, p. 421.

5 Lowndes, 'On Banners and Banner-Making', p. 173.

6 Diane Atkinson, *The Suffragettes in Pictures* (London, 1996), p. 163.

7 Woolf, 'The Post-Impressionists', review of *The Post-Impressionists* by C. Lewis Hind (London, 1911), *E*, I, p. 379.

8 'Jacob Tonson' [Arnold Bennett], 'Neo-Impressionism and Literature' (1910), *Books and Persons. Being comments on a past epoch 1908–1911* (London, 1917), pp. 284–85.

9 Woolf, 'Books and Persons' (1917), *E*, II, p. 130.

10 Woolf, 'Pictures and Portraits' (1920), *E*, III, pp. 163–64.

11 Gillespie, *The Sisters' Arts*, p. 1.

12 Ibid., pp. 2, 277–83.

13 See also Mary Ann Caws, *Women of Bloomsbury: Virginia, Vanessa and Carrington* (London, 1990); Jane Dunn, *Virginia Woolf and Vanessa Bell: A Very Close Conspiracy* (London, 1990; 1996).

14 Bridget Elliott and Jo-Ann Wallace, *Women Artists and Writers: Modernist (im)positionings* (London and New York, 1994), p. 60.

15 Jan Heinemann, 'The Revolt against Language: A Critical Note on Twentieth-Century Irrationalism with Special Reference to the Aesthetico-Philosophical Views of Virginia Woolf and Clive Bell', *Orbis Litterarum* 32 (1977) 212–28; John H. Roberts, '"Vision and Design" in Virginia Woolf', *PMLA*, LXI (1946) 835–847; Jonathan R. Quick, 'Virginia Woolf, Roger Fry and Post-Impressionism', *The Massachussetts Review* 26 4 (1985) 547–70.

16 David Seed, 'The Vision of the Artist: Painting and Experimentation in the Fiction of Virginia Woolf', *Proceedings of the English Association North* 5, (1990) p. 41.

17 Frank Gloversmith, 'Autonomy Theory: Ortega, Roger Fry, Virginia Woolf', *The Theory of Reading*, ed. Frank Gloversmith (Sussex, 1984), pp. 159–60.

18 Marianna Torgovnick, *The Visual Arts, Pictorialism and the Novel: James, Lawrence and Woolf* (Princeton, 1985), p. 62.

19 Elliott and Wallace, *Women Artists and Writers*, pp. 56–89.

20 Desmond MacCarthy, 'The Art Quake of 1910', *The Listener*, 1 February 1945, p. 123.

21 Robert Ross, 'The Post-Impressionists at the Grafton: The Twilight of the Idols', *Morning Post*, 7 November 1910, 3; J.B. Bullen (ed.), *Post-Impressionists in England* (London and New York, 1988), p. 100.

22 Ian Dunlop, *The Shock of the New. Seven Historic Exhibitions of Modern Art* (London, 1972), p. 120.

23 George Dangerfield, *The Strange Death of Liberal England* (London, 1936), pp. 63–64.

24 Dunlop, *The Shock of the New*, p. 132.

25 Frances Spalding, *Roger Fry: Art and Life* (London, 1980), p. 139.

26 Dangerfield, *The Strange Death*, pp. 138, 141, 152, 153.

27 William C. Wees, *Vorticism and the English Avant-Garde* (Manchester, 1972), p. 20.

28 Bullen, *Post-Impressionists*, p. 15. See also Spalding, *Roger Fry*, p. 136ff.

29 See, William Greenslade, *Degeneration, Culture and the Novel 1880–1940* (Cambridge, 1994), pp. 129–133.

30 Ebenezer Wake Cook, 'The Post-Impressionists', *Morning Post*, 19 November 1910; *Post-Impressionists*, ed. Bullen, p. 118.

31 Ross, 'The Post-Impressionists at the Grafton: The Twilight of the Idols'; *Post-Impressionists*, ed. Bullen, pp. 101, 103.

32 Ibid., p. 104.

33 Cook, 'The Post-Impressionists'; *Post-Impressionists*, ed. Bullen, p. 119.

34 Spalding, *Roger Fry*, p. 139.

35 Ross, 'The Post-Impressionists', p. 102.

36 For example, P.G. Konody, 'Art Notes: Post-Impressionism at the Grafton Galleries', *Observer*, 13 November 1910, p. 9, and the anonymous review in the *Daily Telegraph*, 11 November 1910. See Spalding, *Roger Fry*, plate 46, p. 135.

37 Unsigned review, 'Paint Run Mad: Post-Impressionism at the Grafton Galleries', *Daily Express*, 9 November 1910; *Post-Impressionists*, ed. Bullen, pp. 105–106.

38 Ibid.

39 Wilfred Scawen Blunt, *My Diaries: being a personal narrative of events, 1888–1914* (London, 1932), entry for 15 November 1910; *Post-Impressionists*, ed. Bullen, pp. 113–114.

40 Quentin Bell, *Virginia Woolf: A Biography* (London, 1972), I, p. 170.

41 Ibid., p. 168.

42 Max Nordau, *On Art and Artists*, trans. W.F. Harvey (London, 1907), pp. 29, 236–37.

43 Fry, 'Retrospect', *Vision and Design* (London, 1920), pp. 192–93. See *RF*, p. 158.

44 S.K. Tillyard, *The Impact of Modernism 1900–1920. Early Modernism and the Arts and Crafts Movement in Edwardian England* (London and New York, 1988), p. 110.

45 Ibid., p. 102; Tillyard cites 'E.S.', 'Post-Impressionism', *Westminster Gazette*, 21 November 1910, p. 3.

46 Ibid., pp. 102–103.

47 Ibid., p. 104.

48 Ibid., p. 113.

49 Lowndes, 'Gauguin – A Personal Impression', *The Englishwoman*, 9 (1911), pp. 183–84. This is the only suffragist review of the exhibition I have been able to find.

50 Dunlop, *The Shock of the New*, p. 146.

51 Bullen, *Post-Impressionists*, pp. 29–31.

52 Christina Walshe, *Daily Herald*, 25 March 1913; Spalding, *Roger Fry*, p. 139.

10 Romantic to Classic: Post-Impressionist theories from 1910 to 1912

1 Alan Bowness, 'Introduction', *Post-Impressionism. Cross-Currents in European Painting*, Royal Academy of Arts, London 1979–80, Catalogue (London, 1979), p. 9. Bowness also points out the instability of the term, Post-Impressionism, which has since come to describe a much broader (and contradictory) range of art.

2 Benedict Nicolson, 'Post-Impressionism and Roger Fry', *Burlington Magazine*, 93 (1951), p. 13.

3 Dennis Farr, *English Art 1870–1940* (Oxford, 1978), p. 201.

4 Nicolson 'Post-Impressionism', p. 15. Nicolson notes that Fry was later to experience 'a lapse in memory' concerning the content of the show: significantly he elides the 'romantic Rouault'. See also, Fry, *Vision and Design* (London, 1920), p. 159.

5 MacCarthy, 'The Art Quake of 1910', *The Listener*, 1 February 1945, p. 124.

6 MacCarthy, 'The Post-Impressionists', *Manet and the Post-Impressionists*, 8 November to 15 January, 1910–11, Grafton Galleries, Exhibition Catalogue (London, 1910), p. 8.

7 Ibid.

8 Paul Gauguin, Letter to Emile Schuffenecker (1888), *Theories of Modern Art. A Source Book by Artists and Critics*, ed. Herschel B. Chipp, p. 60.

9 MacCarthy, 'The Post-Impressionists', p. 9.

10 Jean Renoir, *Renoir, My Father* (1958), trans. Randolph and Dorothy Weaver (London, 1962), p. 185.

11 MacCarthy, 'The Post-Impressionists', p. 9.

12 Ibid., p. 10.

13 Bowness, *Post-Impressionism*, p. 9.

14 See Spalding, *Roger Fry: Art and Life* (London, 1980), p. 117.

15 Roger Fry, review, *Athenaeum*, 13 January 1906; quoted by Woolf, *RF*, p. 112.

16 Fry, Letter to the *Burlington Magazine*, *Letters of Roger Fry*, ed. Denys Sutton (London, 1972), vol. 1, p. 299. The *Burlington Magazine*'s 'Unsigned review' of the exhibition is reprinted in *Post-Impressionists*, ed. Bullen, pp. 41–44.

17 Fry, *Vision and Design*, p. 23.

18 Spalding, *Roger Fry*, p. 119.

19 Farr, *English Art*, p. 201; Nicolson, 'Post-Impressionism', pp. 12–13; Denys Sutton, *Letters of Roger Fry*, vol. 1, p. 40; Bowness, *Post-Impressionism*, p. 9; Bullen, *Post-*

Impressionists, pp. 8–9; Jacqueline V. Falkenheim, *Roger Fry and the Beginnings of Formalist Art Criticism* (Ann Arbor, 1980), pp. 18–19.

20 Meier-Graefe, *Modern Art: Being a Contribution to a New System of Aesthetics* (1904), trans. Florence Simmonds and George W. Chrystal (London, 1908).

21 Wees, *Vorticism and the English Avant-Garde*, p. 21. See also, Douglas Cooper, 'The Post-Impressionist Phase', *The Courtauld Collection* (London, 1954), p. 51; Spalding, *Roger Fry: Art and Life*, p. 133.

22 Falkenheim, *Roger Fry*, 19.

23 Ibid., p.18.

24 Meier-Graefe, *Modern Art*, I, pp. 267–68, 325.

25 Ibid., p. 204.

26 Meisel, *The Absent Father*, p. 137, speculates that this terminology has its roots in the writing of Walter Pater.

27 Meier-Graefe, *Modern Art*, I, pp. 205, 207, 212.

28 Ibid., II, pp. 60, 62.

29 Ibid., pp. 63–64.

30 Cooper, *The Courtauld Collection*, pp. 51–52.

31 Maurice Denis, 'Cézanne', trans. Roger Fry (1910), *Post-Impressionists*, ed. Bullen, p. 63.

32 Ibid., p. 75.

33 Habermas, 'Modernity – An Incomplete Project', *Postmodern Culture*, ed. Hal Foster (London and Sydney, 1985), p. 4.

34 Denis, 'Cézanne', p. 65.

35 Ibid., pp. 69–72, 72–73.

36 Nicolson, 'Post-Impressionism', pp. 12–13 (my italics).

37 Denys Sutton, *Letters of Roger Fry*, vol. I, p. 40, quotes Nicolson's line as ' "it bore out what Meier-Graefe *and* what Denis had written." ' (my italics). Intentional or not, this misquote makes for a very different emphasis in Sutton's interpretation of Fry's early formulations.

38 Falkenheim, *Roger Fry*, p. 20.

39 Meier-Graefe, *Modern Art*, II, p. 53.

40 Ibid., p. 54.

41 Woolf, Letter, December 1907, to Violet Dickinson, *L*, I, p. 320.

42 Nicolson, 'Post-Impressionism', p. 15.

43 Ibid.

44 Falkenheim, *Roger Fry*, p. 22.

45 See *Post-Impressionists*, ed. Bullen, pp. 120–24, 129–34, 147–51.

46 Falkenheim, *Roger Fry*, pp, 18, 23.

47 Ibid., p. 23.

48 Fry, 'The Post-Impressionists – 2', *Post-Impressionists*, ed. Bullen, p. 131.

49 Falkenheim, *Roger Fry*, p. 23.

50 Clive Bell, 'The English Group', *Second Post-Impressionist Exhibition*, October 5– December 31, 1912, Grafton Galleries, Exhibition Catalogue (London, 1912), p. 9.

51 Compare references to 'significant paint' and 'significant form' in A.C. Bradley, 'Poetry for Poetry's Sake' (1901), *Oxford Lectures on Poetry* (London, 1909), pp. 15, 19.

52 Bell, 'The English Group', p. 10.

53 Ibid., pp. 10–11.

54 Ibid., p. 11.

55 Ibid., pp. 11–12.

56 Fry, 'The French Group', *Second Post-Impressionist Exhibition*, p. 13.

57 Ibid., pp. 14, 15.

58 Ibid., p. 16.

59 Ibid., pp. 16–17.

60 See Nicolson, 'Post-Impressionism', p. 15.

61 Boris Von Anrep, 'The Russian Group', *Second Post-Impressionist Exhibition*, pp. 18–21.

62 Bell, *Art* (London, 1914), pp. 7–8.

63 Ibid., pp. 292–93.

64 Ibid., p. ix.

65 Dunlop, *The Shock of the New*, pp. 156–7. See also *RF*, p. 156.

66 D.H. Lawrence, 'Introduction to These Paintings' (1929), *Phoenix, the Posthumous Papers of D.H. Lawrence*, ed. Edward D. Macdonald (London, 1936), pp. 565–66.

67 Tillyard, *The Impact of Modernism*, pp. 53–54, 55, xviii.

68 Ibid., p. 48.

69 Ibid., p. 183.

70 The Omega Workshops were set up by Roger Fry in May 1913. He employed several artists to design and make painted furniture, decorated ceramics, screens, murals, and printed fabrics. See, Anthony d'Offay Gallery, *The Omega Workshops: Alliance and Enmity in English Art* (London, 1984); Judith Collins, *The Omega Workshops* (London, 1983); Fiona MacCarthy, *The Omega Workshops: Decorative Arts of Bloomsbury* (London, 1985).

71 H.G. Wells, *Joan and Peter. The Story of an Education* (London, 1918), p. 6. See, Woolf, 'The Rights of Youth' (1918), *E*, II, p. 297.

72 Lowndes, 'On Banners and Banner-Making', p. 174.

11 The new prismatics: Virginia Woolf, Vanessa Bell and English Post-Impressionism

1 Woolf, 'The Post-Impressionists' (1911), *E*, I, p. 380.

2 See also *L*, II, p. 230.

3 Vanessa Bell, unpublished memoir of Roger Fry; Gillespie, *The Sisters' Arts*, p. 16.

4 Simon Watney, *The English Post-Impressionists* (London, 1980), p. 137.

5 Ibid.

6 Christopher Reed, 'Through Formalism: Feminism and Virginia Woolf's Relation to Bloomsbury Aesthetics', *Twentieth Century Literature* 38, 1 (Spring 1992), p. 23.

7 Fry, 'Mr MacColl and Drawing', *The Burlington Magazine*, XXXV (1919), pp. 84–85.

8 Reed, 'Through Formalism', p. 24.

9 Charles Mauron, *The Nature of Beauty in Art and Literature* (London, 1927).

10 See James M. Haule, '"Le Temps Passe" and the Original Typescript: an Early Version of the "Time Passes" Section of *To the Lighthouse*', *Twentieth Century Literature* 29, 3 (Fall 1983).

11 McLaurin, *Virginia Woolf: The Echoes Enslaved*, p. 79.

12 Fry, 'Plastic Colour', *Transformations* (London, 1926).

13 Ibid., pp. 218, 220.

14 Ibid., p. 219.

15 Ibid., p. 222.

16 Watney, *The English Post-Impressionists*, pp. 140–141.

17 Erwin Panofsky, *Meaning in the Visual Arts* (New York, 1955); Watney, *The English Post-Impressionists*, p. 81.

18 Watney, *The English Post-Impressionists*, p. 81.

19 Dunlop, *The Shock of the New*, pp. 123–131; Farr, *English Art*, pp. 21–47, 189–230; Wendy Baron, *The Painters of Camden Town 1905–1920*, Christies (London, 1988).

20 Farr, *English Art*, p. 46; Farr cites Sickert's advice as recalled by Ethel Walker, quoted in John Rothenstein, *Modern English Painters: Sickert to Smith* (London, 1952), p. 79.

21 Walter Sickert, 'Camille Pissarro', *A Free House! or the Artist as Craftsman*, ed. Osbert Sitwell (London, 1947), p. 141.

22 Baron, 'Sickert's Attitude to his Subject Matter', Appendix to *Sickert* (London, 1973),

23 Watney, *The English Post-Impressionists*, p. 134.

24 See Louis Fergusson, *Harold Gilman: An Appreciation* (London, 1919); Watney, *The English Post-Impressionists*, p. 129.

25 Anna Greutzner, 'Two Reactions to French Painting in Britain', *Post-Impressionism. Cross-Currents in European Painting*, p. 178.

26 Rozsika Parker and Griselda Pollock, *Old Mistresses: Women, Art and Ideology* (London, 1981), p. 170.

27 Vanessa Bell, Memoir VI; Spalding, *Vanessa Bell*, pp. 36–37.

28 Watney, *The English Post-Impressionists*, p. 40.

29 Spalding, *Vanessa Bell*, p. 124, also suggests possible resemblances with Piero della Francesca's *Madonna della Misericordia* and Matisse's *Nu de dos III* (the latter perhaps being influenced by Bell's painting).

30 Caws, *Women of Bloomsbury*, p. 110.

31 Watney, *The English Post-Impressionists*, p. 80.

32 Ibid., pp. 80–81.

33 Spalding, *Vanessa Bell*, p. 126.

34 Ibid., p. 105.

35 Vanessa Bell, quoted Spalding, *Vanessa Bell*, p. 106.

36 In fact, Frantisek Kupka is credited with the first fully abstract painting, *Amorpha, Fugue in Two Colours*, which, according to Susan Compton, 'caused a sensation at the *Salon d'Automne* [Paris] in 1912'; and she notes that 'there was more popular discussion of this painting than it received in serious reviews. It was featured in a

Gaumont newsreel, released throughout Europe'. Compton, 'The spread of information leading to the rise of abstract art in Europe', *Towards a New Art. Essays on the background of abstract art 1910–20*, The Tate Gallery (London, 1980) pp. 188, 189.

37 The Tate *Abstract* is Bell's most impressive 'in this style', according to Watney, *The English Post-Impressionists*, p. 100.

38 Ibid.

39 This part of the letter is not included in *VB*, but it is quoted by Spalding, *Vanessa Bell*, p. 126.

40 Watney, *The English Post-Impressionists*, p. 94.

41 Spalding, *Vanessa Bell*, p. 171.

42 Caws, *Women of Bloomsbury*, p. 168.

43 For Dunn, *Virginia Woolf and Vanessa Bell*, pp. 157–58, 'the circle of the empty tub' suggests 'barrenness'.

44 Watney, *The English Post-Impressionists*, p. 103.

45 Caws, *Women of Bloomsbury*, p. 176.

46 Ibid., p. 154.

47 Gillespie, *The Sisters' Arts*, pp. 108–09.

48 Ibid., p. 111.

49 Dunn, *Virginia Woolf and Vanessa Bell*, p. 157.

50 Gillespie, *The Sisters' Arts*, p. 173.

51 Elliott and Wallace, *Women Artists and Writers*, pp. 61, 89.

12 'Her pictures stand for something': Woolf's forewords to Bell's paintings

1 Gillespie, *The Sisters' Arts*, p. 72.

2 See Chapter 10.

3 *Oxford Classical Dictionary* (Oxford, 1949), p. 683.

4 Eliot, *The Waste Land*, lines 98–103, *The Complete Poems and Plays of T.S. Eliot* (London, 1969), p. 66.

5 Ovid, *Metamorphoses*, VI, line 577, trans. Frank Justus Miller, Loeb Classical Library (London, 1926), vol. I, pp. 328–9.

6 Jane Marcus, 'Liberty, Sorority, Misogyny', *The Representation of Women in Fiction*, ed. Carolyn Heilbrun and Margaret Higonnet (Baltimore, 1982), pp. 60–97; *Art & Anger: Reading Like A Woman* (Columbus, 1988), p. 215.

7 Ovid, *Metamorphoses*, VI, lines 574–75, vol. I, pp. 328–29.

8 Catherine King, 'Feminist Arts', *Imagining Women: Cultural Representations and Gender*, ed. Frances Bonner et al. (Cambridge, 1992), p. 176; Rozsika Parker, *The Subversive Stitch: embroidery and the making of the feminine* (London, 1984), p. 201.

9 Tickner, *The Spectacle of Women*, p. 52: E. Dusédau, postcard, 'Beware of Suffragists' (c.1909).

10 Robert Graves, *The Greek Myths* (Harmondsworth, 1955), Volume I, p. 166.

11 John Keats, 'Ode to a Nightingale', *Keats's Poetical Works*, ed. H.W. Garrod (London, Oxford, New York, 1970), p. 207.

12 Woolf, 'Poetry, Fiction and the Future' (1927) [Reprinted with minor variations, as 'The Narrow Bridge of Art'], *E*, IV, pp. 428–40.

13 Bell, 'The English Group', pp. 10–11.

14 Fry, *Transformations*, p. 189; quoted McLaurin, *Virginia Woolf*, p. 87.

15 [Charles Marriott], *The Times* Friday 7 February 1930, p. 12.

16 Spalding, p. 235: 'Her great distinction lies in her reticence and frankness.'

17 David Dowling, *Bloomsbury Aesthetics and the Novels of Forster and Woolf* (London and Basingstoke, 1985), p. 101.

18 Plutarch, *Moralia*, 346F, trans. Frank Cole Babbitt (London, 1936), vol. IV, p. 501.

19 Gillespie, *The Sisters' Arts*, pp. 73, 74.

20 See also, 'Pictures and Portraits', *E*, III, p. 163: 'But it is not our business to define what sort of words they are; we are only concerned to prove our unfitness to review the caricatures of Mr. Kapp.'

21 Gillespie, *The Sisters' Arts*, p. 50.

22 *The Times*, Tuesday 13 March 1934, p. 12.

13 *To the Lighthouse*: purple triangle and green shawl

1 Stevenson, *Modernist Fiction*, p. 163.

2 McLaurin, *Virginia Woolf*, p. 90.

3 Patricia Laurence, *The Reading of Silence: Virginia Woolf in the English Tradition* (Stanford, Calif., 1991), p. 36.

4 See Spalding, *Roger Fry*, p. 128.

5 Eliza Haywood, *The Female Spectator* (London, 1771), I, p. 179.

6 For a more orthodox, Neoplatonic, reading of Post-Impressionist colour in this novel, see Jack F. Stewart, 'Color in *To the Lighthouse*', *Twentieth Century Literature* 31, 4 (Winter 1985) 438–58.

7 William Empson, 'Virginia Woolf', *Scrutinies by Various Writers* II, ed. Edgell Rickword (London, 1930), p. 207.

8 Jane Goldman, 'Metaphor and Place in *To the Lighthouse*: Some Hebridean Connections', *Tea and Leg-Irons: New Feminist Readings from Scotland*, ed. Caroline Gonda (London, 1992), pp. 137–56; see also Elissa Greenwald, 'Casting Off From "The Castaway": *To the Lighthouse* as Prose Elegy', *Genre* (Spring 1986), pp. 37–57.

9 Moore, *The Short Season Between Two Silences*, p. 62.

10 Love, *Worlds in Consciousness*, p. 70.

11 Stella McNichol, *Virginia Woolf and the Poetry of Fiction* (London and New York, 1990), p. 93.

12 Peter Knox-Shaw, ' "To the Lighthouse": The Novel as Elegy', *English Studies in Africa*, 29, 1 (1986), p. 33. See also Stevie Davies, *Virginia Woolf: To the Lighthouse* (Harmondsworth, 1989), pp. 100–39.

13 Knox-Shaw, ' "To the Lighthouse" ', p. 50.

14 John Dryden, however, does elegise a woman painter-poet in 'To the Pious Memory of the Accomplisht Young Lady Mrs Anne Killigrew, Excellent in the two Sister-Arts of Poësie, and Painting. An Ode', *The Poems of John Dryden*, ed. James

Kinsley (Oxford, 1958), vol. I, pp. 459–65. He refers to painting as 'the large Demains which the *Dumb-sister* sway'd' (line 100).

15 See Knox-Shaw, '"To the Lighthouse"', p. 32.

16 Yet in another sense we might see elegy as about that very crisis in language: that is, it cannot substitute what is lost: the dead, *pace* Vanessa Bell, are not raised.

17 See Knox-Shaw, '"To the Lighthouse"', p. 34, on the 'rupture of pastoral concord'.

18 An old 'Recipe for Pastoral Elegy' (1738) advises the elegist to 'Blast an old oak or two': see, *The Pastoral Mode: A Casebook*, ed. Brian Loughrey (London and Basingstoke, 1984), p. 66.

19 Annabel Patterson, *Pastoral and Ideology. Virgil to Valéry* (Oxford, 1987), pp. 50–51: Petrarch's second Eclogue (lines 2 13, 19–21) stands as the origin of this tradition.

20 Margaret Drabble, 'Introduction' to Woolf, *To the Lighthouse*, ed. Margaret Drabble (Oxford, 1992), p. xv, alerts us to a biographical reading which may support this idea of Ramsay's solar identity, when she reminds us that George Meredith 'created a fictional portrait of Leslie Stephen as Vernon Whitford, "Phoebus Apollo turned fasting friar", in his novel *The Egoist*, 1879'.

21 Beer, 'Hume, Stephen, and Elegy in *To the Lighthouse*', *Essays in Criticism*, XXXIV (January 1984), pp. 43–44, and McLaurin, *Virginia Woolf*, p. 186, disagree.

22 See Erich Auerbach, 'The Brown Stocking', *Mimesis: The Representation of Reality in Western Literature* (1946), trans. Willard R. Trask (Princeton, 1953), p. 525ff.

23 Knox-Shaw, '"To the Lighthouse"', p. 41, on the other hand, makes the distinction that 'where Lily presents Mrs Ramsay in her painting as a 'triangular purple shape' Virginia Woolf presents her as a "wedge-shaped core of darkness"'. But he rightly adds that she is also presented 'as a being who is shaped by the pressures of history'.

24 'The Fisherman and His Wife', *Grimm's Household Tales with the author's notes*, trans. and ed. Margaret Hunt, with an introduction by Andrew Lang (London, 1884), volume I, pp. 78–85. The text quoted in *To the Lighthouse* matches this edition.

25 Ibid., pp. xxxv–xxxviii.

26 Knox-Shaw, '"To the Lighthouse"', p. 45.

27 Grimm, *Grimm's Household Tales*, p. 78.

28 Shakespeare, Sonnet 98, lines 13–14, *The Sonnets*, ed. John Dover Wilson, Second Edition (Cambridge, 1969), p. 51.

29 Knox-Shaw, '"To the Lighthouse"', p. 50.

30 This echoes Sir Edward Grey's famous remark in the pre-war dusk of August 1914: 'The lamps are going out all over Europe; we shall not see them lit again in our lifetime.' Quoted John Buchan, *The People's King, George V: A Narrative of Twenty-Five Years* (Boston, 1935), p. 98.

31 Sue Roe, *Writing and Gender: Virginia Woolf's Writing Practice* (Hemel Hempstead, 1990), p. 64, supports this view in her biographical reading: Lily 'represents an alternative' to Mrs Ramsay whose 'model, Julia Stephen, was active in the Anti-Suffrage Movement'.

32 Moore, *The Short Season Between Two Silences*, p. 85.

33 Reed, 'Through Formalism: Feminism and Virginia Woolf's Relation to Bloomsbury Aesthetics', *Twentieth Century Literature* 38, 1 (Spring 1992), p. 30.

34 Milton, *Lycidas*, lines 139–41: 'Throw hither all your quaint enamelled eyes,/ That on the green turf suck the honied showers,/ And purple all the ground with vernal flowers.' See, Davies, *Virginia Woolf*, p. 117.

35 Andrew Marvell, 'The Garden', line 48, *Complete Poems*, ed. George deF. Lord (London, 1984), p. 50. See Davies, *Virginia Woolf*, p. 8.

36 Maria DiBattista, '*To the Lighthouse*: Virginia Woolf's Winter's Tale', *Virginia Woolf: Revaluation and Continuity*, ed. Ralph Freedman, p. 166.

37 See Milton, *Lycidas*, lines 4–5: 'And with forced fingers rude,/ Shatter your leaves before the mellowing year.'

38 See DiBattista, '*To the Lighthouse*', p. 167; Pamela J. Transue, *Virginia Woolf and the Politics of Style* (Albany, NY, 1986), p. 91.

39 Milton, *Lycidas*, line 193.

40 Gayatri Chakravorty Spivak, 'Unmaking and Making in *To the Lighthouse*', *In Other Worlds: Essays in Cultural Politics* (London, 1988), p. 45, honours this line 'as an attempt to articulate, by using a man as an instrument, a woman's vision of a woman'.

14 *The Waves*: purple buttons and white foam

1 A version of this chapter was published as ' "Purple Buttons on Her Bodice": Feminist History and Iconography in *The Waves*', *Woolf Studies Annual* 2 (1996) 3–25.

2 For example, Woolf's Hogarth Press published *Our Freedom and its Results by Five Women*, ed. Ray Strachey (London, 1936).

3 Christine Bolt, *Feminist Ferment: 'The Woman Question' in the USA and England, 1870–1940* (London, 1995), p. 101.

4 Woolf, 'Introductory Letter to Margaret Llewelyn Davies', *LAW*, pp. xv–xxxix (reprinted elsewhere as 'Memories of a Working Women's Guild'). Woolf's article was first published in the *Yale Review* (September, 1930) with a number of differences also kept in reprints by Leonard Woolf.

5 Transue, *Virginia Woolf and the Politics of Style*, pp. 132–133.

6 Karen Smythe, 'Virginia Woolf's Elegiac Enterprise', *Novel: A Forum on Fiction*, 29, 1 (Fall 1992), p. 73; Hermione Lee, *The Novels of Virginia Woolf* (London, 1977), p. 168; Eric Warner, *Virginia Woolf: The Waves* (Cambridge, 1987), p. 96.

7 Michael Rosenthal, *Virginia Woolf* (New York, 1979), p. 147.

8 Joan Bennett, *Virginia Woolf: Her Art as a Novelist* (Cambridge, 1945), p. 105.

9 Roe, *Writing and Gender*, p. 115.

10 Ibid., p. 106.

11 Zwerdling, *Virginia Woolf and the Real World*, p. 12.

12 Ralph Freedman, *The Lyrical Novel: Studies in Hermann Hesse, André Gide, and Virginia Woolf* (Princeton, NJ, 1963), pp. 244–70.

13 Lee, *The Novels of Virginia Woolf*, p. 159.

14 Daiches, *Virginia Woolf*, p. 111.

15 Avrom Fleishman, *Virginia Woolf: A Critical Reading* (Baltimore, 1975), p. 151.

16 Moore, *The Short Season Between Two Silences*, p. 120.

17 Warner, *Virginia Woolf*, p. 97.

18 McLaurin, 'Consciousness and Group Consciousness in Virginia Woolf', *Virginia Woolf. A Centenary Perspective*, ed. Eric Warner (London and Basingstoke, 1984), pp. 28–40.

19 Ruotolo, *The Interrupted Moment*, p. 172.

20 DiBattista, *Virginia Woolf's Major Novels: The Fables of Anon* (New Haven, 1980), pp. 159–60; Alice Jardine, 'Pre-Texts for the Transatlantic Feminist', *Yale French Studies*, 62 (1981), pp. 231–35.

21 Frank D. McConnell, ' "Death Among the Apple Trees": *The Waves* and the World of Things', *Bucknell Review* XVI (1968), p. 26; Jean Guiguet, *Virginia Woolf and her Works*, trans. Jean Stewart (London, 1965), pp. 37, 378, 379.

22 McLaurin, *Virginia Woolf*, pp. 77, 79–80, 81–82, 84; Jack F. Stewart, 'Spatial Form and Color in *The Waves*', *Twentieth Century Literature*, 28 (1982), pp. 90–91, 93, 103.

23 McLaurin, *Virginia Woolf*, pp. 128–48.

24 Marcus, 'Britannia Rules *The Waves*', *Decolonizing Tradition: New Views of Twentieth-Century 'British' Literary Canons*, ed. Karen Lawrence (Urbana, 1992), pp. 138, 150, 146.

25 Ibid., pp. 159, 140.

26 Tickner, *The Spectacle of Women*, p. 208.

27 Ibid., pp. 259–60.

28 Gillian Beer, 'Introduction', *The Waves*, ed. Gillian Beer (Oxford, 1992), p. xxxi.

29 Judith Lee, ' "This Hideous Shaping and Moulding": War and *The Waves*', *Virginia Woolf and War: Fiction, Reality, and Myth*, ed. Mark Hussey (Syracuse, NY, 1992), pp. 191–92.

30 Stuart Hampshire, 'Virginia Woolf', *Modern Writers and Other Essays* (London, 1969), p. 45.

31 John Mepham, 'Mourning and Modernism', *Virginia Woolf: New Critical Essays*, ed. Patricia Clements and Isobel Grundy (London, 1983), p. 142.

32 Freedman, *The Lyrical Novel*, p. 246. For the Grail connotations of Percival's name, see Beverly Ann Schlack, *Continuing Presences: Virginia Woolf's Use of Literary Allusion* (London, 1979), pp. 126ff.

33 Moore, 'Nature and Community: A Study of Cyclical Reality in *The Waves*', p. 234, calls Percival 'a comic god of the sun' who 'must constantly be destroyed'.

34 Schlack, *Continuing Presences*, p. 128.

35 J.W. Graham, 'Point of View in *The Waves*: Some Services of the Style', *University of Toronto Quarterly*, XXXIX (1969–70), p. 316.

36 Milton, *Lycidas*, lines 168–169.

37 T.E. Apter, *Virginia Woolf: A Study of Her Novels* (London and Basingstoke, 1979), p. 132.

38 Fontenrose, *Python*, p. 14; and Chapter 8 above. See also Jean Alexander, *The Venture of Form in the Novels of Virginia Woolf* (Port Washington, 1974), p. 15.

39 Patrick McGee, 'The Politics of Modernist Form; Or, Who Rules *The Waves?*', *Modern Fiction Studies*, 38, 3 (Autumn 1992), p. 638.

40 Stewart, 'Spatial Form and Color', p. 94.

41 For comparison between Rhoda and Rachel Vinrace of *The Voyage Out*, see, Laurence, *The Reading of Silence*, pp. 123ff.

42 Moore, *The Short Season Between Two Silences*, p. 129.

43 DiBattista, *Virginia Woolf's Major Novels*, pp. 159–60; Minow-Pinkney, *Virginia Woolf and the Problem of the Subject*, p. 180.

44 Atkinson, *Suffragettes in the Purple, White and Green*, pp. 18–22, 80.

45 See, Tickner, *The Spectacle of Women*, pp. 9, 74, 84; *LAW*, pp. 65, 99; Jean Gaffin and David Thoms, *Caring and Sharing: The Centenary History of the Co-operative Women's Guild*, Second Edition (Manchester, 1993), p. iv.

46 Margaret Llewelyn Davies (1861–1944) was General Secretary of the Women's Co-Operative Guild 1889–1921. Woolf, *L*, II, p. 76, confesses to Davies, who became a close friend: 'I become steadily more feminist . . . I wish I could borrow your mind about 3 days a week.' See also *L*, II, p. 105: 'I enjoyed [the 1916 Women's Guild] Congress enormously. I thought yesterday morning was better almost than I had ever heard it. They are really wonderful.'

47 Atkinson, *Suffragettes in the Purple, White and Green*, p. 79.

48 Tickner, *The Spectacle of Women*, pp. 210–11.

49 Mary M. Childers, 'Virginia Woolf on the Outside Looking Down: Reflections on the Class of Women', *Modern Fiction Studies* 33, 1 (Spring 1992), p. 66.

50 J.W. Graham, 'MSS Revision and the Heroic Theme of *The Waves*', *Twentieth Century Literature*, 29 (1983), p. 314.

51 Atkinson, *The Suffragettes in Pictures*, p. 117.

52 Tickner, *The Spectacle of Women*, pp. 57, 126, 57.

53 Shelley, 'The Question' (1820), lines 9–40, *The Complete Works of Percy Bysshe Shelley*, ed. Thomas Hutchinson (London, 1927), pp. 608–09.

54 Ibid., lines 18, 23.

55 Shelley, 'Arethusa' (1820), *The Complete Works*, pp. 605–06; see Schlack, *Continuing Presences*, p. 124.

56 See Ovid, *Metamorphoses*, v. 572ff., pp. 279–83.

57 Shelley, 'Arethusa', lines 37–54.

58 See Ovid, *Metamorphoses*, p. 283; Pausanias, *Description of Greece*, v. 7. 2, trans. W.H.S. Jones (London, 1918), vol. 2, p. 415.

59 Milton, *Lycidas*, lines, 85, 132–33.

60 See Pausanias, *Description of Greece*, VI. 22. 7–10, vol. 3, p. 141.

61 Graves, *The Greek Myths*, vol. I, p. 86.

62 Tickner, *The Spectacle of Women*, pp. 93, 125–26.

63 It may also suggest 'foam-born' Venus/Aphrodite: see *Oxford Classical Dictionary*, p. 67; Graves, *The Greek Myths*, vol. I, p. 39.

64 James Naremore, *The World Without a Self: Virginia Woolf and the Novel* (New Haven, 1973), p. 183.

65 Woolf, *The Waves: The Two Holograph Drafts*, ed. J.W. Graham (London, 1976), Draft II, p. 642.

66 Schlack, *Continuing Presences*, p. 116, also notes 'myths of pursuit and seduction' in connection with Jinny.

67 Ovid, *Metamorphoses*, V, lines 631–635, pp. 280–83.

68 Henry Thornton Wharton, 'Life of Sappho', *Sappho: Memoir, Text, Selected Renderings, and a Literal Translation*, Third Edition (London, 1895), pp. 17–22; Ovid, 'Sappho to Phaon', *Heroides*, XV, *Heroides and Amores*, trans. Grant Showerman (London, 1931), pp. 180–97. See also Woolf, 'On Not Knowing Greek', *CR*, p. 39: 'Sappho leapt off a cliff.'

69 Wharton, *Sappho*, p. 8.

70 Ibid., p. 19.

71 See Woolf, 'The Intellectual Status of Women' (1920), *D*, II, p. 340: Woolf greatly admires Sappho and the 'social and domestic freedom of Aeolian women'; and she talks, *L*, IV, p. 140, of Sappho not as 'a unique writer but supported by many other poetesses', and, *AROO*, pp. 164–65, as 'an inheritor as well as originator'.

72 Annette Oxindine, 'Sapphist Semiotics in Woolf's *The Waves*: Untelling and Retelling What Cannot Be Told', *Virginia Woolf: Themes and Variations: Selected Papers from the Second Annual Conference on Virginia Woolf*, ed. Vara Neverow-Turk and Mark Hussey (New York, 1993) p. 172.

73 Beer, *The Waves*, ed. Gillian Beer (Oxford, 1992), p. 256.

74 Flint, *The Waves*, ed. Kate Flint (Harmondsworth, 1992), p. 236.

75 McLaurin, *Virginia Woolf*, p. 137.

76 Love, *Worlds in Consciousness*, p. 81.

77 Laurence, *The Reading of Silence*, pp. 169, 174.

78 Minow-Pinkney, *Virginia Woolf and the Problem of the Subject*, p. 145; McLaurin, *Virginia Woolf*, pp. 81–82, 84.

79 Garrett Stewart, 'Catching the Stylistic D/rift: Sound Defects in Woolf's *The Waves*', *English Literary History*, 54 (1987), p. 453.

80 Woolf, sketch (c.1928–29), *The Waves: The Two Holograph Drafts*, Appendix A.1.

81 It also resembles a natural solar phenomenon known as the 'green flash' or 'green ray' or 'green segment'. See, M. Minnaert, *Light and Colour in the Open Air*, trans. H.M. Kramer-Priest, rev. K.E. Brian Jay (London, 1940), pp. 58, 59, 60.

15 Conclusion

1 Rita Felski, *Beyond Feminist Aesthetics: Feminist Literature and Social Change* (London, 1989), p. 179.

2 See Elizabeth Heine, 'Virginia Woolf's Revisions of *The Voyage Out*', *The Voyage Out*, ed. Heine (London, 1992), p. 439.

3 'Slater's Pins Have No Points', *Forum* (1928), reprinted elsewhere with 'Moments of Being' restored to the title. See Susan Dick *CSF*, p. 306.

Index